Letters from Kenneth Burke to William H. Rueckert, 1959-1987

LETTERS FROM

KENNETH BURKE

──── TO ────

WILLIAM H. RUECKERT, 1959-1987

Edited, with an Introduction by William H. Rueckert
Transcribed from the originals by Barbara L. Rueckert
Foreword by Angelo Bonadonna

Parlor Press
West Lafayette, Indiana
www.parlorpress.com

Parlor Press LLC, West Lafayette, Indiana 47906

S A N: 2 5 4 - 8 8 7 9

Library of Congress Preassigned Control Number (PCN)

2002113512

Letters from Kenneth Burke to William H. Rueckert, 1959-1987 /
   edited by William H. Rueckert
Includes index.
1. Burke, Kenneth, 1897-1993 — Correspondence. 2. Rueckert,
   William H., 1926 — Correspondence. 3. Authors, American—
   20th century—Correspondence. 4. Criticism—Literary. 5.
   Rhetoric. 6. Bonadonna, Angelo.

ISBN 0-9724772-0-9

Parlor Press LLC is an independent publisher of scholarly and trade
titles in print and multimedia formats. This book is also available in
cloth, as well as in Night Kitchen and Acrobat eBook reader formats,
from Parlor Press on the WWW at http://www.parlorpress.com. For
submission information or to find out about Parlor Press publications,
write to Parlor Press, 816 Robinson St., West Lafayette, Indiana, 47906,
or e-mail editor@parlorpress.com.

For Barbara, who faithfully transcribed all of these letters from the originals.

CONTENTS

FOREWORD

Some More of the Many Kenneth Burkes: The Burke-Rueckert Correspondence

Angelo Bonadonna

". . . to have such friends as thee art"

Dear Bill Rueckert,

Never, never before in all my life have I been in such a godam tangle . . ."

Thus Kenneth Burke opens his letter of June 18, 1962. He continues:

> Every single paper I try to dispose of involves my finding some other pages that got misplaced. I still have to send in expense accounts for various items, mark a set of final exams, acknowledge various kicks, compliments, inquiries, etc. And the mere attempt to set my room in order, so that it doesn't look like the portrait of acute mental unbalance will in itself take several days.

> So what do I do? Your letter arrives, I pour myself
> a drink of bourbon, push aside some piles of trash to
> make room for the near-collapsing typewriter—and
> smack out some lines.

Of all the moments in the hundreds of letters of Kenneth Burke to William Rueckert—and those moments are varied, even for the Protean Burke—this is my personal favorite. What an honor it must have been for Bill Rueckert to be placed in Burke's "bourbon cluster," to be his hookey from what he later calls the "Disorder Among My Papers," to be his untanglement, to be, in a word, his friend.

And of all the reasons to read the correspondence, this is the most compelling—to catch a glimpse of Burke the Word-man as Burke the Word-man/friend. Burke the friend is available elsewhere, of course, the most notable place being the Cowley correspondence, which chronicles a great intellectual friendship, and more closely and over a longer period than most such correspondences. But Burke and Cowley were peers and colleagues; Burke and Rueckert, besides their rather distinct professional roles, were separated by a generation. While the dynamics of a peer relationship involve intimacies, conflicts, and mutualities of a very revealing intensity, the ambiguous relationship of a colleague/mentor to his colleague/protege, a kind of relationship so common in intellectual circles, allows for a wholly different kind of connection and mode of expression. Burke, for instance, acted as Rueckert's sponsor from time to time, submitting his name for awards, contacting publishers, and offering advice on how to negotiate "the Slave Market in December" (9/22/1963), (the MLA Convention). Indeed, the shrewdness of Burke's coaching on issues of professional style and tone and his skill at "networking" so evident in the letters might well give question to the received view of Burke as an outsider to the academy.

More so than for mentoring, though, Burke uses the letters as a kind of writer's journal, outlining the many talks and essays of his very productive late period. Contentwise the letters are full of Burkology, and there are several projects to be done here, for instance, juxtaposing the way Burke represents his projects in the letters with his other representations available elsewhere. In tone, the letters are poignant, often suddenly so, but their dominant mood is playfulness. Burke plays his typical epistolary games with return addresses, salutations (one sequence of three letters opens "Dear Bill"—"Dear Billiards"—"Dear Pool"), datelines, and closings. Most are written in Burkese, a hodgepodge of English, East Coast dialect, Yiddish, Shakespeare, *ablaut* forms, joycing, and various other kinds of uncategorizable play.

The proportion of these three elements—work, play, and poignant emotion—is just such as defines an intimate friendship. In this regard, the letters, for all their diversity individually, are rather redundant as a whole. Collectively the letters stand as but a single utterance, a thirty-year enactment of an attitude, the attitude of affectionate gratitude for friendship. As we eavesdrop year in and year out, we hear Burke repeating, if only implicitly, "Thank you, Bill, for understanding and appreciatively so. Thank you for reading, writing, and speaking—for verbalizing, or co-verbalizing—in a mode not merely competent, but resonant, deeply so, with my own life's project of humane, linguistic quizzicality." To put it in Burke's explicit words, from the letter in which he reacts to the "stupendous job" of Rueckert's *Critical Responses to Kenneth Burke*: "You have been devoted to this job. Vexing though it necessarily was, you did it. In brief, you allowed my particular morality-of-production to tie in with yours" (5/5/1969).

Perhaps the best illustration of Burke's gratitude comes in the letter in which he announces that his "darling snooze has a vexing symptom" (3/10/1967). Burke seems aware that his "sweetest Other," his wife Libbie, is suffering the disease that would ultimately take her from him, and the hint of despair here is reinforced in many letters to follow that chronicle his adjustments to what he calls the "one dirty deal in [his] life" (11/25/1973), Libbie's "clearing out" before him.

Burke's tone is at once melancholy, cautiously hopeful, and angry. The letter is actually full of rage, perhaps a natural deflection of the anger at Libbie's condition. The targets of the anger are the Johnson administration, a recurring whipping post in the letters of the late 1960s, God, and a particular "damfool," with whom Burke had argued but to no avail:

> If he decides that your position is such-and-such, and
> you go and show by a specific passage in the text that it's
> not your position, the guy blunts off like a clam (except
> that a clam knows its business—and I greatly respect a
> clam, and some day, I hope, I'll be allowed to clam up
> for good, and not hang on for ever being tortured by a
> Gawd that loves not only me but great saviors like the
> current administration than which nothing ever more
> persuasively stank to high heaven). (3/10/1967)

In the swirl of rage, despair, exasperation, hope, and irony that Burke sets into motion in this letter, he concludes, "Jeez, I realize all the more what luck I had in being allowed to have such friends as thee art. Please always count me in" (3/10/1967).

"HOLLA!"

Lest we overemphasize the goodwill and friendliness of the letters, we need but linger a bit more on their sharper moments. Burke's letters, both published and unpublished, contain some of the finest vituperation in the language, and this correspondence does not disappoint in this regard. In general, Burke never wanted for something to lash out against. He was an individual who not only had enemies (or "enemas," as he picturesquely put it on May 5, 1967), but one who cherished them—even to the extent, when times got tough and there was a shortage of opponents, he treated his friends as enemies. Rueckert certainly is a target from time to time. For instance, in the letter that immediately precedes the friendship letter I cited above, he chides Rueckert for his pedagogical irresponsibility in using for class "that fuzzy book of Frye's as a text. I saluted it originally as a kind of conceptual fun. But I never for one moment thought that anybody as astute as you could put kids to work on it. Jeez, learn me, boy, learn me! And I pray, give me some examples of how *you* use it, in *your* work" (2/26/1967).

Rueckert insists on using Frye and Burke offers to get him psychoanalyzed, the first of several such offers. When Rueckert is late writing a promised review, for instance, Burke offers to raise the money for the psychoanalysis to get at the root of Rueckert's "Phartisan Review complex" (1/13/1968). And later, in response to Rueckert's advocacy of a critical theory that would too unproblematically treat "written history" as an "ultimate grounding," Burke writes, "Once again I beg you to go get psychoanalyzed, and to ask your doctor that he help you find out why you refuse even to recognize what Poor Ole Honorary Rejected Father (Kink Leer) Burke has been talkink about [. . .] Wadda woild!" (2/11/1968).

But the target of targets in these letters, as elsewhere, is Sidney Hook, the enemy par excellence, Burke's sole purpose, it often seem for striving on and on. April 27, 1970: "I don't know what to say. Apparently I'm gwanna die with my boots on. Wouldn't it be wonderful if, in a classroom, after just having said, 'Pardon my French, but that filthy hatchet-man, Shitney Hook . . .' and I passed out, while all present saw a dove fly out the window?"

From May 12, 1970:

> In the meantime, I have read your student's lively, amusing dialogue. It was good clean intelligent fun— and please tell him I said so. But there was one almost unforgivable mistake.
>
> I refer to the places where I address Hook as "Sidney." If your student really understood my essence, he'd know that I could at best address the guy as "Hook." But I'd feel more like myself if I just introduced hit-and-run expressions such as "by hook or crook." And, around the house, he is fondly referred to as "Shitney." Otherwise, all is O.K.

August 8, 1974: "There's only one thing I can promise for sure. I will put off slicing my jugular vein as long as there's not a grave by Shitney Hook for me to piss on."

The combative spirit was not confined to Burke's side of the correspondence. Rueckert's first letter to Burke—indeed his first sentence—voices a complaint. Rueckert explains that he is writing a book on Burke's literary and critical theory and he wants to know where "that perpetually 'forthcoming' *A Symbolic of Motives*" is. Burke, ever the agonist, could only have been delighted by such an approach—which, to my mind, *enacts* a compliment rather than merely delivers one. That is, the letter opens on the slope of benevolent antagonism rather than mere verbal flattery, and in doing so it enacts the same attitude of dialectical co-haggling that characterizes the correspondence with Cowley, Williams, Hyman, Duncan, and a host of Burke's other close intellectual friendships. "I grow uneasy," Rueckert writes. He later concludes: "I do hope this letter will reach you at a time when you are not so busy (say with the proofs for *A Symbolic of Motives* or one of the other three or four books you seem to be writing simultaneously) [. . .] meanwhile I will continue racing my first child to completion (8/4/1959).

Burke's first word of response was "Holla!"—that omnipresent Shakespearean exclamation of surprise and repartee that in itself so well characterizes Burke's mental acuity. *Holla!*—a word collapsing passion and action into one, a Burkean "title" indeed, and one that goes a long way, perhaps, to explaining the insomnia that the man was renowned for and that is such a recurrent theme of the letters. "Holla!" Burke writes, "If you're uncomfortable, think how uncomfortable I am. But I'll do the best I can by you and the baby" (8/8/1959).

He apologizes, explaining that the "damned trilogy has become a tetralogy" (8/8/1959)—and in a long first letter of roughly a thousand words, he discusses his plans for the *Symbolic* ("Yes all the things you mention shd. go into the Poetics"); he describes his current formulations of dialectic in an article he'd just finished writing called "Body and Mind"; he shares his hopes to do a section on "comic catharsis"; he cites three or four books by others relevant to Rueckert's project; he offers to "ship off . . . some multilithed copies of three things I did at the Center for Advncd Std in Bhvrl Scncs some time back," among which was a first draft of the *Poetics*; he explains his understanding of the term "rebirth" (in Rueckert's proposed title, *The Rhetoric of Rebirth*) to be but a rhetorical term for the principle of development or transformation often called dialectic"—all of these comments culminate in his reflection, "Jeez, when I think of how sick of myself I get now and then, I tremble at the thought of your six-year vigil. But inasmuch as every-knock-is-a-boost, maybe we might both survive your ordeal" (8/8/1959).

They did, and at a tenor and pitch that is remarkable for its consistency. This first letter—with its familiar tone, its succinct excursions into theory, and its generosity—is paradigmatic of the entire correspondence. In looking at the later letters one is hard-pressed to find a variation in tone or depth of connectedness. This is not to say the friendship did not develop. Rather, I would suggest the friendship is entered upon at full speed on both sides, like synchronized gears (pardon the metaphor, O shade of Burke), and it maintains a steady epistolary pace throughout, till May 25, 1987, the date of the final letter, and the eighteenth anniversary of Libbie's death. Burke concludes his correspondence to Rueckert, much as he had begun it—ending it in fact with the same word with which he had begun:

> One thing after another intervened, and every one brought up stuff I wanted to talk about to you. And now, this being a big weekend, my nonagenarian garrulity is peopled by both new doings that are notable.

. . . sudden chance to get this letter mailed in NYC
this morn. Holla!

Many "Holla's!" intervened, and whether they all mean the same
thing or something different in context is an interesting question. What
changes and what remains the same throughout the correspondence?
One thing is certain: By the end, Burke was still "sick of himself"—in
the best sense of that term—and Burke had clearly "mellowed"—in the
best sense of that word, which is to say he had "ripened without rotting,"
just as he had always hoped.

Walpurgisnacht at And/Or And/Or Elsewhere

An introduction to this collection would not meet its essential obliga-
tion if it did not share a wide sampling of Burke moments, presented by
one of his favorite techniques, the "hit-and-run Walpurgisnacht style" (5/
25/1963), the fragmentary jottings that in the fashion of the last chapter
of *Towards a Better Life* "sometimes sum up what has gone before,
and sometimes make new stabs" (6/18/1963). Thus:

On observing that the year 1961 looks the same when turned upside
down: "Obviously that's the kind we need" (1/7/1960).

On the beauty of nature: "One should give thanks by simply rotting"
(1/291963).

On history: "Does everything just go down in history?" (5/11/1978).

On himself: ". . . when I am on especially familiar terms with myself, I
speak of me as 'Kennel Bark'" (10/20/1960).

On the American Southwest: "Everything lives on the edge of disaster,
and in that respect it flatters me into loving it as an honorifically stylized
portrait of mine own present moods" (1/10/1967).

On critical practice: "A critic doesn't experience too much trouble trying
to meet another critic halfway. But if has just spent ten weeks trying to
meet a whole tangle of critics halfway, it's like firmly grasping a handful
of tacks" (8/5/1963).

On Pittsburgh: ". . . I don't see why you shouldn't like it there, except in the technical sense that everyplace is a vale of tears" (May Day 1970).

On ambition: "[A]las! no problems of career can ever be settled. The goads of career are like trying to go on counting and counting until you have got the number that is beyond the possibility of adding 'plus one'" (6/19/1977).

On life's busyness: "Just at present, I'm almost nightmarishly tangled—and the nightmares of an insomniac are mussy indeed, particularly the ones when he's wholly awake" (4/1/1962).

On departmental limitations: "Using linguistics to solve the problems of Rhetoric is like trying to pack twenty people into one phone booth" (2/10/1967).

In response to an editor's wish that Rueckert's "brilliant analysis" might answer how Burke's "antecedents and background . . . prompted [him] to take up the lines of inquiry that . . . [he] so ingeniously developed":

> Jeez. Here's betting twenty to one that your book doesn't answer his question! The answer would have to deal with the ways in which a sickly kid raised in a rundown suburb of Pittsburgh and with an almost hysterical fear of death developed pig-headedness and got bumped, and has always beena mixture of asseveration and uncertainty. (7/29/1960)

On "The Kiss" (4/4/1974):

> I went to the party, taking a bottle, and had a good time. I left as an old man on the drunken side—and [Marsha] was so pityingly sweet, she kissed me goodnight. I think she was saying in effect, "You were peddling your wares quite assertively, as you should. But 'neath it all you are an old man near death. By my kissing you on the way out you are proclaimed to be not a dirty old man but a sweet old man who needs just such kinds of graciousness as I, in my role of hostess, enact towards you." Or I could be insulted, if I so decided, or got decided for me. But of course I warnt.

And finally, on life: "I WANT OUT"—Burke states so flatly on December 23, 1968. But he had started saying goodbye long before and his leave taking throughout the letters, so prolonged as it is and so rich in its decay seems comparable to the long glorious decline of a fine wine. Neither really declines; they mellow in that fine Burkean sense.

SCHOLARLY USES OF THE BURKE-RUECKERT CORRESPONDENCE—AN EXAMPLE

The Burke-Rueckert correspondence provides a rich, fertile field for future Burke studies. Scholars will find references to every imaginable Burke theme. In the early letters we see Burke charting his struggles with the *Symbolic* (eventually dubbed the "Sin Ballix"); his expansion of the *Motivorum* from a trilogy to a tetralogy; his dichotomous views on catharsis/dialectic; his method of conducting critical reviews; and so on. Many of the attitudes and ideas addressed here are available elsewhere in the Burkean corpus. What may generate more immediate attention from scholars is Burke's reflection on the themes of his remarkably productive late period, including his characterization of the relationship of "dramatism" to "logology"; the development of his "Bodies that Learn Language" formula; his take on postmodern language theory (e.g., as "Marcel Marceaus in reverse," who see "us as all words, no body" [12/8/1982]); and his development of the Super-Nature/Counter-Nature dichotomy.

A personal anecdote suggests the potential of the letters for advancing Burke studies: I first read the letters some months after Burke's death, just after Barbara Rueckert had completed her generous and most competent act of transcribing the correspondence into a digital archive. I read the letters with hopes of finding validation for some of my arguments in the dissertation on Burke's theory of comedy I had just completed. That dissertation, incidentally, had sprung up in response to a parenthetical comment Burke himself made to me in the once piece of correspondence I received from him, in a letter dated "V/ii/89." (I note with some playful one-upmanship that, although Bill Rueckert's correspondence with Burke covered nearly 30 years, and consists of hundreds of letters addressing every imaginable life/professional/literary situation of two very engaged thinkers, my one letter is more recent than his latest letter.) I had sent Burke a copy of *Counter-Statement* and asked him to autograph it. Burke, on the verge of his 92nd birthday, wrote back:

> If I sign my name slowly, it isn't mine. And if I sign it
> as I used to, it now becomes a bit illegible. So I com-
> promise (ever the compromiser) by signing it several
> times.

Burke thus returned my edition of *Counter-Statement* with three sig-
natures on the title page. But it was his phrase, "ever the compromiser,"
that caught me—and almost became a mantra for me. I read and reread
the books and articles through the genius of this idea, and I ultimately
spun out a reading of Burke in terms of a theory of comedy constructed
as a cycle of terms implicit in the idea of "compromise."

In turning to the Burke-Rueckert correspondence, I was both pleased
and a little disappointed when I discovered the phrase "ever the compromiser" in the letter of December 17, 1966, as a relatively "young"
Burke refers to himself as "[e]ver the aging compromiser." I have since
discovered the phrase used by Burke in other contexts; but this early
usage indicates Burke's way of latching onto and living with key defining
principles in the varied contexts of ongoing developments.

More to the specific purposes of my dissertation, the Rueckert letters are sprinkled with references to Burke's fiction as relevant to his
criticism. For instance, on October 12, 1972 he writes: "I consider
TBL [*Towards a Better Life*] the ritualized expression of what I develop
analytically in my criticism." The collection's final letter (5/16/87) presents a notion that, had I access to it in my dissertation defense, might
have shortened the proceedings considerably. There Burke gives me an
author's imprimatur to think things through exactly as I had attempted,
namely to treat Herone Liddell, the "little hero" of *The Anaesthetic Revelation of Herone Liddell,* as the comic corrective to John Neal, the pre-
cipitously tragic hero of *Towards a Better Life*:

> I'm delighted with your having dragged a class through
> TBL. And I have been taking notes for quite some time
> with the trick conceit that I would round out my opus
> totum by a tract on that, perhaps with the story of my
> operation (the last piece in my *Collected W.O.* volume
> ["The Anaesthetic Revelation of Herone Liddell"]) as
> a kind of sequel.

I present this anecdote simply as an illustration of the *responsiveness* of
the letters to the critical needs or agendas of scholars. Bill Rueckert himself has commented that my "reader's response" to the correspondence

is characterized by significantly different themes and emphases than his readings. Other variations would be true of course for readers interested in other topics. Part of the variability stems from the nature of reading as a *performance*, to use a Burkean figure (2/4/1978), whereby any given text is considered to be a set of instructions, as variably interpretable as is a musical score. As the letters of this correspondence are "played" by various scholars, we will undoubtedly hear a range of tunes. Even so, it is certain that the "score" itself will command increasing respect for all the possibilities it will generate. These letters present the rich deployment of a great mind in various moods of relaxation and intensity, and personal and intellectual friendship over several decades. As such, they will generate new readings of Burke, even as they are employed to substantiate perspectives and conclusions already in place.

"SOMETHINKS IS GOING ON . . ."

Ultimately, the letters present us with many Burkes, most of them familiar, but all of them somewhat eye-opening for their new context. If Henry Bamford Parkes was right in 1938 when he said, "One might sum up Mr. Burke's ideal [of social life] by saying he would have liked to live in Confucian China," these letters present this Confucian mind in its musings on John Glenn, Lyndon Johnson, Richard Nixon, Malcolm X, Watergate, Reagan, feminism, homosexuality, dishwashers, wall-to-wall carpeting, technology, and much more. The letters help us enjoy Burke's "Last Phase," with all expected wryness and not a little pathos, as we glimpse the Word-man responding to and counter-attitudinizing the turbulent and accelerating developments of the latter part of the twentieth century.

On every page, we find Burke "[s]till somehow, like a damfool, hoping somewhat" (10/24/1978). And ever-present are the implicit and explicit appeals to his friend, playful always, but serious too: "Anything you could say to make life more worth living would be appreciated" (8/5/1974).

In characterizing his "winding up" mode, Burke himself stated to Rueckert, "You could do it as no one else could . . ." (1/7/1985). In all, the range and depth of the Burke-Rueckert correspondence confirm that there could never have been a more appropriate author than Bill Rueckert to write the essay he titled: "Some of the Many Kenneth Burkes." Burke's response to that essay provides a most inviting introduction to the collection that follows:

By heck, your new stuffo in your book anent my Sickly
Selph, and your friendly exercising in the *Representing*
volume do make it look as though somethinks is going
on. Thanks slavishly. (6/20/1983)

There are some "thinks" in these letters, to be sure. Somewhat after
the fact, I join Burke in saying "thanks slavishly"—to Bill Rueckert and
Burke's literary executors—for making this remarkable collection available to the present and future generations of Burke scholars.

Angelo Bonadonna
Chicago, Illinois
May 14, 2002

INTRODUCTION

William H. Rueckert

PART I — THE HISTORY

My correspondence with Kenneth Burke began in the summer of 1959. I was finishing the first draft of *Kenneth Burke and the Drama of Human Relations* and wrote to Burke to ask him two questions: (1) about the status of *A Symbolic of Motives* and (2) about what he was working on at the time of writing. I pointed out that I was trying to finish the book I was writing on him before my first son was born in early September. As it turned out, my son won the race and was born on September 7, 1959 in Urbana, Illinois. Burke answered my letter at once and sent me copies of those parts of *The Rhetoric of Religion* that he had finished, which was all but the final chapter, "Epilogue: Prologue in Heaven," as well as a copy of "Poetics, Dramatistically Considered." From that point on, our correspondence was more or less continuous until his last letter to me on 16 May 1987. Actually, the correspondence was continuous until 1984/85; then there was a two-year gap, before the last letter. Burke was 90 when he wrote final letter to me. Nothing obvious happened to bring our correspondence to an end: it just stopped. He was preoccupied with other things from then until his death in 1993 and was being looked after by other people who took good care of him, and being lionized by the speech communication people who could not seem to get enough of him, even in his final declining years.

These 262 letters tell their own story, which is primarily Burke's story. Burke was a wonderful correspondent. He took letter writing seriously, as is obvious from this correspondence, just as it is from the Burke-Cowley letters and from the many other long-term correspondences that Burke carried on over the years during his long life.

For Burke, a letter was a formal occasion. Letters had a set form, which he always followed. They had a date and a location. There was a salutation, and an opening or beginning of some kind. There was the main body of the letter, followed by some sort of way out or closure. There was a signoff, followed in Burke's case, by his trademark "KB." Letters were an act of language. You didn't just write a letter, you composed one. That meant that letters had style or, in Burke's case, a Burke style. He was a very playful letter writer and loved tinkering with the language and the different parts of the form of the letter. He was always making up his own way of spelling words to make puns. After a while, I developed a term for this feature of Burke's letters, calling it Burkespells. He liked nicknames and had ones for all the members of his family and most of his good friends and enemies. It took him a long time to come up with one for me, but he finally settled on Billions, and Billions I was in his letters to me to the end. Libbie was Shorty, Anthony was Butch, Michael was Unc, his older daughters were Dutchy and Hap. He had nicknames for friends and enemies alike. Sidney Hook was always Shitney Hook, because he wrote a negative review of one of Burke's early books and Burke sustained a lifelong animosity toward him. The degree of his animosity is indicated by the number of times Burke returned to vilify him in his letters to me and his determination to piss on Hooks's grave if ever he got the chance.

As one would expect, there were certain recurrent subjects to which Burke returned. Here are some of them: his body and his health, his work and how it was going, responses to his work by friend and foe. Bad reviews of his books really set him going, as did the absence of reviews of a given book. It would be something of an understatement to say that alcohol was important in Burke's life, as it was for many other writers of his generation—Faulkner, Hemingway, F. Scott Fitzgerald, Hart Crane and many others. Burke had an amazing capacity for alcohol and an obvious need for the kind of relief and/or stimulation it provided him. Burke often mentioned his fellow critics and kept careful track of their reputations and achievements in relation to his. This was especially true for such writers as Northrop Frye, whom Burke thought was overrated, Marshall McLuhan, Buckminister Fuller, N. O. Brown, and other critics who came to fame during Burke's lifetime. Burke was generally paranoiac about his work and jealous, in a petty way, of the kinds of reputations some of his fellow critics achieved. After Libbie was diagnosed and they knew that the course of her illness was irreversible, she became a constant reference in his letters, long after she died and Burke was trying to cope with his loss and loneliness. Burke referred often to my work on him and was always anxious to correct what he took to be my wrong-headed interpretations of some of his major points.

When I say that these letters tell their own story, I mean that they tell Burke's story during this crucial period in his life from age 62 until 90—the period during which Burke finally came into his major and well-deserved fame and recognition of his achievement as a writer and thinker. Burke was literally a self-made man and wrote and thought his way to fame. His long career was a function of his incredible energy, willpower, and his drive to achieve something important and to leave a significant body of work behind him. Even in his nineties, Burke was still looking (searching) for a new breakthrough, a final definition that would sum up the human condition, a universal definition that would give him a way to account for as much of the human drama as possible. His definition of humans as "bodies that learn language" comes close to serving him in this way, as did logology, the principal methodology of his later years, and his many comments about our tragic condition and the need for comic criticism as a way to cope with this condition.

All of this is well-documented in Burke's letters to me, especially in his many comments on his own work after Libbie died and he was on the road so much, lecturing and teaching all over the United States, being lionized and made much of wherever he went—except, it seems, the one time he went to Europe to lecture soon after Libbie died and spoke to a Spanish audience that knew little of his work and less English. It was his only trip to Europe.

These letters are best read in chronological order so that one can follow the relationship that developed between us over the years and so that one can follow Burke's development in his later years as he finished his work on Dramatism, which he began in the early forties, and started working out Logology, in *The Rhetoric of Religion* in the late fifties. The culmination of Dramatism came in *Language as Symbolic Action* (1966). After that, Burke began working out the implications of logology as a theory of language and as a methodology for the analysis of acts of language. Burke's letters to me during the sixties and seventies chart his attempts to arrive at a series of final, summings-up based on both dramatism and logology. These attempts at summing up can be found in Burke's late essays, a selection of which will soon be published by the University of California Press. The letters also chart his continued struggles to finish his *Symbolic of Motives*. As his letters make clear, the longer he struggled with it, the more diffuse it became until finally, even Burke was ready to give up on it and put it in the hands of others. As David Cratis Williams has made clear in his essay on this subject in *Unending Conversations* ("Toward Rounding Out the *Motivorum Trilogy*: A Textual Introduction") and as I try to make clear in my own essay on the same subject in the same volume,* it is never really clear just why Burke had so much trouble with this project which, for all intents and purposes, was complete and ready for publication by 1957. Burke's letters to me—and others—are filled with references to the *Symbolic* and to his continued intentions to finish it—way into the eighties.

These letters tell us a lot about Burke. For a long time I was afraid that publishing them would be an invasion of Burke's privacy. But Burke was a public figure and he must surely have known that whatever documents he left behind would eventually be made public and that his life would be carefully scrutinized by the many scholars working on the archives. Much of what is in these letters is not private in the sense that a series of love letters would be. Many of the letters tell us important new things about Burke that will eventually contribute to our overall knowledge of who this great man was and how his amazingly resourceful mind worked. In fact, just a study of what he did with the letter as a form and as an exercise in style can tell us a lot about how his mind worked—sober and sometimes somewhat tanked.

If you really want to know the secrets of Kenneth Burke, you have to study his novel, *Towards a Better Life* (1932). He knew that his real self was hidden away in that novel; and as he points out in one of his last letters to me, one of his final projects was to have been a last attempt on his part to crack the secret of his own self as he had hidden it away in that novel, behind the disguises of his fiction. Burke dedicated this novel *To Libbie* by hiding the dedication in the first letters of the paragraphs of the Preface to the first edition of the novel. Burke was never able to leave this novel alone and went back to it again and again, and to the unsent letters written by its protagonist, John Neal. I'm not sure that the many letters he sent me will reveal his secret self to us; but they do tell us a lot

---

* "Kenneth Burke's 'Symbolic of Motives' and 'Poetics, Dramatistically Considered." *Unending Conversations: New Writings by and about Kenneth Burke.* Ed. Greig Henderson and David Cratis Williams. Carbondale: Southern Illinois University Press, 2001.

about him and one of the important relationships in his life (and mine) that lasted for a lot of years—through the years that saw the publication of *The Rhetoric of Religion* (1961), *Language as Symbolic Action* (1966), his connection with the University of California Press (the work of Bob Zachary) that at one time had all of Burke's books in print at the same time, his discovery by the speech communication people, which transformed their discipline, the formation of the Kenneth Burke Society, the many awards he received honoring his work, his many honorary degrees (for a man who never even got a college degree), his steady productivity until about 1984, when new editions of *Permanence and Change* and *Attitudes Toward History* were issued by the University of California Press, and, closer to home, the sickness and death of Libbie in 1969; and in my case, the birth of all four of my sons between 1959 and 1970, my divorce and remarriage, my numerous job changes, my many public talks about Burke at national conferences and Modern Language Association meetings, many of which he attended, the great pleasure of having my university (Rochester) award Burke an honorary degree; and finally, the publication of my books and articles on Burke and the recognition they brought me.

All of these things are in the letters, as are the many references to most of the political events of those years. Burke hated the Vietnam war and everything that was part of it; he had a special dislike for President Nixon and was always upset and angry because of the destruction that our government was allowing to be done to the environment, not just in Vietnam, but in our own country and elsewhere in the world. But, as I have said, the letters tell their own story and I hardly need to rehearse it here.

PART II. SOME LETTERS TO KENNETH BURKE

12 May 1999

Dear Burke,

I've been rereading your letters to me—all 262 of them—written between 8 August 1959 and 16 May 1987. My purpose in doing this was to use the letters as the basis of a talk to be given at the upcoming meeting of the Kenneth Burke Society in Iowa City. But I could never work out anything that satisfied me about the letters, so I wrote another talk. Then, when it was done and sent off to my designated reader, Angelo Bonadonna, a way to do the letters finally occurred to me; it was the device you used in *Towards a Better Life*—the unsent letter—which I have used before to different ends. Once this way of doing things occurred to me, I was off and happy to be able to use the many pages of notes and fragments of commentary I wrote for the talk that never came off.

After I had reread your letters many times and carefully analyzed them for their form and style, I discovered that you had established a set form for your letters, which you repeated over and over again, with the variations coming in stylistic changes or in the different ways you managed the fixed parts of the form. I documented all of this, treating the letters as texts and arrived at some interesting and often amusing results, the main points of which could be summarized as follows: you liked fixed forms with variations, and had a restless, playful mind with regard to how you handled both the form and the language or style of the letters. In some ways, the most interesting salient characteristic of your letter style is the way in which you played with the spelling of hundreds of ordinary words, to create new words out of old ones, as in yestiddy for yesterday. Sometimes you punned, but usually you just played around with sound, sense, and sight as in Gaytie's *Faust* for Goethe, or in Backert for Rueckert and Billions for me, Bill, or Ignatz de Burp for yourself. But more on this later.

I realize that now that I have started this, there will be a problem with it, this fiction, which will result from a kind of absurdity because you wrote the letters and here I am telling you what you already know you did in them. Unless I shift to the importance and significance of the letters for me and other Burkeans, there is no way to get around this apparent absurdity except by concentrating on your favorite conception of criticism, which was that it should convey useful and not always obvious knowledge, both about the nature of form and style of the text as a structure of terms, and about the content—what the text does and says. So that is what I will do.

Avanti,
Billions

14 May 1999
Grounddown Island

Dear Burp,

Here are some comments on the form of your letters. Like everything else in your letters, the form provided you with an occasion for play—or fun and games with the language, especially anent your sickly Selph, your aging body and the perpetual jam of work you were always in. Oof, you would write, what a jam I am in. You always seemed to get unjammed in time to give your talk or get an article done, so after reading all of your letters to me a number of times, I decided that you liked to keep yourself in a state of induced hysteria or semi-hysteria because you worked best that way and because you could later relieve that hysteria with your medicayish, alky.

But to the form of the letters, which provide a classic example of permanence and change. The basic form of your letters never changed during the 25 years we corresponded, though the way you filled in that form varied considerably. Every change and variation had to be deliberate and testified to the conception you had of a letter as symbolic action. You clearly always thought of letters as a personal communication from one person to another. You really believed in letters and wrote a prodigious number of them to a great variety of people. So far as I know, you always answered inquiries from people like me—and there must have been hundreds over the years. You also handled your own so-called professional correspondence, which must also have been considerable—especially in the years after Libbie's death.

To the form of the letters. All of your letters were dated and located. If you were away from Andover, as you were for long stretches of time—say at Washington University or Yaddo or Western Washington, Penn State, or Emory or Harvard or Stanford or in Florida, your locations were mostly always straightforward, but if you were home in Andover (And/Or), your locations were often very playful and added a dimension to a specific letter it would not have had otherwise. Here are some examples of how you located yourself in your letters to me: aside from And/Or, you used clutcher's gulch, copesmithery, Nixon's nook, Han ging on (for hanging on), and others that referred to your own condition or to political events during the Vietnam war, an event that maddened you more than most other political events of your time.

Here is a list of the different ways B. located his letters to me over the years: Heresome, and da Capo, Pesthaven, Parturition, Hastyville, Ad Interim, Nixonheld, Back at the old stand, Paraphernalia, Verlorenberg, Worer Binich, self talk, lone noisings, yasnaya Polyana, slumpwump, Olde Stand, last stand, Gatesville, Onwards, Outwards, and Up, Under New Management, Nixon Nook, Heavingscote, How Afford Ford, the copesmithery, clutchers Gulch, 07821, Lingerlag 07821, Han Gin Gon,

07821, Ever onwards, Lingerlag Lane, From the same old Severe Monastic Cell, still somehow clinging on, Groove 154-07821.

What are we to make of all these renamings of your Andover location except to point out what you surely knew when you chose them: that each represented your mood or state of mind on the specific date and time when you wrote the letter. Having gathered them all together like this, I'll study them to see if anything more significant occurs to me, meanwhile,

Avanti,
Billions

18 May 1999
Grind me down

Dear Ignatz,

You were also always careful about your salutation. In my case, I went from Mr. Rueckert, to Bill R., to William Haitch (your way of doing H in anybody's name), to Bill. I was Bill for a long time until some point in 1974, you decided it was time to name me in a way that suited you and you began a series of experiments until you hit on Billions, which I remained to the end. I was B. for a while, Billify, Biller-killer-diller, Burpius Billions, Billiards, Billyrus, Billoxi, and finally variation on Billions—such as Billions & Billions & and Billions, or More and More Billions. It took Burke fifteen years to decide that I was worthy of a nickname—that is, of being renamed in his own terms, as he did so often with so many ordinary words in his letters and members of his family.

I knew I was going to run into trouble with this unsent letter device, slipping from you to he without even being aware of it when trying to avoid the absurdity, even within this rhetorical fiction, of telling Burke what he did when it is obvious that so self-conscious a writer as Burke knew full well what he did. Letters were a serious business with Burke and he took a lot of care with them.

18 May 1999
Aqua Vista, NY

Dear Burpius,

You were 72 in May of 1969, the same year and month that Libbie died. I think of this often because I am now 72 and my wife, Barbara, is 70. That whole sequence of events from Libbie's "vexing symptom" while you were in California to its diagnosis in 1967 while you were at Harvard, to its inevitable conclusion two years later in May, 1969 is the only truly personal event in your life that I have ever allowed myself to dwell on. There were other personal moments, of course, as when you came to get your honorary degree at the University of Rochester, or came to stay nearly a week in Saratoga Springs while I was working for Empire State College and we made a couple of TV programs together; or when I visited you in Andover with my first wife, Betty, various sons (my house full of Swedes you called them) and my dog, Burke. Libbie, of course, was always there also and we even visited a last time when she was near the end, though you warned us it would be painful—and it was. Such a wonderful person, who understood you perfectly and knew exactly how to get along with your often difficult behavior. Those were memorable visits; I had spent much of my life reading the words of others and never putting the words together with a living person. But there you were, the words in the flesh. Meeting you did not change my way of reading your words, but it certainly enriched my life in ways quite different from your words.

I think of you often during my 72nd year. Libbie died thirty years ago this year.

20 May 1999
Groundround

Dear Burps,

Helndamnaysh, KB, why did you fabricate all those Burkespell words—hundreds of them if the notes I took are correct. Was it just another way to play with words, as cummings often did in his poems, and you sometimes did in yours; or must we look beyond that for some deeper significance involving the power of making new words, or the Joyce factor, as in *Finnegans Wake.*

Clearly, I could go on like this for many more pages, but, again, it's all *in* the letters and I am mostly just having fun, as Burke did, playing around with his playings around. So, I will leave them to the reader to discover and enjoy as I did over the years, and let various readers answer this last question about why you did what you did to the language. Something significant could obviously be made of it.

Farewell,
Billions

PART III. BEYOND THE WRITTEN WORD

These letters take us into a dimension of my relationship to Burke that went far beyond his written work—or where it started out back in the late fifties, though our relationship was always closely tied to his work, to his books and essays and to his place in the intellectual and cultural life of his times. The letters tell the story of our developing human relationship even without my half of the correspondence. This relationship was extremely important to me and had a significant effect on my personal life, how I conducted my life, and how I used my mind in my professional life. It was hard not to succumb to the power of Burke's intellect and way of looking at things, especially for someone like me whose mind was saturated with Burkean perspectives, by incongruity and otherwise.

Reading, writing about, and corresponding with Burke changed the way my mind worked. What Burke mostly taught me was how to use my mind with maximum efficiency; more than anything else, he taught me about irony and comedy and how to discount the foolishness and bureaucratic nonsense that prevails in so many phases of our lives. Here is one of Burke's definitions of irony that has stayed with me as part of my equipment for living: "Irony is an adjustment in the agent, not a change in the scene or other agents. Irony is an attitude, not an action." Burke was self-taught and had many of the failings or limitations of the autodidactic; but he also escaped the institutional limitations that are part of any formal education, and that freed his mind for the many radical insights that characterize all of his thinking.

Also, he mostly lived away from urban centers, though he worked in NYC for many years, and never shared the values of the urban intellectuals such as the "Phartisan Review" critics who never understood the motives of this twentieth-century (or was it nineteenth-century?) romantic idealist who was always saved from sentimentality by his belief in the rational powers of the mind and his devastating sense of irony. But like many great thinkers, Burke was not able to escape the paranoia about his own work which tended to obscure his ability to judge his achievement in relation to that of his peers. This limitation shows up clearly in his letters to me (and others) and we have to learn to discount it.

We all still have a lot to learn from an approach like Burke's, with its profound humanistic values and nature-centered ecological view of technology. He did not live to see what the electronic revolution (the WWW, the Internet, the fantastic power of computers) has done to the way we live and think about the world we are creating and destroying, but he anticipated some of it, and his work is still a corrective to the excesses of hypertechnologism, which it still (and even more so these days) behooves us to acknowledge and be wary of.

Bill Rueckert
April 23, 2002
Fairport, NY

POSTSCRIPT: A NOTE ON LIBBIE'S LETTERS

In my file of letters from Kenneth Burke, there were 17 letters from Libbie Burke, KB's second wife and the sister of his first wife, Lillie. These letters began after we first visited the Burkes in Andover in 1963 and end shortly before Libbie died in May 1969. Her last note was dictated after she lost the use of her arms. She acknowledges receiving a copy of *Critical Reponses to Kenneth Burke*, which I dedicated to her.

Libbie wrote wonderful letters and it was tempting to include all of them. But I have only selected those parts which relate directly to KB, plus a few passages about the course of her fatal illness, from the first symptom of it to their stay in Brooklyn, a period Burke writes about in his long, "Eye Crossing" poem. These excerpts from Libbie's letters have been inserted at the appropriate chronological points between letters from Burke. I have identified any references that are not self-explanatory.

LETTERS
FROM
1959 TO 1969

4 August 1959
212 Hessel Blvd.
Champaign, Illinois

Dear Mr. Burke,

For some years now I have been at work on a study of your literary theory and critical, to be entitled *The Rhetoric of Rebirth*; and now as I drive towards the completion of the study, towards the completion of the fifth and last chapter, dealing primarily with that perpetually "forthcoming" *A Symbolic of Motives*, I am getting a little uneasy about that book, for though I am fairly certain what will be in it, I am not positive, and, of course, I have no idea as to what order the various published "fragments" of the book will assume when the book is put in final form. Beyond this, I have no idea as to what as yet unpublished material will be included in the book: you have long promised us a systematic and detailed study of Coleridge (promise made in PLF), a detailed and systematic study of Freud (promise made in one of the essays published since 1950), a detailed study of one of Hemingway's stories (promise made in Postscript to the Negative), the rest of the poetics and theory of tragedy, of which you say the "Oresteia" essay is a part (and of what I assume "the Poetic motive," "Catharsis" and "Symbol and Association" are parts).

So what I am really asking about is (1) when on earth is that perpetually "forthcoming" *A Symbolic of Motives* forthcoming; will it be soon enough so that I can wait for it before I complete my book (which will be, if I don't wait, this fall, early); if the Symbolic is not forthcoming soon, would it be too much trouble for you to send me a list of exactly what will be included in the book, and some idea of the structure of the book. Since the final chapter of my study is to deal with "the dramatistic theory of literature," and will attempt to systematize what I take to be your final view of literature, I would be mightily disturbed to find out, after I was done, that some crucial part of the whole had been omitted by me through a sin of omission.

Since I have invested nearly six years in you and this book and have, contrary to what you are always saying in some footnote or other, read all your works through at least three times, usually more, and have, even, rather quixotically, read you through backwards just to check your "entelechy," I would be most appreciative if you would write answering my questions about the Symbolic, even sending whatever material you think might be helpful to me.

Just to satisfy your curiosity, my credentials are as follows: I did all of my graduate work at the University of Michigan where, though not under the direction of your old friend and admirer, Austin Warren, I wrote a doctoral dissertation on your literary theory and critical practice (1956). Presently, I am an instructor in the English department at the University of Illinois, which seems to be some kind of Burke center. Though I have not met Miss Hochmuth, and never knew Miss Holland, I have read their work on you; I do, however know Kerker Quinn, and have promised to review the Symbolic for him if and when it ever comes out.

I do hope this letter will reach you at a time when you are not so busy (say with the proofs for *A Symbolic of Motives* or one of the other three or four books you seem to be writing simultaneously) that you cannot find time to answer it; meanwhile, I will continue racing my first child to completion and hope that I will hear from you in time to avoid any really stupid sins of omission or commission.

Sincerely,
William H. Rueckert

Andover, New Jersey
August 8, 1959

Dear Mr. Rueckert,

Holla! If you're uncomfortable, think how uncomfortable I am. But I'll do the best I can by you and the baby.

One trouble is: The damned trilogy has become a tetralogy: Grammar (built around "substance"); Rhetoric (built around "identification"); Poetics (built around "catharsis"); Ethics (built around the negative, as per my articles in *Quarterly Journal of Speech*, 52-53; my article on *Faust*, in *Chicago Review*, Spring 55 also indicates a bit of this, as does my piece on language in *Modern Philosophies and Education*, edited by Nelson B. Henry). One problem in Poetics volume is to decide whether I should leave it in one sequence, or also insert various incidental pieces (which otherwise I'll collect in a separate volume). The Ethics also is scheduled to contain a batch of "devices" that I never published except for a few samples on the pages I have marked in the enclosed offprint from the *Journal of General Education*. (Incidentally, an excellent book by Erving Goffman, presenting material of this sort from the more exclusively sociological angle, has recently appeared in the Anchor series. Title: *The Presentation of Self in Everyday Life*. He refers to some of my similarly minded items in the Rhetoric.)

The unfortunate thing has been that some other possibilities turned up—and I couldn't resist tracing them down. (along the lines indicated in my article in *Daedalus*, Summer 1958).

I'll try to ship off to you some multilithed copies of three things I did at the Center for Advncd Std in Bhvrl Scncs some time back. (First drafts of Poetics, and the items on Genesis and St. Augustine mentioned in the *Daedalus* excerpt. They're all lousy with misprints. I'll try to correct some of the worst, but I may not get around to that. And in any case, though you're welcome to quote anything, please check with me finally. For some of the errors are quite misleading.)

Yes, all the things you mention shd. go into the Poetics, though I shall probably use but a part of the "Symbol and Association" item. That stuff in Accent on Imitation also figures. The Coleridge article is written, but developed an extra angle which I still have to revise.

At the moment, for a vacation (home after a bustling year), I have been indulging myself, puttering around with an article called "Body and Mind." I don't know just where it fits—but in general I think of it as a sequel to the Q. Jrnl of Sp articles. I'm asking just where "body" figures and just where "words" figure in this business of being a symbol-using animal. I mean: I'm trying to work out a *dialectic* of such comings and goings, though not wholly unaware of its necessary limitations, even at best. I hope to get that finished during the dog days, then to do the final bits on the Poetics. I hope to do a section on comic catharsis, for instance, though the general lines are already indicated in the Kenyon article. And I hope to make clearer the relation btw. dramatic catharsis and Platonic (dialectic)/transcendence, though I think you'll agree that I have already indicated the main lines in that connection.

Jeez, when I think of how sick of myself I get now and then, I tremble at the thought of your six-year vigil. But inasmuch as every-knock-is-a-boost, maybe we might both survive your ordeal.

(Didn't I meet you somewhere along the line? At Northwestern, maybe?)

The item concerning the variations on the negative in the Hemingway story would probably fit better in the Ethics volume.

As for your proposed title, *The Rhetoric of Rebirth*: it is a good title. However, I'd look upon "rebirth" as itself but a rhetorical term for the principle of development or transformation often called "dialectic." So I take it that what you are dealing with here is the relation btw. Burke's dialectic and his rhetoric. Or am I guilty of o'ersimplificaysh?

If you have spotted the various things scattered around in magazine articles, as you apparently have (and here's hoping you didn't miss "Thanatopsis for Critics: A Brief Thesaurus of Deaths and Dyings," in Oct. 52. no. of Essays in Criticism), and when you get these items I am sending you, I don't think there's anything else essentially, except maybe a few minor points in this article I'm now writing (points mainly concerned more with language in general than with poetics in particular, though the Poetics dimension also figures).

Meanwhile, many thanks for your suffrage and your suffrance. Please give my best regards to Kerker Quinn, and to Miss Hochmuth when you meet her. Also, I wonder if you know Mary Jane Aschner (who teaches, I think, in the Education dept.).

Sincerely,
Kenneth Burke

Maybe I shd. add: I treat the negative under Ethics because of the close relation btw. character and the thou-shalt-not's. And inasmuch as the negative is a wholly linguistic invention, I take it that the keystone of the entire edifice is No.

You also mention Freud. Some of my material on that subject will probably be used in this "Body and Mind" item. Recently I reviewed Philip Rieff's book on Freud. I liked it a lot, but to my great disgust I never got around to saying the things I wanted to say about it. Other things I have read recently on the same subject are: Norman Brown's *Life Against Death* and Erich Wellisch's *Isaac and Oedipus*. Wellisch would fit with the Oresteia material, Brown's chapter on Luther would go well with the material on "The Thinking of the Body" (in the Ms I am sending you, though a bit of it showed in the Kenyon piece on Catharsis).

If you are writing to Austin Warren, please do give him my friendliest greetings.

Andover, New Jersey
September 10, 1959

Dear Mr. Rueckert,

I started to write you on Labor Day—but in the light of the race btw. your book and your papahood, I decided against such a conceit. Also, as one who is five times a father, ten times a grandfather, and now somewhat belatedly an advocate of birth control, along with a firm, ill-natured conviction that publishing houses are the death of literature, I am quite confused about all such matters.

I haven't yet read Lewis's new book, but I know his general slant. He was at Bennington for a time. And only a short time ago I suicidally o'ercaroused at his place in Princeton. (he now teaches at Rutgers.)

I'm sorry you didn't turn up at Indiana.

Somewhere, I have extra copies of my "Notes on the Litry Life." I'll send you one if I run across them. It's just a bit of cavorting, an after-dinner talk.

As for your problem about titles: Why not use 'em both—as title and subtitle?

I'd be much interested in seeing your review of Knox's book, and a copy of the talk you mention.

I enclose copies of some Flowerishes you might be interested in taking a glance at.

But to the grind, while my desk is a shambles, and developments internationally seem to be Laos-ing things up.

Sincerely,

K.B.

Kenneth Burke

Bennington College
Bennington Vermont
1/7/60

Dear WHR, or Witcher, or punwise, Wager,

Begad, I survived this term. But how about the next? (It begins on March 8th. In the meantime, I have to contend only with my own dirty in-fighting. And on that score I'm a killer.)

I was bepuzzed to hear about Lewis's vast silence. And I'll be much interested in hearing whom they turned to next.

Meanwhile, many thanks for the MS. (Incidentally, under separate cover I am sending you some post-mortem items that I thought you might care to consider in a footnote.)

My book on The Rhetoric of Religion (sic) is scheduled to appear on June 14th, under the sign of the Beckoning Beacon. Though they have also signed a contract for a paperback ATH, I don't know when they plan to issue it. If all goes as planned, I'll sign another document soon for the Poetics material (though I'm being a bit coy, since other notions keep cropping up, so that I can't be sure of getting the damned thing finished by any specified date.)

I find myself all steamed up about a kind of Ave Atque Vale course I want to give next term, on "presuppositions and implications," starting perhaps with some stuff on Poe.

Do send word when you know how your course eventuated. And the book, too, naturally! And know of best regards for 1961 (I see some great observer noted that the year looks the same when turned upside down. Obviously that's the kind we need.)

Sincerely,

K.B.

19 May 1960

Dear Mr. Burke:

The book is at last done—about a month ago—and my son did indeed beat me by quite a few months, for he was born on 7 September (labor day, so you could have punned after all). The book is presently being typed; a colleague will then read it; I will then make final revisions and submit it to the press here. If they accept it, it will be published in about a year—which would mean either next spring or a year from this fall, probably the latter.

Would you care to read it before publication? I ask for a variety of reasons. My own conclusions about your work are, as you might imagine, fairly well fixed at settled at this point, but if you really thought that in some of the things I say I am absolutely wrong or wrong headed, I might certainly consider some modification. Or, should you care to comment at places where you feel I am wrong or the treatment inadequate, I would certainly include such comments in the notes. The other reason I hesitate to mention, but since it might interest you, I guess I will. The person you cite as your "authoritative" spokesman in the "Modern Philosophies and Education'" piece, Marie Hochmuth, happened, by a fluke, which was none of my doing, to read the talk I gave on your work here last year to the department. I submitted it to *Accent* for publication and, before they rejected it as too general, one of the editors gave it to Miss Hochmuth to read. To put it mildly, she tore it to pieces, partly because she either did not know or forgot why it was written and to whom it was addressed, and partly because she seems not to have read those parts of the Poetics which you have so far published. I have no bone to pick with Miss Hochmuth, though her attack on my talk seems to me unjustified and in many places either wrong or ignorant. Perhaps she has only concerned herself with your rhetorical theories and has ignored the poetics. I will send you a copy of the talk as soon as my typist gets to it and you can judge for yourself. Miss Hochmuth also refers *Accent* to George Knox's book as being good. So I will send you my review of that book (I enclose it). Anyway, all of this having happened, you might like to read the book before I let it go, finally, to a publisher. If so, let me know and I will send a copy when I have made my final revisions.

Another matter came up while I was finishing the book which I think might interest you. It occurred to me that a Kenneth Burke reader might be a very useful kind of book to have around and that some commercial publisher might be interested. If I did the book, I would obviously select in accordance with my own interpretation of your work as I present it in my book; in fact, a Reader would be a nice companion to my study for I could include in it the main texts I discuss and essays where you apply the theories and methods I discuss. It would offer the public an opportunity of having representative selections from all your work gathered together in a single volume. By all your work, I mean stories, poems, reviews, literary pieces, and the like, arranged so as to suggest your range, your development, and the coherency of Dramatism itself. I have not decided definitely to go ahead with the Reader, partly because I want to get the book off my back first; but I thought I would consult you about it and see (1) if you approved, and (2) if you had any publisher in mind. Is Prentice Hall to publish the rest of the Tetralogy? Might they be interested. I thought of the various publishers of paperbacks who would do such a book as one of their originals: Anchor, Meridian, Grove, and the like. I also thought of Hermes, Chicago and Harvest (or was it Vintage) might be interested since they published you in paperback editions. Let me know what you think.

For the moment, that seems to be all. I apologize for the long silence. A first child seems to have so absorbed and occupied me, I let many things slide. I also apologize for not sending the two pieces, especially since you so kindly sent me what I asked for so promptly.

Sincerely,
William H. Rueckert

Andover, New Jersey
June 18, 1960

Dear Mr. Rueckert,

Felicitations on your double papahood. I have always found it helpful to shift back and forth between the two kinds of troubles, each the cure for the other.

As for my nebbing in the book: I think it would be better if, with my usual shrinking-violet self, I demurely let you have your say as you would have it.

Judging by your review of Knox's book, I gather that you are aiming to spin things from a generating principle. And that seems to me ideal. You may in general have in mind the same generating principle as I do, you may have a different one. But I'd like to neb out, and wait and see. I liked your approach to the problem, as indicated in your review, though I do feel that Knox merited a bit more charity than you granted him. And in any case, here's earnestly hoping that your vast labors will be rewarded at least with publication.

Meanwhile, I do hope that you will send me a copy of the moot talk you mention. Some time back, an editor asked me to suggest the name of someone who might contribute an article on my work *in general*. I had thought that you might be the person, and that this article might be the right item. But then there followed the Long Silence (the which I wholly understand, since such are my ways, too). If you will send me the item, along with permission to submit it to said editor in case I think it would meet his particular requirements, I'll gladly, etc.

As for a Burke Reader: It has been suggested. And in case you continue to feel like doing it, your low-down on my Self might prove that you are the one to consult. As for Prentice-Hall, jeezoos keerist, no! I finally got clear of that outfit (a copy of the correspondence might amuse you at some later date). Hermes would be out, since the mazuma is lacking. But there are other possibilities, though for the time being they should be allowed to mellow. ("mellow" : "ripen without rotting.")

Meanwhile, I'm sorry to say: In putting my Logology stuff into final shape, besides an introductory section built around nine analogies btw. logology and theology, I have done a (tentatively) final section, a "Prologue in Heaven" detailing a dialogue btw. The Lord and Satan. (The intermediate sections are the Aug. and Genesis items, slightly revised.) The form is like that of the first long essay in PLF, followed by the "satyrplay" on "Electioneering in Psychoanalysia." But there's a diplomatic problem in this case, since my disportings might seem somewhat on the side of sacrilege. I'm still not sure. But in any case, I want to make it clear that the dialogue between The Lord and Satan in purely imaginary.

Sincerely,
K.B.

[Postcard, postmarked June 20, 1960]

Dear Mr. Rueckert,
I meant to add:
I wonder if you have seen the section on "Kenneth Burke's Theory" in *Roots for a New Rhetoric,* by Daniel Fogarty, S.J., Teachers College Studies in Education, Columbia. And the chapter, "Kenneth Burke's

Terminological Medium of Exchange," in *Psychoanalysis & American Literary Criticism,* by Louis Fraiberg (Wayne State U. Press). And if there's time to use it, I must send you a copy of an article on folklore and poetics I'm publishing in J. of A. Folklore this wint.

K.B.

23 June 1960

Dear Mr. Burke:

I am delighted with your decision not to neb in the book. I thought I had better ask, though.

I am now putting the thing in final shape: revising the first part of the first chapter, over which I have broken my brains about ten times; meditating on the introduction; making minor stylistic revisions; doing the footnotes and bibliography, and the like. There is still time to use stuff in the fifth chapter, so if you have an available copy, I would indeed like to see the piece on folklore and poetics. I aim to have the book out of my hands and to the press by the end of the summer, so if some new point appeared in the folklore piece, I would have time to work it into the final chapter.

The talk is back from the typist and, after proof reading, I will ship it off to you. Do what you like with it. The talk has (1) the limitations of a talk addressed to a mixed audience, most of whom knew little about you and (2) the limitations of being the agency by which I was given my trial by fire before the department. If you think said editor might be interested, by all means submit it. I will try to make sure the copy you get is clean.

Fraiberg and I happened to be in graduate school together and to write our dissertations under the same man (Norman Nelson). Then I thought he was somewhat wooden and, save for a couple of startling insights, think his essay on you somewhat wooden. He seems to have a rather limited or excessively rigid notion of what constitutes an affinity between your work and that of Freud and other psychoanalysts. He seems, also, to be unfamiliar with your work after 1941; and to have worked only with your specific references to Freud rather than with your system as a whole. Yes, I probably was a little hard on Knox; I was actually much harder at first, but the editor of JEGP toned the whole review down. Perhaps I have invested too much and have the blindness that goes with over-commitment. I tried hard to be fair to Knox; but the books still strikes me as incoherent, ripped off as it were too soon before it had settled into a coherent interpretation. My other objection to Knox's book (not in the review) was that he seemed critically naive, really unaware of the major critical issue raised by your work or, for that matter, by anyone's critical system. Have you read R. Williams' review, in *Criticism*, I (Winter, 1959), 80-82? He is more unkind than I. Or M. Worth's review, in *Prairie Schooner*, XXXIII (1959), 2-3, where she talks of your "peeping thomism"? Maybe I'll ask whoever publishes my book to send Knox a review copy so he can have his say in return.

I have not read the Fogerty piece, but will. I didn't even know of it.

A couple of technicalities. I have used material from the Genesis, the Augustine, and the Poetics pieces you sent me. I do not think there are any misprints in any of the passages I have used, but do you want me to copy them off and send them to you to check? In the bibliography, I have referred to these essays simply as unpublished material, though parts of the Genesis piece and portions of the poetics draft have been published. In the bibliography, I described the Poetics tract as an "incomplete draft" of *A Symbolic of Motives*. Is that Correct? A couple of other questions: Could you tell me the date when you delivered the talks on Logology at Drew so I can at least place the Genesis and Augustine pieces chronologically; and, if the publisher agrees, I would like to include as a frontispiece (or whatever it is called) a picture of you, preferably the one which was on the flyleaf of the Whitman book you contributed to. Could you tell me how I might get a reproducible copy of that picture—or do you object to it? The picture seems to fit my image of you.

I would still like to [do] the Burke reader but will let it "ripen without rotting" for a while.

Sincerely,
William H. Rueckert

Andover, New Jersey
July 20, 1960

Dear WHR,

Now, after the three talks at Georgetown ("Drama," "Dramatism," "Logology") and a week-end of charming but permissive parents (with correspondingly uncharmingly permitted offspring), I am happy to say that there seem to be no more major assignments until school resumes in the autumn.

I finally got around to sending your piece to McWms. Though I had minor bleats, all seemed to me excellent in its main lines. So I'm hoping that he will take up from there. (He is usually away at this time of year, so developments may be belated.) I have asked him to get in touch with you direct. Ideally, however, I yearned for a section briefly characterizing the slant or contents of each book.

I trust that, by now, you have recd. the folklore-vs.-poetics piece from Stanley Hyman, who saluted my formalism but has written a folklorist attack upon the book itself (a review to be published in *Commentary*). I don't yet know what he has said, though I expect to receive a copy of his asseverations soon.

Yes, Fraiberg seems to have stopped too soon. But in one notable particular I can't reasonably object. I am only now getting around to attempts at a systematic distinction btw. psychoanalytic and Dramatistic concepts of "symbolic action" (or rather, a *head-on* distinction btw. 'em)—and I guess that that's my job rather than hisn. In any case, psychoanalytic rhetoric is so much milder than the political rhetoric I once used to suffer when accused of heresy, by comparison I almost felt as though Fraiberg and I were pals. What a gentle hatchet man he is, as compared with a reviewer like Hook!

I missed the lady who referred to my "peeping thomism." I must look that up, and see what legs she has to stand on. In the meantime, wd. say: the concept, like the clitoris, is a cute invention.

If you feel that the quotations from the multilithed pieces make sense, I see no need to type them out for further consultation, etc. Recently, I submitted to Beacon (who had evinced interest) revised versions of the Aug. and Genesis items, preceded by an essay "On Words and The Word" and followed by a "Prologue in Heaven," a dialogue between The Lord and Satan concerning The Lord's prescience with regard to what he was in store for, if he carried out his plan to create a symbol-using animal. I'll try, before long, to send you copies of the introductory essay and the concluding "satyr play." The Augustine and Genesis talks I gave on April 30th and May 9th, 1957. The one "On Words and The Word" was given late in 1956. I can dig out the exact date if you need it. A trip to Florida intervened, I recall. I haven't yet heard how Beacon fares with these items. (There are some prior morbidities to do with the fact that they want to publish a paperback edition of ATH—and the state of the negotiations with Mrs. Ligda is beyond my confused abilities to fershtay, though I hope that things will be cleared up soon.)

As to the picture you ask about: I lent the original to an outfit in NYC—and to date I haven't succeeded in getting it back. But I'm still trying, and may recover it after all. On that point, more later. I think your suggested placing of the Poetics ms. would be ok.

And now, to wind up with some hit-and-run comments on your highly competent essay:

P. 2. 4 lines from bottom. "language becomes the ultimate reduction." This could be misleading, if the reader forgets your earlier point about *animality.* However, I see that, on 3tp, you add the necessary corrective!

3btm. Your statement slights fact that I wd. *start* with hortatory negative and *arrive at* the propositional negative. Your way of saying things suggests the opposite route.

p. 4, middle of page. "are graded," etc. Didn't something go wrong with his sentence?

After fooling with "hierarchic" and "hierarchical" for a while, I made the emancipatory discovery that "hierarchal" and "hierarchally" sound less like hiccoughs. Hence, I'd prefer "hierarchal psychosis."

8 btm. "an imitation of the possession or ownership tension" is literally correct, but sounds a bit sociologese stylistically.

12tp. "that poets are blessed with a superior way of knowing." I'm a bit wishy-washy on that point. My primary category for the discussion of poetry is *action* rather than *knowledge.* And I believe that, even in the very act of symbolizing something correctly, a poet can be astoundingly the victim of his failure to see what he has said. Somnambulism takes hold of us all, including the poet. And sometimes we are awake at the point where he is asleep.

14. "Burke has almost literally derived an image of man and his ways from literature itself," etc. In my early books, yes. But in my later books, I have tried to modify this position somewhat. For I decided that it opened me to the charge of "aestheticizing the non-aesthetic." My three talks at Georgetown last week were built somewhat with this problem in mind. I tried to show what *transformations* are necessary in one's terminology as one goes from "drama" to "Dramatism," and so, on to "logology" (my cut into the "mythology" line). My "logological" definition of man (as per back jacket of new edition of ATH) is meant to be wholly *literal,* whereas the early slogan of "poets all" was metaphorical. I

should *contrast* it with my treatment of "perspective" in P&C. The step in general is from "metaphor as perspective" to "presuppositions and implications of a terminology." Incidentally, I have noted somewhere: the Bible's view of man is "bookish."

15tp. "that poetry must take over the functions previously performed by religion." Not quite. I have tried to show that religious coordinates give us insight into poetic processes. But, for better or worse, poetry holds out neither the absolute promises nor the absolute threats of religion.

21btm. Of Venus and Adonis. "An interpretation more remote to the facts of the poem can hardly be imagined." Right. But I should say in my defense I picked this poem precisely because I had always read it in terms of sexual courtship. In fact, I still remembered my horny hours when I first came upon it as an adolescent. So I thought I'd try the most unlikely case of all, to see how it might yield socioanagogically.

22. "the principle of hierarchy ... is what he starts from and ends with." In one sense, I wholly agree with this statement. In another sense, I should build *formally* from my theory of form as the arousing and fulfilling of expectations (with the stress upon hierarchy arising when I tracked down the implications of this definition).

Though perhaps I am not the one to judge, I think that your essay is quite clear and comprehensive. And the few comments I have offered are not important, so could be ignored—but they occurred to me as I read, so I put them down.

Here's hoping that McWilliams finds your pages useful for his purposes. Meanwhile, many thanks indeed for your skilled exposition.

[Carbon of letter to Kenneth Burke from Carey McWilliams, Editor, The Nation, sent to William Rueckert.]

July 26, 1960

Dear Mr. Burke:

Thanks very much indeed for sending us the article by William Rueckert. Although it is a brilliant analysis, it presents some problems because of its length. However, I want to hold it until Bob Hatch gets back from vacation so that we can discuss it in terms of possibly using it in the fall book issue.

Reading it makes me want to see his book. I am anxious to learn what he has to say about how your work relates to various aspects of the American tradition—what it was about your antecedents and background that prompted you to take up the lines of inquiry that you have so ingeniously developed.

Thanks again for keeping my original inquiry in mind.

With you I will probably be voting for the Vegetarian candidate come November.

Best wishes,
Carey McWilliams
Editor

Mr. Kenneth Burke
Andover, New Jersey

P.S. Mr. Rueckert: I assume that you have no objection if I hold the piece for a few weeks. When is the book going to be published, and who is doing it?
C. McW.

Andover, New Jersey
July 29, 1960.

Dear WHR,

Though McWilliams may have written you, just to be safe I'm dashing off a quickie to report a letter I recd. from him.

"Brilliant analysis … presents some problems because of its length" … wd. hold until Hatch gets back from vacation, "so that we can discuss it in terms of possibly using it in the fall book issue." Then: "Reading it makes me want to see his book. I am anxious to learn what he has to say about how your work relates to various aspects of the American tradition—what it was about your antecedents and background that prompted you to take up the lines of inquiry that you have so ingeniously developed."

Jeez. Here's betting twenty to one that your book doesn't answer his question! The answer would have to deal with the ways in which a sickly kid raised in a rundown suburb of Pittsburgh and with an almost hysterical fear of death developed pig-headedness and got bumped, and has always been a mixture of asseveration and uncertainty.

I trust that you have received the essay on Folklore that I asked Stanley Hyman to forward to you. I'd be grateful for the return of it when you are through with it. (Or no, come to think of it, I guess I don't need it now. I'll let you know if I need it later. It's to appear in Journal of Am. Folklore late this year.)

I still haven't been able to get an answer from the outfit that has the photograph—but I go on trying. I don't yet have free copies of the other two essays ("On Words and The Word" and "Prologue in Heaven").

Have just been reading *The Power of Satire,* by Robert C. Elliott. It's a good book on which to hang a sermon.

Best wishes.

Sincerely,
K.B.

Bennington College
Bennington, Vermont
10/20/60

Dear WHR,

My salute to the finished book. And as for the dog, I guess I'm enough of a cynic to "identify with" dogs (as they say in sociologese). Indeed, at times when I am on especially familiar terms with myself, I speak of me as "Kennel Bark."

I finally pried that picture out of the outfit that had borrowed it. So I should be able to let you have it when you need it. But I have another use for it in the meantime.

You are welcome to the three multilithed items. (You might do as the University library at Indiana did. I gave them a set, and later I learned from one of my students that they were being used for scratch paper. But the staff had only worked partway through one, and he got the other two.) As for poetry-folklore item, I could use that—so, if convenient, would you please return that item?

Any time you cared to list a typical set of resistances from your Studententum, I'd be most interested in seeing it. Kicks are always helpful. It's the silent and inert who raise the trouble for one's asseverations.

Q: Am I o'erladen with toil? A: I most decidedididly am.
Meanwhile, best luck (and what a messy page!)

Sincerely,

K.B.

Bennington College
Bennington, Vermont
B.C. 1/30/61 A.D.

Dear WHR,

Helndamnaysh! I'm sorry to learn of your vexations with regard to your problem-child. It occurred to me that, in a sense, you are in double jeopardy with a book like that. First, you encounter resistance from readers who resist me. And next, if you find a reader who is favorably disposed towards me, he may have own ideas as to how the job "should be" done.

Also, you seem to have felt that, once you had finished the book, the only thing still to be done would be to show it to a publisher and let him publish it. Yet it isn't often, surely, that one's first book is taken by the first outfit that has a look at it.

And for God's sake, even as a conceit, pass up that outlaw thought about the "hidden tape recorder"! Fantasies of that sort haint good for the soul.

I doubt whether Beacon would be a good place at the moment. But they have now signed me up for the ATH paperback and the Logology hard-cover (publication date June 14th). They are willing to sign for the Poetics material now, but I don't want to sign until I am nearer to my last final definitive decisions about the material—for otherwise my damned contrariness may lead me to work on everything else under the sun but that. Also, they have expressed a willingness to get out a book a year, if I go ahead and clear up the other stuff now in its 2/3 stage. If, after a couple of my projects, they are not bankrupt, and your Ms is still looking for a home, that might be the time to knock at their door. I doubt whether the time is ripe now, as regards any out-and-out commercial publisher. But use your own judgment, in case you'd like to try 'em anyhow.

McWms should have let you know months ago, one way or the other. And I think that you should certainly write and ask him, sweetly, what the heck. The ideal article for *his* purposes, I think, would be along the lines of the recipe you give in your first set of "objections."

In the meantime, here's hoping that your trials of authorship are being lightened by the joys of pedagogy. I shall most certainly be interested in hearing how your charges conducted themselves. You do seem to have given them a good work-out. Kill-or-cure basic training, like the eight weeks one of my sons has just been through, in the army? Leaving them more trim than they're ever likely to be again, all the rest of their lives?

Circa half of my precious winter offage is over. I have taken many notes, but finished *nothing*. I have commissions for two articles on which I could really make some money (at minimum of ten cents a word); so, of course, my godam ornery Ucs has got me to working on everything but those. And the problem is still more diabolically complicated by the fact that, as soon as I sit down with a firm decision to work on one of them, I begin to think of the other, and that's enough to take the steam out of my efforts on either.

But I have a chance to get this mailed, so I desist. Best greetings— and felicitations indeed on the charming young-un!

Sincerely,

K.B.

Andover, New Jersey
August 25, 1961.

Dear Wm Aitch Are,

Jeez, 'twas the merry month of May when last our paths crossed.

You were regretting that you had tried to see Burke-trying-to-sell-Burke. Or, as you put it, you had put "all your brains in an unmarketable basket."

As a student of catharsis, I can only remind you: If anything goes wrong, you can blame it on me. So what more do you want?!

Meanwhile, wd. say: I wish you had sent me the report of your class. Naturally, I was much interested.

In particular I was interested in the problem of your best student, about whom you wrote: "The paper would, I think, have been a joy to you simply because of the skill with which some of your central ideas and methods were applied; it would have brought you up short as well,

I think, for it also illustrated some of the shortcoming of so thorough an analysis as your theory and method encourages. Some of his remarks were so thorough, so involved, so involuted, so concerned with the dialectics of guilt and purgation that you could not see the poem for the analysis."

That had me worried, for one major reason: I wondered whether you were going at my approach correctly. The *first* thing I require of any analysis is that the student give us the from-what, through-what, to-what of each item he considers. This admonition should in itself be enough to make sure that the poem doesn't get lost in the analysis. (I mention the point in PLF. And I think I already sent you my sample analysis of Joyce's *Portrait*. My essays on *Julius Caesar* and *Othello* should also illustrate this matter.)

Ennihow, here's hoping that all goes well with you. My *Rhetoric of Religion* (several parts of which you already saw in earlier drafts) has now been printed. (Official publication date: Sept. 8.) Somebody ought to importune you to review it.

I am now striving valiantly to finish my Poetics by the end of the year. Problem is to work in a lot of new stuff I did last term at Bennington (along with my revision of the earlier material). A week or so ago, I was verbalizing in Chicago, and now I'm back with the self-wrestling.

Here's hoping that you're positively rotten with success.

Sincerely,
K.B.

The Nation
333 Sixth Avenue
New York 14, N.Y.
October 20, 1961

Dear Mr. Rueckert:

I'm afraid it is true that we won't use your essay on Burke. I have read it several times and several times have been on the point of writing you to suggest ways of condensing it to the scope of our magazine. But I don't really believe it can be done and have therefore repeatedly put it aside. This, I know, is discourteous and I apologize.

On the other hand, I would very much like to have from you a review of the forthcoming book. This might run to 1000 words and could perhaps embrace at least an outline of what you say in the longer piece.

The problem with Burke is that explanations of his system become almost as rigorous as the system itself. I don't know how this can be overcome but it makes difficulties for a magazine of general readership.

Sincerely yours,
Robert Hatch
Literary Editor

Mr. William H. Rueckert
212 Hessel Blvd.
Champaign, Illinois
rh:ms

Andover, New Jersey
December 9, 1961.

Dear Bill Rueckert,

My God, the WHR family has had its fill of troubles. May all by now be peace and placidity once more. And may your son also get free of that dreadful post-Manichaean heresy, the contra-logical belief in the extra-symbolic existence of the negative. But it is, alas, only too true that psychogenic illnesses, among which asthma is often included (I incline to think, correctly) are clear evidence of the ways in which man's greatest invention can come to operate troublesomely. But I can be doubly sympathetic because I have some kind of respiratory attacks that make me fight so hard for breath, I begin to fear that I might split apart my lungs. I get them sometimes after several hours of insomnia. Alky is a remedy of sorts, but what will remedy the remedy? I have a theory that, if about once a week, I unwind with Nembutal, then I can start over, and only gradually get myself tied into knots again. The regimen works somewhat. (Perhaps as a hangover of my early training in Christian Science, I try every way possible to avoid taking any medicine *regularly*. Every damned one of them, I am certain, builds up troubles in one spot while easing them in another. Also, although not knowing it for a fact, I take it for a sound rule of thumb that medicos get cutbacks from pharmacies for the dopes they prescribe, they're so/not too modest about trying things. If I'm wrong in this notion, then please don't set me right. For I shall lose my faith in human nature. However, I naturally also take it for granted that such a rule of thumb would not apply in all cases, and is rather on the ambulance-chasing side of the profession.)

And jeez, I'm sorry to hear that your Ms still suffers from acute Burke disease. (I wonder, by the way if the thing you sent to The Nation got lost, and they're afraid to say so lest you charge them a million dollars for negligence. Again, you see, I reveal my profound faith in human nature.) And I'm sorry to hear that Champaign seems to you rather like flat near-beer. Heck, insofar as you get a chance to teach what you want to teach, is there really any major beef to be registered? But in any case, it's good to know that thoughts on E. B. White have brought you a New Sunniness. And, as regards the entanglements of analysis, it is true, alas, that anything can serve as a way into everything. But though analytic procedure is by definition piecemeal, it must also have its corresponding modes of synthesis (a kind of synthesis that is intrinsic to the resources of *categorizing* and *attitudinizing*). I wonder whether you happen to have seen my splotch anent concerns of this sort in the Oct. number of Poetry. (Doesn't all summarization, as when saying what *kind* of thing something is, automatically serve to put Humpty Dumpty together again, so far as the requirements of our bizz are concerned?)

Yes, I'd be much interested in your wife's elucubrations on Whitman. In the light of his leanings, I should think that his views of the Fairsex short-changed them a bit. (Incidentally, I have three bleats on Whitman: the item in the volume edited by Hindus, the pages near the beginning of ATH, and a batch of notes which I have used for lectures but have not yet written up into an article. The notes develop farther the sort of things I took up in the Hindus collection. They are an early concern with such notions of "prophesying-after-the-event as I discuss in the piece in Oct. *Poetry.* I figger out how Whitman's poetry "ought to be," in the light of his method. Then I check my "prophecies" by consulting the text—and, surprise! they prove to have been correct. Roughly, I'd assume that Woman for Whitman was the mamma type—and when he thinks of women as sweeties, they'd tend to fade into his "democratic" delight in the thoughts of gents as sweeties.)

Gossip column: My friend Stanley Hyman writes me that there's a recently published book by one Robt. E. Lane, the Liberties of Wit (Yale), dealing with various of us with varying pluses and minuses. I have been shopping around in Daniel Aaron's Writers on the Left—and it seems to me a quite decent effort to get things straight whereas discussions of that era are usually trying to twist things one way or another. René Wellek's reference to me on p. 109 of his article on lit. crit. (in autumn number of Yale Rev.) goaded me to lay aside my book and write a long, unwieldy answer. Though I wrote it without hopes of publication, I sent a copy to the editor, John Palmer, and he has written saying that he may be able to print it in the spring issue. I just got wind of an article on "Covenant Theology," in Commentary for July. It looks as though it may be fittable by me into such speculations as in RR on Genesis; so I have ordered a copy, in hopes. I have done a bit of barnstorming lately, and have some more scheduled for spring. Shall probably be living near Princeton during Jan-Feb-March, though not in connection with the University. Haven't yet seen a single line on RR in the reviews, but I know of some items that have been done or are on the way. I begin seriously to doubt whether I shall meet my self-imposed deadline for completing the revision of my Poetics material. (I had vowed to get it done by Dec. 31st, 11:59 P.M.) Just went to a doctor and found that my blood-pressure is up again. In some respects, final revision can do one more damage than first drafts. It's a continual forcing oneself to go slow when one wants to race ahead. Hence the e'er-present invitation to blow one's top.

Meanwhile, best regards indeed—and may family and projects flourish.

Sincerely,
K.B.

31 January 1962

Dear Burke,

Thanks, first of all, for the two letters—loot letters they should probably be called; I have not yet heard from either of the giveaway groups yet, but should hear within a week from the ACLS and in April from the G people. Apologies, second of all, for the l-o-n-g silence, but I have —quite literally—been working my ass off, usually in the same rather hard chair, first of all revising the manuscript from beginning to end for the U. of Minnesota Press and, monomaniac that I am, writing the first sixty pages of the Wescott book. The manuscript was finished around the first of November, has been copyedited at the Press, is now on its way back to me to be checked over, then goes back to them, then off to the printer. They are apparently now going to get it into print with all dispatch, though I do not know when. I have signed the contract, and aside from all the proof reading that remains, have only to get all my permissions to be done with it. I can't say that I am sorry—to be done with it—though I am happy to have written it (even though sorry it is not as good as it would be if I started now to write it anew) and grateful to you for having written the books that contributed so largely to my education—said without sentimentality, I hope, and anyway, sentimental or not, it is true. I keep forgetting that you have not read any part of the book, so at least I have that to look forward to—or maybe it is the other way around, though perhaps that is really the final blow: after having written all that stuff, then to have to read about it.

I have held off writing hoping either to hear that you were back in Andover or waiting to get a warm Florida address. But with the Press moving so quickly, I'm getting antsy about the permissions, and so will trust the letter to the mails and assume that it will find you. I'm confused as to who I write to get permission to quote from material which you have copyrighted. Specifically, I have quoted from *Towards a Better Life, Counter-Statement,* Second Edition, *Permanence and Change,* Revised Edition, and *A Book of Moments,* and *The Rhetoric of Religion.* You hold the copyright to all of these books. Can you give me permission to quote from them, or am I to write to Harcourt, Brace, Hermes, and Beacon for it? I have also quoted from *Poetics, Dramatistically Considered,* but I believe you gave me permission in one of your letters to do so. If you are, as they say, the permission granting agent, the Press wishes to have a particular form signed, which I will send you. If not, then I write to the various publishers, which would seem like the sensible way to handle it.

We are all reasonably well here and hopeful of getting some of that loot money so we can get the hell out of this place for a year, probably to the West Coast, for a long rest in more temperate climates. We are expecting another baby in late February or early March (naturally, since I am trying to write another book) and so are anticipatory. It looks now as if, after my sabbatical, we will (I will, professionally, that is) be leaving this prairie pest hole, for the English Department rather shockingly (since I have done all the work and more than meet their stated requirements) did not promote me to associate professor. Since their attitude toward me has been clear all along, I was shocked (as were all of my friends) but not really surprised, since others before me (good men all, I tell myself) have received the same treatment and have, fortunately for them, left in various states of rage and frustration—not at leaving, but at the place, the department because it says one thing in print and then the HEAD, after having thrown up a murky fog of democratic mumbo jumbo, does as he pleases and has his full professors approve it. Though I am not a vengeful or revengeful person at all, I shall probably devise some subtle professional revenge for the Head, not necessarily because I wanted to stay here—which I didn't really—but because principles have been violated, again and again, and good men (I am not now thinking of myself) have been made to suffer cruelly and immorally. In some ways, my not being promoted was a very good thing, for we will now definitely leave and all of us will be happier for it, for we have never done anything but hate this place, for its geography, for its failure to move in the right direction, or at least in some liberal direction, for its orthodoxy (most members in power are church-going Episcopalians and one is a Baptist who leads revivalist meetings), and for its uncanny ability to lose or fire or attempt to break all of its odd balls, radicals, eccentrics—"trouble makers," it calls them. So much for the "brute realities."

One funny story and then I must go on to the rest of the permissions. One of my students—in fact one of the most brilliant students I ever had—was sent a copy of the Meridian *Grammar and Rhetoric*. He read much of it and went into shock (due to the excitement); he then, like all good converts, started lending the book around, mostly to his teachers in the Russian Department. The result, he reports, was nothing short of sensational. That department here is very "scholastic," conservative and historically oriented. Your two books, apparently, caused a furious and prolonged debate (apparently in the best sense) among the members of the department. As usual, the division was sharp: outrage and excited praise. I have not had a report since the initial uproar, but will report any later developments. In my student, at least, you have someone who read you carefully and uses you intelligently.

I hope you are enjoying or enjoyed the "warm south." We are freezing here.

[signed] Bill R.

Kingston, New Jersey
2/20/62

Dear Bill Rueckert,

This is a quickie to say Thankus most zestfully, as per Other Side.

Have been racing around like an unindignant Fury (than which what could be more unanchored?).

Was glad indeed to get your wife's bright note, with documents. And shall answer ere long. (May I call her Wilhelmina?)

The last I heard from Stanley Hyman, he was getting all set to do a report on your Wolume. He offered to subcontract—but I'm so damned run-ragged, I couldn't negotiate. (Jeez, given the state of the world, mebbe I should admonish that the offer was a wisecrack!)

Meanwhile, would depose: If your book is as to-the-point as that review, then I'm sure that S. Hyman, who is both perceptive and just, will decidedly yea-say.

May Glenn get back (all is still in-the-interim), may the National Psyche expand accordingly, and may the shitty progress Towards Globalism be effectively resumed.

Sincerely,
(signed) K.B.

[Copy of letter to Carey McWilliams, The Nation.]

Box 143
Kingston, N.J.
Feb. 20, 1962

Dear Carey McWilliams,

After much thrashing about, through several nights and across several states, I finally got the opportunity to read Rueckert's review. And bejees, I owe a debt indeed both to you as editor and to him as exegete.

No author could properly ask for a more expert summary of his tangled text. And though I know of other reviews on the way, I am to you indebted for the first statement of my case.

I enclose herewith czch from the Self-Love Department, requesting some issues of the numero (?), to be used for buttonwholing purposes.

Incidentally, I had missed that inside info about me and God. But inasmuch as I sometimes fondly refer to myself as Kennel Bark, I assume that God was putting on dog. (Also, Rueckert once wrote me that he had a dog named "Burkey.") And I could fall back on the middle ages, which treated *any* summarizing work as an *analogy* to the "divine." Ditto, the Platonic Upward Way, towards higher levels of generalization.

* * *

Meanwhile for shame! Even as I write these lines, about me, meself, and I, work comes from the air as regards our astronaut's launching. Is it humanly possible for us in the realm of "action"" and "words," to keep up with the powers of "motion" (this mighty New Birth that may blow us all to hell)?

Physicality, yes. Animality, yes. Symbolicity, yes. But what of Globalism? Can we be equal to that? For most of us, I guess, it's All or None. If my devices have any ultimate value, it should be because they're Towards Globalism (though my studies have convinced me that "Towards" is a shit-word).

In any case, I O U.

Sincerely,
Kenneth Burke

24 February 1962
212 Hessel Blvd.
Champaign, Ill.

Dear Mr. Burke,

Your note that you liked the review (I managed to, I should say, my wife—and she says, no, you may not call her Wilhelmina—managed to —make out the carbon of the letter to McWilliams with breathless intense excitement) has given me great pleasure and satisfaction, more even than the actual publication of it, which was intense, or the unexpected $25 they paid me for it. I was sorry Hatch would not give me 500 more words, for I felt badly about not discussing the rectilinear-cyclical idea (logologic?) which you work out in both the Augustine and Genesis essays. I felt especially bad about this because the reading of the Genesis essay when it first came out produced one of those great synthesizing experiences for me in my own study of your work, and much of it centered around the cycle of terms implicit in any substance-cluster, but especially the Order, Hierarchy, Negative cluster. Oh well, another time, maybe—or perhaps sometime that wretched manuscript of mine will be published and I can have my say there.

About the manuscript—Rueckert's folly, or Rueckert's interrupted verbal drama—the bad luck that has dogged it from the beginning continues. At Minnesota, where it still is, it gathered dust for a great many months (about five, I guess) on the desk of the first reader who just couldn't seem to get around to it—I can't say that I blame him, really—while he settled into a new house, read proof on his own book, etc. and the editor of the press and I exchanged witty notes wondering why it was all taking so long. After SEVEN months, I finally wrote, firmly but nicely, suggesting that it had been rather a long time and perhaps they could set a deadline for that reader and come to a decision one way or the other. (I hope it was not Mr. Hyman, for I respect his work and would value his judgment—so may he be the second, not the first reader.) Anyway, it finally got back from the first reader with a "sketchy but favorable" report, and recently sent to a second reader, and will be reported back to me one way or another in March. The editor at Minnesota wryly suggested that I was lacking somewhat in "maturity,"—i.e., I was an eager, young scholar—for if Burke is for eternity, what difference could a few months make? I didn't point out that if someone didn't hurry up and publish that damn book, I would have to write a whole other chapter to cover the stuff you have just or are about to or will soon publish.

Meanwhile, after fighting our way through most of the fall and the multiple physical maladies that characterized it, we push forward, my son wheezing away, my wife back taking courses, my nervous, aging dog expectant every moment that something wonderful will happen, and me (I?) at the moment, in a great burst of energy, making new verbal dramas, short ones this time, one on "James Joyce and the Morality of Self," one on the symbolism of the wych-elm in Forster's *Howard's End* (I Indexed the term), one coming up on "Symbolic Action in the Heart of Darkness," and another on the early novels of Cozzens, but mostly on *Castaway,* and mostly on purgative function of that work for Cozzens, and mostly on the body as focal motive in Cozzens.

Monday, 26 February

By way of conclusion, the latest (today) report from Minnesota on the manuscript is that it is back from the second reader, but, like the first one, this report is "sketchy" and the director of the press feels that he must have a third report, so, etc., apparently ad infinitum, though they promise "speed."

Assorted concluding remarks. I (also) spent most of Glenn's day with the radio on, in a trance-like state so intense that if I did not have a carbon of it I do not think I would even remember the letter I wrote to Twayne Publishers suggesting that I might be just the man to write one of their volumes in the series on British and American writers (K. A. Porter, I suggested).

I did not make up the rumor about God: it came to me from a rather reliable source, very roundabout, and ultimately directly from Bennington. I always thought it was kind of nice, for true or false, it is (was) true in essence of the stuff you were writing then.

I am in a mild flu-trance at the moment and think it best just to end this. Oh yes, one other thing: I did get some pretty good papers from my honors students last semester, but a change of emphasis in the course (from my study of you to my in progress study of the disguises of fiction) produced a change in the papers so that, though the best ones make use of many ideas and methods of yours, not one of them is a pure application of Burkean ideas and methods. The one that is closest to being pure is so badly written I wouldn't inflict it on anyone. One that is close (purgation and redemption in Faulkner, the women as purgative-redemptive symbols) is also not very well written and I hesitate to send it on. So, though I took the trouble to get carbons this time, I don't really have any papers as good as the two from last year that I mention (the ones on Hart Crane and T. Williams).

Sincerely,
[W.H.R]

Box 143
Kingston, New Jersey
March 1, 1962

Dear Bl Rckrt,

Oof! did my naming propensities get smacked down! So, then it's "nay Wilhelmina."

This is frantically a quickie. (I'm trying to prepare simultaneously for two talks, both nearly upon me, each different—and, as you might expect, I keep taking notes on something aside from both.)

Meanwhile (but psst! don't tell 'em I said so, since I guess this is an ongtra noo sorta thing), Hyman wrote me that he thought the book "excellent" and "told Minnesota to publish it." However, he registered some murmurs (which would probably involved a bit of revision), though the sort of things he mentions look to me as though they could be done rather easily by mere omission or mere specification). By omission I have in mind his reference to some "repetitious" passages. And by specification I have in mind your failure at times to distinguish btw. your illustrations and mine. Changes of the first sort should certainly be made, if he is correct—and promblely he is. And I personally would favor changes of the second sort, as you shd. get credit for whatever is yours. Incidentally, Hyman was obviously the *second* reader. For I know he received the Ms. only recently (a) He is a fast worker. (b) Bennington is having its long winter vacation.

But I am bepuzzed at the thought that they feel the need of still a third reader. Conceivably they might this time be asking for a more specific kind of judgment. For instance: "If the book is accepted, just what particular passages would you want changed, and how?" But I make this suggestion without the slightest inside info, or the slightest idea as to how their press proceeds.

More as soon as poss. For some obscure reason which I both welcome and grumble about, in the last several months I have been receiving a considerably increased no. of requests to lecture, participate in conferences, etc. While greedily accepting most of them, I keep half-hoping that I'll soon fall back into my usual sparse pace, though your review might, in the end, make things even "worse" for me. Just at present, I'm almost nightmarishly tangled—and the nightmares of an insomniac are mussy indeed, particularly the ones when he's wholly awake.

In any case, here's hoping that "Rueckert's Folly" will turn out O.K. after all.

Sincerely,

K.B.

Andover, New Jersey

June 18, 1962

Dear Bill Rueckert,

Never, never before in all my life have I been in such a godam tangle. Every single paper I try to dispose of involves my finding some other pages that got misplaced. I still have to send in expense accounts for various items, mark a set of final exams, acknowledge various kicks, compliments, and inquiries, etc. And the mere attempt to set my room in order, so that it doesn't look like the portrait of acute mental unbalance, will in itself take several days.

So, what do I do? Your letter arrives, I pour myself a drink of bourbon, push aside some piles of trash to make room for the near-collapsing typewriter—and smack out some lines.

I have been chasing around the country, peddling my wares under various conditions. Fortunately, the episodes seem to have all gone well, some of them very well. Otherwise, I don't know how I could ever hope to get my stuff rearranged in intelligible files, etc. For there's a murderous kind in my godam back—and I feel so suicidal from sheer Disorder Among My Papers that I'd welcome the end forthwith if it weren't for some stupid, automatic prejudice against being dead just yet.

As for RR: except for your handsome paean in *The Nation*, and a friendly but brief and admirably self-contained item by Marie Hochmuth Nichols in the Q. J. of Sp., I know of not one single other published statement. I have recd. some friendly acknowledgements from private letter-writers—but damned few of them; though a charming letter from John Crowe Ransom recently (and still, bejeez, unacknowledged), helps reassure me, as did your song, that my belief in the book is not sheer fancy. I know of another review (highly expert and favorable) that is to appear some day in an academic gazette. The editor of a litry quarterly wrote me that he had farmed the book out for review and that a review was still being promised. And I was assured of a friendly comment in another quarter, except that the friendly reviewer happens

to be the sorta guy who just never gets around to finishing things like
that. But beyond that I know nothing except (and you'll agree that it's
always dangerous when an author falls into this groove!) I heard a lecture
by a bastard distinguished theologian recently, who struck me as having
swiped the book for the glory of God and sans to mention me (the high
moral principle doubtless being that he should modestly accept the revenues in the name of God, while making sure that no credit to a heathen
ever sullied the purity of his racket.)

I'm glad to hear that you got the Texas *Graduate Journal.* The amusing thing is that, since I nominated three or four recipients, I have
ceased getting the gazette myself, though I am happy to learn that they
are now anointed with Texas Oil (than which does anything have more
pungency?). As for the recommendaysh to the Behavioral Center: Yes,
I nominated you, and I'm happy to learn that the next step has been
taken. You stressed, I hope, the ways in which your concerns have either
a sociological or a methodological angle (along with their humanistic
slant). That's about where I stood there. The next thing is to get some
more votes by former Fellows. You're now in line for processing; but
you can wither on the vine (or am I most disastrously mixing my metaphors?) unless other old-timers add a word in your behalf. On the other
hand, the young-uns can't expect to have the scattering of backers that
one can expect of oldsters and middlesters, yet the Center wants a high
representation of youngsters. (The year I was there, the distribution was
about one-third for each age-group. And later the Trustees rebuked the
Administraysh for not having had more young-uns. So, I'd assume that
you don't need as many votes as are needed by a middlester and an oldster whom I also nominated, while also making it clear that I was nominating for these various levels.) Frankilee, I was so grateful to the place,
and I worked so hard when I was there (and they knew I was grateful
and they knew I worked hard), I dare think that my nominaysh will
count as much as one nominaysh can.

It would be good if you did a book on Glenway Wescott. (Incidentally, I was on a program with him a coupla weeks ago, in Wisconsin of
all places.) He has done some excellent work. There's probably only one
reason why so handsome a man didn't marry; namely: because he didn't
want to.

I think there were other bits of the Sinballix published. But the only
spot I think of at the moment is the item in *Kenyon,* Summer 1959. And
an item that wasn't in the multilithed Ms., but that I am going to use in

some form, is the piece on Poe in *Poetry,* Oct. 1961. I think I'll end by plumping in a big way for the *principle* I there propound.

I'm sorry that Minnesota still keeps us dangling like a kind of participle. But that's how life is, me frenn. Recently an old pal of mine struggled to get me endowed with an honorary degree, but he finally wrote in fury to say that it went to a G. E. vice president instead. He was apparently surprised, but I wasn't. And that's why I'm not unduly O'erwrought about the o'erlooking of RR (though naturally, at any time of the day or night, smiling through my bourbon, I'm willing to admit that there are baystards everywhere you turn, and that I've suffered them aplenty, my only point being that I'm still not allowed to spend full time feeling bitter, though I have resolved that I'll henceforth knife any crook I can knife quickly).

Duncan is apparently going strong. He's going to teach next year in, yes, Texas.

Please tell thy Better Half I'd agree with her view of Wilson. He has kept bubbling, and even his journalistic worst is superior journalism. (And summers among these unsorted piles that tower about me and about me in my study, there is a set of cards that she sent, anent I believe Walt W. and his habits—and you jes watch and see: If I can but manage to live for another coupla months and get this room back into order, I'll find that Exhibit A, and depose accordingly.

Bstlck.

Sincerely,

K.B.

Do you see *The Nation* regularly? I did a mildly stinko review of Empson's *Milton's God,* that shd. appear there soon.

And I swear in the name of Jeezoos Keerist: If you address me once more as "Mr. Burke," I'm not going to answer your letter.

K.B.

4 July 1962
212 Hessel Blvd
Champaign, Illinois

Dear Burke:

A fantasy on hierarchic themes: set in the heat oppressed midlands; fantasizer: one whirring, partially burdian (typographical pun), burkian agent, somewhat beaten down from above by the unrelenting sun who (which) punishes people for living in reclaimed swamps, and somewhat [repeated because it is a recurrent junk word in all of Glenway Wescott] torn apart by the apparently unreconcileable demands of a course on tragedy, a book on Wescott, family life, and deep residual yearnings for to get the hell out of this pest hole for the summer (or forever); time: a ritualistic holiday, celebrated with great pomp and fanfare, and many explosions.

The fantasy is rather short because it is quite hot, and the atmosphere is very explosive.

"And I swear in the name of Jeezoos Keerist," he said, calling upon one of the terms from the top of the hierarchy, and punning backwards, across religious lines, upon the name of another from the top of another hierarchy, appropriately enough for this particular day, a thunder thrower: "If you address me once more as Mr. Burke, I'm not going to answer your letter," finishing it off with a threat of punishment, which is certainly appropriate to, or consistent with allusion to and oath-makings from terms at the top of the hierarchy. BANG, as the mind, working in the old hierarchic grooves, began: Dear Mr. A household god addressed in the same way old familiar way as one's new rather tiresome dog, upon whom one uses the same (but emptied) hierarchic—BANG—oaths. Dear KB; Dear Kenneth (BANG BANG BANG) [Zoos without the jeez just got me]. When this good, tried, true, and faithful god has lived in our house all these years, as part of the psychic reality of the establishment, in the cells, in the blood; when he has been absorbed but not necessarily humanized or familiarized; to get out of those old grooves takes some doing, to change the form of address is to change the substance of the relationship, and this is liable to take some doing, especially for a person who, after nearly eight years has not yet been able to decide what names to call his mother and father-in-law. Ah, the psychoses under the aegis of Hierarchichus, in whose name you should have sworn in the first place; and the uneasiness in the approach, for reasons beyond the naming of them, masked and placed in a fantasticus on hierarchic themes, spun out, banged out and a fourth and fifth, in a hot month that produces the physiological, neurological counterparts of the psychoses of Hierarchichus. (And my son, my son, choking and screaming, deep in the terrors of an asthmatic seizure, more mysterious, almost, than the p's of H.) On the fourth, fifth, and sixth now, for all the obvious reasons, and getting too far away from the generating idea, impulse, and moment. The fantasticus has lost its force, somewhat, though it has probably made its point, and at eight in the morning of the third day, what more can be asked of it? Henceforth it shall be Burke, Sir, no man's enemy, forgiving all—even—but hierarchichus, its negative inversion in my particular case (with apologies to Auden). As I think about it, though, this is not a case of inversion, really, but part of my birthright as a symbol-user, which it is my right or duty or inescapable fate to transcend by the very means which caused it. FIAT. A change of terms is a change in the form of the address, every image or term containing or expressing implicitly an attitude toward what is addressed in the term. With this pithy verbalization I will bring this symbolic action to a close. Exodus that donkey-term "Mr. Burke" with his burdens, out into the hot midlands to perish in the lands from whence he came. If it were spring, the fantasizer said, there would be rebirth; but there is bourbon, only I'm not much given to it, and anyway it's rather early in the morning, and Glenway, that golden boy without a violin waits for his share of my symbolic acts, and my future says: mount that hierarchy by verbal acts.

So, descending from the realms of fantasy, I remain, in the terms of undress,

Sincerely and purgatively yours,
[K.B.]

And/or
7/30/62

Dear BillR,

Big day for us both. Your book has been accepted, and my *Rhetoric of Religion* got a long, sustained treatment in a publication of vast nation-wide circulation. The best way I can think of, to convey quickly the infectiously persuasive style of the report, is to quote this account of my

"Prologue in Heaven": "At the end of the book, through the word-act unity of a dialogue, he tries to exemplify his total procedure." This rousing article (and you mustn't miss it!) appears in the *Review of Religious Research*—and runs to no less than 399 words.

As you well say, *Onward*. (To look back would be sickening.)

Ennihow, I am happy to hear that you will have graduated from the vexations of non-publication to the vexations of publication. We are so constituted that we always think of that step as a relief, so I guess it is.

I saw quite a bit of Arrowsmith some years in NYC (if he is the Arrowsmith who was connected with the lil mag, *Chimera*). No, my remarks may have been misleading. I saw him a few times during the three months or so I was in NYC one winter. I thought that we got along well, but later he seemed to be otherwise-minded—and I don't happen to have followed him recently. (Or am I getting mickest-uppest, and was he only with *The Hudson Rev.*?)

As for your elucubrations on *Othello*; Anything connecting words with shit (or, or as you delicately put it, "alchemy") seems feasible to me.

In the meantime, thank God for thine elation. I am in the godamnest slumpy-wumpy of my career (or do I mean my careen?). My motto has always been: Ambulando solvitur. But some physical disabilities have been interfering with my perambulating, hence reminding me of a Flowerish I worked out years ago: "It is solved by the ambulance." A most benign offer has been extended to me for next spring. But just when I could be mellow, am I to find that I might be in radical disrepair? The dreadful thing is that such vicious irony seems so "right" to me. Bah!

I winced indeed at your reference to your boy's battles for breath. The religious tell us that a kindly God (kindly in ways we do not understand) can credit such suffering to the account of some other person, so that it isn't wasted. One can imagine it going to pay off for some wealthy crook who holds the mortgage on the church. Let's hope that your boy's troubles were only a reflex of your entanglement—and that now he can BREATHE. Let's hope for this other kind of story. (This analogy doesn't exactly not raise problems! The analogy is not between you and a wealthy, mortgaging-holding crook, but between a general state of stoppage and a general state of release.)

As the fella sez, ONWARD!

Sincerely,
K.B.

For meditative purposes, I enclose a graphic representation of my Definition of Man.

Bennington College
Bennington, Vermont
10/6/62

Dear BillR,

This is a quickie to say that I was delighted to sing in thy behalf to the ACLS, and I'll be glad to do ditto for the Guggy.

Sorry I was slow in answering your letter. But it came just when I was in the midst of preparations for some sessions here (where I'll be until about the 25th or 26th).

At the moment, am in a picturesque tangle of unfinished business. So this is just a note done in hasty wasty, to reassure you that, so far, your case has been duly processed.

More anon. Meanwhile, here's hoping you can cut in one some of that mazuma.

Sincerely,
K.B.

Route 1 - box 327 AA
Englewood, Florida
Yearsend, 62

Dear Bill R,

Delighted to hear tell of you, and to have the good picture of No. 1, who seems incipiently a masterful man. I only regret that the parents didn't also get into the act.

We are on a key here, in the Gulf, slated to linger until mid-March, when we migrate back north in time for me to do a ten-week stint at Penn State (a course in contemp. lit. crit.).

Already I'm behind schedule. I was to have finished a review by the time the whistles blew this eve, whereupon all would be free for me to swing into the last final ultimate work on the Poetics. But it'll be a few more days, alas, before I am back in the particular tangle.

I forget whether I told you: I received the inquiry from the Guggy outfit, and sang my song in they behalf. (But now I remember that I did tell you.)

How goes it with the book on you-know? Still cussin, or is it out of the road?

I chased around one devil of a lot this autumn. I even got bright enough to pick up a lecture engagement on the way south, so that our traveling expenses were covered, plus quite a bit more.

We are about 20 yards from the beach, with only an empty lot twixt us and the sea's infinity. And though there was a picturesque cold snap (as you doubtless read in the papers), it cut little ice with us. For there has been a squandering of sunlight, and every day we have taken a four-mile walk on the beach.

. . . .

Next morning. Another cold snap has moved in. But again, with brilliant sunlight. Incidentally, I have assembled another batch of verse. It includes a poem on Cummings (eight type-written pages) which has been accepted by *Poetry.* For the first piece I did a longer one which, for want of a better title, while working I tentatively called "Introduction to What?"—and now I'm wondering whether I shd. call the whole batch, *Introduction to What: A Second Book of Verse.* And the Secretariat-Culinariat-Aesthesiat Dept. is lettering some more Flowerishes.

meanwhile, novannually flourish.

Sincerely,
K.B.

Psst. Indiana U. Press tinkers with the idea of a Burke Reader, to be edited by Stanley Hyman.

Route 1- Box 327 AA
Englewood, Florida
January 5, 1963

Dear Bill R,

Gladtuh hear from you.

Give me credit for TBL, and Poetics. Give Hermes Publications credit for C-S and P&C. I suppose you should ask Beacon for permish to quote from RR. (Send me a form for Hermes, and I'll send it on to Mrs. Ligda, with my recommendaysh. Hermes also for BkMom.)

As a natural born suicide who, to his surprise, finds himself five times a father and ten times a grandfather, I salute your forthcoming contribution to the population explosion. The best argument (and I remember it particularly because I was an only child) is the one I remember from my father-in-law (the father of seven), who repeated regularly in my presence, "One child—three fools."

I'm sorry to hear of your troubles with the Establishment, so far as financial matters are concerned. But there's no getting around the fact that one is always better off for such disagreements, so far as matters of character are concerned.

I was amused by the story about the Grammarhetoric. But how come you never exposed the guy to them books?! Wadda woild! In any case, do let me know how it all TRANSPIRES. Incidentally, I wonder whether from the sociological angle, any one out there has seen Hugh Dalziel Duncan's book, *Communication and Social Order* (Bedminister Press). Is it, or is it aint, in the local Baptist-Episcopalian library?

No references to ATH or PLF? ATH wd. be Hermes, PLF wd. be me.

But I would be greatly interested in knowing just what the stew in the Rooshian Dept. hinged on (if a stew can hinge). And Duncan's book might join the fray. (Incidentally, I have been asked to review it, along with books on leisure and aesthetics, for a U. of Wisconsin publicaysh, *Arts in Society*. I had sworn to finish the review before the beginning of this year, with its nice number scheme, but I won't get shut of it until this week-end. But I done tole you that afore.)

As I finish this, another grand, irrevocable sunset is squandering it-self o'er the Gulf, a picture in our window. A splendid act on the Old Man's part. His politics don't seem to turn out so well, but He should be satisfied with many of His natural marvels.

> Holla!
> Sincerely,
> K.B.

[Undated Postcard]

Dear Bill R:

Before getting out the Hermes edition of ATH, I got a letter from the now deceased Daniel Mebane, explicitly transferring to me all rights to the book. Mebane had complete authority in this matter. Also, of course, the renewal of copyright for the first edition is in my name. The Hermes edition shd. have been in my name, too; but for reasons best known to herself Mrs. L. proceeded otherwise, without consulting me.

I can't offer legal advice in the matter; but I'll be blamed if I can see how the NR is in a position to ask for one single cent. Also, I think it's quite flimsy of them even to want to.

[Postcard]

Dear Bill R,

This is a quickie to say that NR has no rights to ATH. Dan Mebane transferred rights to me. So, would you please send a form to Mrs. Mil-dred Ligda, Director, Hermes Publications, Box 397, Los Altos, Califor-nia, in re that book. When I get it back from her, I'll countersign it and send you the whole batch.

Incidentally, do please refer to the new Hermes edition, unless the reference is to one of the brief spots that were omitted from the revised edition. (Ditto with regard to the other Hermes reprints, and with PLF.)

In haste, More anon.

> Sincerely,
> K.B.

Route 1 - Box 327 AA
Englewood, Florida
January 29, 1963

Dear Bill R,

Herewith the documents, including those back from Mrs. Ligda who, by the way, greatly favors your title. (Ich auch!) I can send you the ATH one when it turns up later. If the New Republic grants you permission, they don't know what they're talking about.

Incidentally, in recent Kenyon, John Crowe Ransom (who gave the publisher quite a handsome paragraph on RR) has a further generous reference. It will help cancel off, I hope, two other references that didn't turn out so good, but a farthndle on p. 162. Also, I am told that B. De Mott discusses the book in an article or omnibus review in the new Hudson, but I haven't yet seen it.

In the revision of the Poetics, I took out a large portion of the stuffo on "body-thinking" and wrote it up as a special monograph. An editor assembling material on art and psychoanalysis for an issue of The Psychoanalytic Review asked me for a contribution, and I sent him this. A sizable portion (amt. not yet decided) is to appear there. At the moment I am writing up, for possible magazine publication, a talk on my "Definition of Man" which I peddled at various schools in recent months (and am planning to peddle once more, at the U. of Fla. this Feb.)

Don't allow yourself to have too high hopes of a Guggy. Everybody I know, including myself, has a low batting average of successful sponsorships in that quarter. Recently one friend of mine who had sponsored many candidates, and with as high a percentage of hits as I know of, applied for a grant himself, and got turned down! I think there is a might crush of applicants, and your chances are much improved after you have done more publishing.

. . .

Next morn. A great block of motionless sunfilledness, and the sea a mighty dozing lake. Too Arcadian for ideal typewriter weather. One should give thanks by simply rotting. But the good God also dangles the possibility that, by proper application, I can finish my essay on the low-down on man. It has to do with the closing codicil that I added to the definition as given in RR: "and rotten with perfection." But that all fits together, too, doesn't it? On a perfect day, writing on how man's profound yearnings for perfection may lead to his extinction. Perfect! Perfect!

Best regards to all, incl. Burkey the canine Sherlock Holmes.

Sincerely,
K.B.

Route 1 - Box 327 AA
Englewood, Florida
February 23, 1963

Dear Growers and Multipliers,

Felicitations on augmentation! Neither quaint nor quint but Quentin. All hail to the Next Phase.

Meanwhile, when you receive this, I shall probably be asseverating at the U. of Fla. (Gainesville), where I'm scheduled to give one public talk and three seminars. Am a bit uneasy, since I'm a bit rusty. Also, I'm in one of those stages when I"d rather not do much but tinker. (Alas! maybe I'm getting to the stage where I'd rather putter around with projects than slap and bang them into shape.)

Just got proofs of my Cummings poem—so I assume that it will be appearing in *Poetry* soon.

We plan to reach Andover sometime around March 16-17, then to leave for Penn State on about the 22nd. (Course there lasts for ten weeks. Seminar with twelve students.)

Best luck.
Sincerely,
K.B.

Postcard
March 11, 1963
Englewood, Florida

Dear Bill R,

Sorry to hear of your family troubles, and hope all is placid by now. As for Beacon Press, that's the only time they've ever shown any promotional zeal, where RR is concerned, so I'm not surprised that it's promotional zeal in reverse. It's stupid, and in all probability the work of some automatic functionary. If they insist, write it off against all the others. I don't think P-H will be thus excessive. (They weren't with Duncan.)

After leaving here (very soon), we go to Andover for a few days, then to Penn State until after the first week in June, then back to Andover for the summer.

Did you see De Mott's article in the last *Hudson*?

Best luck,
K.B.

525 Glenn Road
State College, PA
May 24, 1963

Dear Bill R,

How go things with self, family, and career?

My sessions here end June 5th, and thereafter we return to Andover. I have one more seminar next Thursday. Otherwise, all is finished but the parties and final papers.

It has been a fairly bustling season, and we've been living in an eleganz modernique house not our style; but since there is radiant heat, at least we haven't made the mistake of keeping the coal in the bathtub.

When appeareth your wolume on Burke and similar psychanda? (Incidentally, I got so disgruntled with Beacon for their treatment of RR, I cancelled my contract with them for the Poetics Ms.)

Here's hoping your long silence means that you've been happily and prosperously engrossed in futurity.

And I wonder if you happened to see my poem on Cummings in the April number of *Poetry*. It seems to have gone well with Cummingsists.

I think I have at last decided how I want to end the Poetics bizz. On a kind of hit-and-run Walpurgisnacht.

Holla!

Sincerely,
K.B.

Andover, New Jersey
June 18, 1963

Dear BillR,

Back at this end of the line, and still trying to untangle the muddle of books and papers that had to do with the sessions at Penn State. (I am a morbid ass who always takes at least fifteen times as much material as he'll have use for. I'll have to learn somehow to get over this damnable compulsion.)

Here's hoping that the news is good about your ailments. Doubtless a term away from the steady grind of the academe will help set you up.

Sure, we expect to be here at least until quite late in the fall, and we'd be glad to see you. We can arrange something definite later on, when you know more about your plans. And we could put you up here, if you don't object to our exceptionally primitive conditions, which are as anti-modernique as an alluvial swamp.

Yes, you can get places for circa $100 a month on the key where we went in Florida, if you stay for several months. Ours was $150. The rent usually includes light and heat, though you have to buy bottled water for drinking ($1 for five gallons). It's about halfway down, on the Gulf side. But you'd have to go still farther south if you wanted to be assured of really mild weather. (One year at Englewood, we didn't miss ten days' swimming all winter; last year we got practically no swimming at all. However, we did get plenty of sunny weather for walking, along more than two miles of unobstructed beach, houses at one end, wild at the other. But there is another gamble: there seems to be an increasing trend towards attacks of "red tide," an organism that can suddenly flourish in one spot or another of the Gulf, killing various quantities of fish. There have been occasions when a nauseous deposit of dead fish piles up on the beach. Also, the damned organism gives off a kind of gas that causes your eyes to burn, along with an irresistible dry cough. There have been several of these invasions in recent years, a couple of them quite bad. We always managed to miss any of the big ones, but there were two minor ones when we were there, and for a few days they were quite irritating.) If you are driving south, you might plan to stop here on your way. At present, except for a few days' trip on a lecture, I am scheduled to be school-free until the end of next January. I'd like to pick up another lecture or two, but otherwise all is as I have hoped for.

I have sworn absolutely to finish the Poetics Ms. this fall. And I don't think I'll knock at any publisher's door until the damned thing is done. I am so counter-suggestive, as soon as I sign a contract I have much more difficulty in finishing a book. Ever since I got out of my contract with Beacon, my hopes for the book have been picking up. And my course at Penn State suggested a kind of bing-bing-bing ending, such as I had vaguely been looking for. It should be the part of the book that is both easiest to write and easiest to read. And fittingly (as with the last chapter of TBL) it will be in the style of notes (quickies that sometimes sum up what has gone before, and sometimes make new stabs).

I still haven't decided whether some of the quickies should be dirty (or at least, teasing). For instance, if a fairly pompous critic informs us that "art throws up value after value," might we not quote this enthusiastically, as a statement about "the emetic function of art?" Jeez, why not? Why not some good clean dirty FUNNN? Or if, after having made me squirm by his suggestion that my theories of symbolic action put Shakespeare, Marie Corelli, and Dashiell Hammet in the same bin, Blackmur then cuts into the act by a slogan about art as gesture, and illustrates the point by the example of a woman paying her fare on a bus, why should I not arise from the grave and tell him to turn over? And so on.

Maybe, if you can drop around, maybe by that time I'll have a chunk of that Finalization lined up, and you might be willing to glance o'er same and divulge how it strikes you.

In the meantime, prombly e'en as I write, you are On the Road, anti-astronauting towards a piece of the good earth still not too much improvedbyprogress.

My only trouble is this: When you come from there to here, it can be but a come-down. But if you had inhaled NYC fumes for a fitting period of time; and if from that experience you had, like us, found this haven fifty miles from town; and if, then I dare think you'd know why we think of ourselves as having beaten some kind of game. Figgger it out along them lines.

At present writing, the field near about us are all smacked into good behavior (thanks largely to the doings of my older son, who came down from Havvud to help us dig ourselves out of the vernal accumulation). And Thepondthedialbuilt is mellow with amplitude. But Science, as you know, has been meddling in a big way, with stupid expertise mussing up ecology, weather, and whatever. So, one can never know to just what lengths Progress will have taken us, come Sept. But if it all is anything like now, I promise you that your "more or less neurotic shyness" will have no meaning. (I mean: Promkly it's just a fleeting impulse to kill somebody—and if only the weather is allowed to behave, you won't have to worry about such things one minute. And ptikly in late Sept. or early Oct., these here rough acres are in song, all kinds of song, whatever kind you would have, and all together. Things are hurrying to get it said before it's all over—and you'd grant them a good grade. But it's too bad you can't be here prezackly now, for after some forbidding days which I accredit to the science-meddlers, all is beauteous in ways that I accredit to Hizonner, whose spring still hatheless springeth.)

Meanwhile, may the Ruecksacks flourish, and may your book on Burke be taken by Hollywood (in case you haven't carelessly surrendered the Dramatistic rights).

Holla!

Sincerely,
K.B.

Andover, New Jersey
June 22, 1963

Dear BillR,

Your book arrived yesterday—and I sailed through it (hoping you would not mind if I just sniffed at the places where you quote).

You have done a valiant job, even unto the sheer machinery (I refer to bibliography and index). I am indeed most grateful to you, for such a happy mixture of industry, perception, and expressiveness in re things to do with the litry output associated with my sick Selph.

Also, I accept your twittings on my more-than-Biblical concern with shittim wood. (However, I feel that your statement of my position with regard to the relation btw. the Trinitarian pathos and the corresponding bathos of the Demonic Trinity—as stated on p. 149, for instance—o'ersimplifies my thoughts on this sumjick. All told, there are: The different kinds of accountancy in solemn tragedy and the Aristophanic guffaw about matters of this sort; the hidden punning ways in which, along with tragic purification by victimage, there run the ways of making the imagery of bodily excretion look "beautiful"; third, whereas in satire such imagery may provide basic material for attacks upon someone or something as "filthy," I accept Freud's observation that man's "primal" and "profoundest" response to his own secretions is in the terms of *love* rather than *insult,* as when Freud says that an infant, in wetting the person who picks it up, is relaxing in confidence and affection. Your statements seem to make the issue look less complicated than I take it to be.)

On p. 155, you say I assume "that everything else has an entelechial motive built into it." I may have misled you a bit here. On this point, I am willing "logologically" to settle for less than Aristotle. Whereas Aristotle would treat even the physical real Dramatistically, I accept my equivalent of the "Cartesian split," whereby persons act and things move (except that I'd have to treat the person, the analogue of the *res cogitans,* as also involving extension, and thus overlapping upon the realm of sheer things as applicable to entities that do not possess the powers of "symbolicity"). Hence I do not claim that the category of sheer motion can be fruitfully analyzed in terms of the entelechy. (I don't say for certain that it *can't* be so analyzed. I say simply that, as I understand modern physics, the gains in that field have been made in terms of sheer motion. Maybe, for all I know, a stone is working like the very devil to be a snootier stone than the one next-door. All I am saying is that, regardless of what goes on in such a field, there is a kind of entelechy atributable to the nature of terminology. And I'll settle for that—owing to my distinction btw. motion and action.)

On p. 172, there seems to be the opportunity for a misunderstanding on the part of the reader. I refer to your two remarks that "Stephen then becomes an extension of Joyce" and "the novel as a whole becomes a symbolic replica of Joyce." You here touch upon something which needs clarifying on my part. Though it is clear that Stephen is in some respect a spokesman for the author, it is also a fact that the novel as a whole represents the author much more complexly (with many more adjectives to the noun and adverbs to the verb). In the case of my own novel, for instance, I remember that I did quite definitely associate myself with John Neal. Yet at many points I deliberately connected him with "facts" that were not true of me. I did not, for instance, marry a woman of means who possessed a herd of cattle which I palmed off as my own, when meeting again another woman whom I had known in the past and who had now fallen on evil days. In many ways I went out of my way to make Neal a heel. And the whole business is the story. Yet the fact remains that this ironic "perfecting" of myself was in some sense "entelechially true." The puzzle comes into focus on p. 146: "I knew there was deceit in using the harsh words only—but unless we adopt a false position, we cannot get our truths stated." Here I was first trying to say, in terms of grotesque tragedy, what I might now say in terms of "comic methodology," when I propose to translate the theological formula, *crede ut intelligas,* into the sheerly logological formula: To say something, you must use some terms to say it with—and since terms have implications, in your very choice of terms you have the technical equivalent of a "belief" in terms of which you may hope to "understand."

On p. 179, you suggested a wrong slant on my use of the term "methodic demoralization." The reader might tend to assume that I am "against" such "demoralization." On the contrary, I am all for it, as long as it is "methodic." In brief, if one can "give oneself" to the book, even as far as sheer lostness, that's the way to do—but one must have a "method" of doing so, since thereby one also has a method for the "recovery" of one's independence. In brief, let oneself be rained on by the full torrent of the terms' complexity; for the rain-drops, despite their merger into the great liquidity of the work as a whole, miraculously also retain their atomistic nature, as "terms" or "words," countable one by one. Your own excellent work-out on Howard's End proves the point excellently. Yet I question whether the reader will read your reference to "methodic demoralization" in a way that gives him right slant on the expression. Mine enemies accuse me of the wrong fault. In effect, they accuse me of being unable to yield (inasmuch as I supposedly approach the work with a scheme already set advance). On the contrary, I am asserting that *this very method* IS a *method of yielding.* The book itself must tell me what goes with what—and I must let it happen. During that stage of total surrender, I am in a state that might be called the technical equivalent of "demoralization." But, thanks to the nature of terms, such demoralization can be *methodized.* For the work is a sea in which each drop, for all its merging into the totality, remains there in its atomistic uniqueness.

There is still a bit of repetitiousness. But that might work out all to the good. For it helps burn a few things in, or gives readers a second chance, in case they didn't get it the first time. (The repetition becomes ironic when, after kidding me for my sturdy turdiness, you re-peddle your own contributions to the mère-mer-merde-etc. complex. But I especially saluted your invention in this regard on p. 224, "it would be foolish—or, perhaps, fecal—for us to deny.")

But the main point is: Although I can't be sure (since I know the material rather better than most people), I have the feeling that you have built the right way, that you have a genuinely integrated presentation of the various concerns. The only further complica—would involve a closer tie-up or tie-in with the fiction, etc. And I wholly agree that you should not have tinkered with that (which might possibly be a job for the self-lurker, if he ever gets around to it, as he does now and then in bits).

You pay me the double compliment of both working hard at the text and being determined to establish your independence. And it seems to me that you have brought out, as no one else did, the rootedness in the *logologizing of theology* (a "fulfillment" which was necessarily more difficult for the earlier writers on this morbid sumjick, since the RR stuff wasn't then available).

. . .

Interruption. Friends turned up. I wish I had a record of my telling them about my gratitude for your doings. That would be the best testimony with regard to my indebtedness to you for your good work.

I incline to think that it is a splendidly muscular job. You have developed from a center that comes dangerously close to dead center. I think you have shown quite a bit of tact in your ways of so developing (though other sonsofbitches might decide otherwise—for who knows?). Possibly, at this time, you're enough like me to loathe everything that had to do with this business you're now through with. If so, it's just as possible that later on you'll not too much mind having gone through this mill.

In the meantime, I thank thee—yes.

Sincerely,

K.B.

More delays. It's now Sunday morning. The only stylistic flurry I noticed. On p. 144, you say "the rape of a white woman by a Negro (or vice versa)," Would not the vice versa be: "the rape of a Negro by a white woman"?

Incidentally, I'm especially glad that you swung into the comic angle at the end. For though I somehow maneuvered myself into a much greater stress upon tragedy than I had originally intended, I consider it a comic observation to note that people feel edified by weeping at a fiction.

. . . More later. I have a chance to mail this in town within a few minutes. The proportions of this letter turned out wrong. I should have stressed the many pages that call for unqualified thanks rather than paying so much attention to some minor hagglings.

. . . Have a nobly earned rest!

Andover, NJ - 07821
July 26, 1963

Dear B&B,

Many thanks for your latest, of the fifteenth inst.

I was most happy to have photos of you-all. If you won't feel insulted, please permit me to say that I think we ought to get along fine. Maybe I'm wrong; but on the basis of the photos I assume that you are a studious couple, with children to match. Most likely BillR is connected with some university, and his BettyR Half is similarly oriented. And the kids look charming, too.

Meanwhile, wd. say:

As things now line up, we expect to be here all summer, except for some days late in August. So, tell us how you incline towards avec, as regards your travelling in these here areas (including, I trust, an arrangement with Glenway W.), and we'll respond accordingly.

We are indeed sorry to hear that your older boy is having some trouble. But, given contemporary progress as it is, God only knows what he is justifiably rejecting. (I say as much because I assume, after much inquiry, that my insomnia comes from the bodily radical rejecting of more godam Inventions in the Food Dept. than you can find in all the length and breadth of The Holy Bible, despite my Fundamentalism. I assume that other Victims of Progress, like your poor kid, are similarly rejecting, though in terms of asthma rather than in terms of insomnia. But in any case, I take it for granted that one must perforce go on getting loaded up with all that the market can bear.

BillR should know: I have received a letter from a good man (head of English Dept. at Penn State) who speaks of his admiration for Bill's book. And, on the basis of a phone call from *Time Magazine* I'd suggest: Bill should make sure that a copy of his book gets to these quarters. (They're doing a piece on lit. crit., apparently trying to undo or outdo the recent splurge in *Esquire*. But I wonder: Will they too build up Wilson, as topsy-wopsy? Or will they, as they should, give info anent *all* the corks on the waves? Incidentally, I wasn't in the morbid picture because, though invited to be there, I was in Floridoah at the time when the stuff was in the works. I'll show BillR the documents, just in case he feels that he bet on the wrong horsicle.)

Meanwhile, as regards your plans for migrating hither, please say when. And know that we'd be delighted to have you here among us.

Sincerely,

K.B.

Andover, NJ - 07821

August 5, 1963

Dear BillR,

Another friend of mine (in whose judgment I place great confidence and who invested in a copy of your book), writes that he finds your opus "really lst class!" (shout his).

Watch us grow.

Meanwhile, I thought I shd. write you about plans for August, so that we don't have trouble getting together.

As things look now, we shall leave here on the nineteenth, and be back on the 25th. And we expect to be here steadily thereafter, at least through October (although I shall be on the way to or from Texas btw. 28th and 31st, in connection with a lecture.)

I had reasons to drive as far as Connecticut; and these potentiated some reasons I had for driving as far as Cambridge; and the drive to Cambridge potentiated some reasons I had for winging up to Maine for a day or two (to a place off the southeast end of Moosehead Lake, in the vicinity of a town called Monson). And so it goes.

Incidentally, I forget whether I told you. In case you have occasion to make last-minute plans for your treck, our phone here is 201-347-3249.

Me—after two months of pointless entanglement, I have begun to slough off my slough. Thus, at last, my desk is cleared up. (Oof, what a morbid sight it had become, with me writing atop the eleventh citee.) I diagnosed my difficulties thus: A critic doesn't experience *too much* trouble trying to meet another critic halfway. But if he has just spent ten weeks trying to meet a whole tangle of critics halfway, it's like firmly grasping a handful of tacks. Their many points left me pointless; their arrows pointing in every direction left me temporarily arrowless. Heretofore my encounters, insofar as we could call them encounters, were one at a time. (From your bibliography, by the way, I discover that a kindly deity had caused me either to miss or to benignly forget several of the attacks on me. Max Black's, for instance, or Hubler's, neither of which I have yet seen.)

Here's hoping you're either curatively rotting, or swinging ahead with your Wescott project. (Or are you, by now, beginning to appreciate the poignant splendor of a sunshine thought I continually recall, from some colyumist whose name I forget, probably FPA: Getting out a book is like dropping a feather into the Grand Canyon and waiting to hear the reverberations?)

Best luck,

Sincerely,
K.B.

Andover, NJ - 07821
August 16, 1963

Dear BillR,

This is a quickie to say: Sure—Fine. And plan to stay here with us for the days you mention, or whatever other ones seem to fit your plan later, and with and/or sans offspring on whichever days also fit your plans.

If you play tennis, bring racket and shoes. If you aren't already too waterlogged, bring bathing trunks in case you might deign to get wet in our small pond (built by a dam paid for by the Dial Award). Otherwise, be prepared for rudimentary living, in a house that has Garden of Eden plumbing, but plenty of bourbon and ice cubes.

I enclose a map for locating our ptikla spot, after you arrive at the larger nearby towns. It is done by the family cartographer, Elizabeth Batterham Burke. And I repeat, our local number is 347-3249 (area code, 201).

We're promantly going ahead with our quixotic plan to trek into Maine for a few days, starting for Cambridge on the 19th and planning to see some people there that evening. Godwillens, we shd. be back here on Sunday aft., Aug. 25th. And I shall hope to have cut down (before your arrival) at least some of the grass that will have leapt up to engulf the joint during our absence.

But when am I going to get an urgently needed haircut? Well, we'll see.

Meanwhile, best luck—and looking forward ...

Sincerely,

K.B.

Your scheme about Glenway Wescott may be the best way, I doan no. But at least I'm sure that if you had known me before writing your book on my mussy Selph, you'd never have written it. Mysterious are the ways of the deity (which, in my *Towards a Better Life*, is spelled diety, thus giving the idea a totemic touch). But back to the grind. Today I hope to finish what I hope will be my final contribution to the Beauty Clinic (for a while at least). It is called Somnia ad Urinandum (which, unless some Latinist sets me straight, I'm taking to mean "Dreams Toward Urinating"). It has to do with observations on dream-analogies caused presumably by pressure on the bladder. (Incidentally, I have been thinking: If Maritain and his followers are correct in warning against the charge of "angelism," the belief that man can attain intellectual purity untainted by body-images, then one can use their own arguments as implying the likelihood of such analogies.) Today I end on some new stuff regarding the Porter Scene in *Macbeth*, a clincher. (I might add, by the way: I rewrote, cut, and better schematized much of the stuff on body-thinking that I had in the early draft of the Poetics. I dropped most of it from the present version of the Poetics proper. And quite a bit is now at the printer, to appear in the forthcoming issue of *The Psychoanalytic Review*.)

K.B.

Andover, NJ - 07821

September 22, 1963

Dear B&B,

Glad to hear that you successfully weathered the traumatic conditions of the Burkes' modus vivendi. And we enjoyed your sojourn. I omitted talk about The Book because, at any given moment, something else always seemed to fit in better. Also, for some time I've been in such a mood of self-cancellation, the only thing that could get me out of it would be a vicious attack on me—whereupon I'd start singing like a lil birdie in the springtime. Insofar as you inclined to agree with me, there was always the risk that I'd "solve" my problems by haggling with you instead of with myself.

By all means, stop in on your way to warmer climes. The time you suggest is about right. Towards the end of the month, I'm flying to Texass for a coupla days, there and then to do my song-and-dance on the Definition of Man. And your proposed itinerary would bring you by here early enough for me to fold back into myself and develop the necessary preparatory glumness for my Return to the Arena, where I will be All Smiles.

I enclose the almost illegible copy of a page that may tell the story. Since you were here, our elder son came home, repaired the putt-putt, and spelled me in laying low the grass behind the house. The "Case History" herewith enclosed celebrates that grand state of affairs. But there was still much slaying to be done, in the field btw. the road and the pond. And I was all set to do it. But one hour after my son left for Cambridge, the godam machine refused to do anything but tantalizingly fart, in response to my attempts at cranking it. Thus, the problem of being a Philosopher in an Age of Run-Down Progress becomes almost insuperable (particularly if we decide to stay here this wint., and I have to o'erlook that uncut field every single day).

The trees are turning. We've had but the first nips of frost. Already I have put on a few of the storm windows. I have cleansed the coal stove in the kitchen, removing previous years' accumulations, in preparation for the as-it-were Vestal fire soon to Be Continuously. And so it goes.

Henry Sams was here last week. (He is the head of the English Dept. at Penn State.) I sang of Bill's great virtues. From something he said, I gather that he'll be at the Slave Market in December, and would be interested in talking with the candidates (though this is more of a surmise than a definitiveness). Ennihow, it's worth keeping in mind, as regards Bill's designs on the Next Phase.

Tonight, my guess is, we have our first big Killer frost. Already there has transpired considerable coloration of leafage. And, despite my theory that I should stay north this wint., in fancy I 'gin respond to auguries of migration. But my Better Half, I whisper encouragingly to the Selph, will help me linger, at least into December—and maybe both of us will want to do something or other from then till February (when by shedyul I must hold forth hereabouts).

Holla!

K.B.

Case History

Bored with
        Build-ups
        Smears
        Bellyaches
        Flatteries
        Threats
        Promises
        Boasts
        Confessions
        Challenges
        Controversies
        Diagnoses
        Dialogues
        Catalogues
        Details
        Generalities
        Market reports
        Petitions
        Protests
        Prognostications
        Questionnaires
        Surveys
        Digests
        Outlines
        Indictments
        Insults
        Inside info
        Official hand-outs
        Apologies
        Things to show how delicate
        Things to show how indelicate
        Songs or anti-songs
        Pomps and circumstances
        People with their hair down
        People with their pants down

Tweet-tweets
Yap-yaps
Klunk-Klunks
Twat-twats
Buzzy-wuzzies
Ringy-dingies
and
Splotch

The poor baystard went out and looked across
A field he had cut with his putt-putt
"Begad, jes look at that!" he said to his Selph—
Then Went Back
Into The House
K.B.

[Postcard postmarked October 12, 1963.]

Dear B&B:

Yes, first part of week is O.K. My trek officially begins on the following Sunday when I take the plane from Idlewild. ... At the moment, I am side-tracked into doing a review of Stanley Hyman's selections from Darwin. ... Weather here still fantastically mild and sunny, but decidedly on the drought side. ... Let us know exact time of arrival. And invite Glenway W. over here if you want. ... Last week, under Bill's guidance, I read the Ford and Max Black reviews. ... I consider the Ford ingeniously unperceptive; and I do wish Bill had quoted Black's characterization of the pentad as "mystical."

Holla!
K.B.

Andover, NJ — 07821
October 15, 1963

Dear B&B,

We have Betty's of the eleventh inst.

Yes. Welkim. Sunday-Monday is quite feasible. It's later in the week that Dr. Jackal must go into Hiding.

Though it's hard to imagine, we envy you that "drenching cold rain." Here the tragically beautiful weather continues.

Incidentally, if you're interested in anything to do with William Carlos Williams, you might bear it in mind that John Thirlwall lives in Riverdale. 4414 Tibbett Avenue. He's now doing a biography of Bill. He and his wife (Fuji) have been out here occasionally. He teaches at CCNY.

I also note that you have Durham on your list. I spoke at Duke, when on the way south last wint., but under the auspices of the social sciences. (To my knowledge, not a single member of the lit. branch sullied himself by attending.) And here's hoping that, while you were at Troy, you drove up to see the campus at Benny Bonnington.

Meanwhile, best luck to all.

> Sincerely,
> K.B.

> R.D. 2, Andover, N. Jersey
> November 7, 1963

Dear B&B,

Many thanks for the pictures. And we're delighted to learn that all went so well at Wescott's. That should compensate somewhat for the turbulently improvised gathering here.

Incidentally, would it be possible for you to lend us the negative of the photograph in which I am facing to one side? We'd promise to take care of it and return it pronto. We think it could serve for publicity purposes, despite the fact that it so clearly displays my criminal ear. I'd be most grateful if we could thus borrow it.

Last week I received a note from Jacob Taubes, who teaches at Columbia. He had seen Bill's book, and proclaims it admirable. I am hoping (though sans any specific assurance to that effect) that there'll be a review of it by Henry Sams in the winter issue of The Journal of General Education.

Editor of *Arts in Society* has invited Duncan to comment on my review. So I assume that he has made the same offer to Kaplan and Kaelin. Having yanked everything one way, I guess they'll yank it back again. Meanwhile, I'm doing (for Grinnell) a piece built around essays on Man and Satan in *Journal of Social Issues,* Oct. 1962. I hope to work out, to some extent, the problem of steering "symbolic action" midway btw. the

Charybdis of neurosis on one side and the Scylla of computer-program-
ming on the other.

At last, the drought is broken. We have had nearly four inches of
rain. And never riotous, so that it all went into the ground.

Holla!

Sincerely,

K.B.

R.D. 2, Andover, NJ - 07821
November 14, 1963

Dear Bill,

Just put on the last shell against the weather (the storm door to the
front porch). It's now quite dark (at 5:15), and there is a slight rustle
of rain that seems to me as though it were all set to end up as our first
snow flurry. Since you left, my nephew came over with his power saw,
and sliced up tree trunks while Butchie and I lopped off the branches.
So we have plenty of logs for the fireplace. And I'm feeling all set up
because I just got unwound from a 30-page article on "Order, Action,
and Victimage" for next January's seminar at Grinnell (atop a discarded
first-draft of 26 pp.). Like that item in *Arts in Society*, it's a restatement
using other books as foils (in this case, two articles on Man and Satan in
The Journal of Social Issues, plus an article which attacked one of them,
the trick being that I first defend the attacked against the attacker, before
registering complaints of my own).

Your letter suggested a million-dollar idea, which I hereby offer
you for nothing. For your book on Wescott, add a bit of preface pretty
much along the lines of your observations about your visit there (except,
of course, the troublous ones). Put it all just that way: You had never
met Wescott before, you were uneasy about the meeting, but gradually
things warmed up, he displayed his great range and charm, etc. I assure
you, it would be an excellent way to introduce your subject, so far as
"reader-reception" is concerned, perfectly effective and perfectly justified. Pool your resources with Betty, for at least two or three thousand
words—and you'll start things with a bang.

If the Penn State deal comes through, by all means take it, even
though at a lesser sum than at most other places. (I doubt whether it
would be much less, if any.) It's a nice town, and Sams is a prize man to
have for a boss. I had some notions about going slower in the buildup

stage, but they were doubtless due to the timidity of age. In any case, I personally think it would be splongdeed if you lined up there, for your next phase. Rochester, by the way, seems to be quite a lively place too. One of the places that's on an upswing. So, all told, those two answers to your five letters strike me as promising indeed.

I just got a fan letter from a dynamic miss who is now in Geneva, and apparently is making herself and me popular by attacking her professors in the name of Boikwoiks. She wants to know what I have written since *RR*. So, after mentioning a coupla articles, I'll tell her about Rueckert. (She begins her six-page, single-space communication thus: "For years now, I have been wanting and meaning to write to you, especially since 1960 when they flatly refused me admission to Bennington, and perhaps my bald statement that I wanted to go there almost exclusively to study under your professorship was a deciding factor in their refusal." Pages 4-6 are copy of a letter to her parents about Burke's Grammar n sech. Jeez, what a responsibility I escaped! But I'll tell her abut you, and we'll see if you can pass her tests. She scares the life out of me, and I'm going to tell her so.)

So far as I could judge, the Texas enterprise turned out oke. Incidentally, I ran across quite a lot of good guys there. (Among them being one who whispered to me that my talk on the Definition of the Hominid had drawn the largest audience so far in their series on criticism n sech.) There's a splendid irony about the place the prevents the faculty from becoming typical Texans. Namely: Though they struck oil on the University grounds, so that the school is stinko rich, the money can only be spent for buildings n sech. The faculty still must relie on crumbs from the state legislature. So they tell you stories about the *decadence* of oil revenues rather than trumpeting them as a triumph of individual genius. However, it is true that, if the faculty must starve, it can starve in palaces. For the only real money in education is in the buildings and the roads—and on that score the place is zooming.

I hope you got (and looked kindly on) my letter requesting the loan of the negative of my sick Selph, to be used for the purposes of the city of publi.

Meanwhile, in my behalf, please fart in the face of any local Lilywhite of which you happen to be in the presence of which, of which.
Holla!

Sincerely,
K.B.

[Libbie Burke. Undated, stapled to a letter dated December 1, 1963.]

Andover

... I am glad that Bill is after KB to finish the big opus. After more than five years waiting for that final finishing touch, I have had to give up even mentioning it! It is extremely difficult for him to decide he is finished with a ms. And particularly one so important to him. The other articles are ways of postponing this final reckoning. Though, I must say, I do like the articles he's done this winter ...

... While on the subject of food: our Catholic Priest friend spent the night with us last night, and he and KB talked and drank all night till six a.m. He had the Eucharist on his mind, and would not talk about anything else, so we spent hours discussing imbibing the body and blood of Christ—and all its ramifications. I got tired of being polite, concealing my feelings about this primitive heathen practice. His idea was that the communicant was not absorbing Christ, but Christ by this method absorbed him—i.e. instead of Christ becoming a part of you, you become a part of Christ. KB made it a little difficult for him to twist everything round about, but he persisted. I went to bed leaving them with their verbal feast. Which they were washing down with good Scotch and Bourbon ...

R.D. 2, Andover, NJ - 07821
Christmas Eve morning, 63

Dear Bill,

This is a quickie to raise an elaborate protest as regards your not going to the slave market. If Sams and the Rochester guy (Hartshorn?— he sent me both an inquiry and thanks for my answer, but his letter is filed upstairs in the cold) have a certain no. of jobs to fill, won't there be a tendency to do the filling on the basis of interviews? And couldn't you have gone around and knocked at other doors?

True, I only attended one of the meetings myself (one year when I was asked to give a paper on James Joyce, on a program with Harry Levin and a beauteous lady's-man from Vassar—I'm not a member, being too pig-headed or something). Yet it seems to me that, under the circumstances, there was a point to your going. Sams definitely told me, when I gave him a sales talk, that he looked forward to seeing you at the show. And Hartshorn certainly wrote a cordial letter acknowledging my bleat in your behalf. I learned, by the way, that he was down to see Blackmur, and doubtless asked for nominations from him.

My won't-play attitude with regard to Faulkner is, I grant, hard to explain. Part of it comes from my violent resistance to violence. Part comes from a tendency I have to resent writers who pander to the very evils they are warning against. (That's a variant of objection No. 1.) I don't like his style, which seems to me alcoholic (I mean alcoholic *at the time*, as distinct from those who swill afterwards or write from a hangover, chastened.) Part is unquestionably due to a feeling (quite unprofessional!) that I'd be unspeakably miserable in Mississippi. I admit, I once had a student who did a special job on *Light in August*. And in the course of guiding her (or, more accurately dragging her) through an analysis of its structure, I became quite impressed with its way of releasing a story (by circling back to the same place, each time with a bit more significant info having been imparted in the meantime). And the characters "derive" in a quite interesting way (using J.C. as terminus a quo.) So, I guess that someday I'll try going through the works (though I must admit, except for this one book which I read super-thoroughly for pedagogic reasons, I have never been able to finish anything by Faulkner, not even a story like "The Bear."

I question your theory as to why I work so much with the Demonic Trinity. But who's to say? I'd tend rather to turn things around, and to say, not that the theories derive from the outhouse, but that my tolerance of the outhouse derives from my theories. (The "idealism of the W.C." is a basic ingredient of our national blindnesses. And in any case, I feel that I have saved my boys from the risk of some stupid local marriage, thanks to this "test" of a TV-trained girl's intelligence.)

Incidentally, if you see the newest issue of the Psychoanalytic Review, it contains a revised section (48pp.) of my stuffo in the Poetics Ms., on Alice in Wonderland, Wagner's Ring, Flaubert's Temptation, Aeschylus' Prometheus Bound, and the "Pure" Poetry of Mallarmé, and the confessions about my stories and verses. Your reviewer friend will probably bust a gut if he sees that. Or the Laurel (Dell) edition of Timon of Athens, with my introducsh.

One other thing, and I'm have done. I have contracted to do (for the International Encyclopaedia of the Social Sciences) a 5000-word article on "Dramatism." I'd be grateful for any suggestions that occur to you, regarding what should be put in or left out.

But the postman is due. And I should get to work. Best regards to the Rueckerts all, from the Burpians.

All hail to thirteenthnight.

Sincerely,

K.B.

R.D. 2, Andover, NJ - 07821

December 31, 1963

Dear Bill,

Two words, to clear off the slate for the year.

I contracted to send you some corrections anent Falconer.

They run thus:

Yes, I did get all the way through *Intruder in the Dust.* I used the paperback edition, advertising "Murder and Violence in a small Southern town." Signet.

Above all, I was struck by the twist in the classic formula, on p. 124: "through the catharsis of pity and shame." And I asked the Selph: "Just what is involved in that shift? Just how many notable differences are there in "catharsis" as so turned?

Why not, for a starter, simply work out a "cycle of terms" implicit in that deflection? There's a whole clutter of words such as: justice, conscience, outrage, pride, expiate, abolish, vindication, vengeance, befouled (125), etc. Why not build a whole set of them (including related imagery, dust, grave, kill, filth, the interesting circular movement on p. 151, etc)? Perhaps featuring the "doctrinal" statement on pp. 138-9? Then, after having worked out the terminology as a directionless *chart,* next show how it works when translated into terms of persons in an irreversible *development*? And, on the side, keep watching for contrasts btw. this kind of line-up and the kinds in Genesis or Grk. Tragedy?

Then, after you have got it all trimmed up in this one case, expand ad lib., by considering F's other books, and asking what should be added or subtracted or modified in each case?

But postman with last mail out this year is due, so I desist.

Best luck.

Sincerely,

K.B.

R.D. 2, Andover, NJ - 07821
March 16, 1964

Dear Bill,

Eight o'clock in the morning. The sun bleeding into the room like a stuck pig. And me so damned sleepy I cd. cry (after a pointlessly insomniac night, I gave up the effort entirely about 4:30, and have been buzzing ever since).

Sorry to hear that the Rochester bizz collapsed. I might be able to find out something this summer (as Slochower's friend, who teaches history of art there, usually turns up at least once). I, incidentally, have just finished an article in which I somewhat take issue with Norman Brown's angle on Freud. ... As for Penn State, it turns out that Henry Sams did not go to the MLA meetings—so you were proved right in not budging from the sewers of Norleans. If Sam's policies prevail, Penn State is in for much enlivenment. But it is true that there is a pretty hard core of sturdy backlog of tenure-clinging deadheads—and far be it from me to underrate the sticking powers of bumps on a log.

I'm glad to hear of the honors done to your book on Burke nsech. I wonder whether any place will weaken and give it an adequate review.

By now you should be sufficiently denicotinized to have far transcended the burlesqued spirituality of smoking. From then on it becomes great fun, despising the whores of the advertising racket who try to hook you.

Your current sense of being "empty" might result from the fact that you had been goaded by some kind of antithesis which Wescott and I happened to represent in your psychic economy. And now that you got both books done, you're at a stopping place, until or unless the antithesis turns up in a new form, or hits upon some likely synthesis. But I do wish I could have sold you on the idea of working with that interesting twist in *Intruder in the Dust*. What a remarkably different set of implications there seems to reside in that distinction (btw. a stress on catharsis via pity and fear for the hero, and catharsis via pity and shame for the black-white issue). And I'm sure that the whole logic of the text could be tellingly "prophesied" from that as the starting point. (Incidentally, I am trying to find time to read a long paper on Crane, written by a teacher who builds his analysis by listing how many principles I operate on, and then ticking them off one by one. The machinery gets somewhat in the way of the analysis; and some of the material I am stressing in the godam Poetics is not, of course, considered. But the guy seems to have been working at the stuff for some time, and to have been teaching along those lines. Another man sends me a long paper by a *highschool* student! That I'll be particularly interested in—though the guy also astutely asks me for advice as to how some of my terminology might be *disguised*, so as to escape the malice of mine enemies, or rather, to help his students escape such malice, when they go on to other classrooms. A good point! I am reminded of the time when a bright student of mine at Bennington went to a meeting of a leftist labor organization, and came back a wreck because of the razzing she got when she avidly began expatiating about "consubstantiality." I said: "Of course! *Their* word is 'solidarity.' My vocabulary is best adapted to showing the internal logic among a whole batch of terms. But in all sorts of local situations, some piecemeal translation is advisable." Any Marxist would raise hell about a "scene-act ratio," unless you talk about it in terms of a "response to the objective situation.")

But what of my terministic problem with regard to the paper I just did on Freud?! It's for a psychoanalytic gazette—yet it's essentially on the theory of symbolic action in general (as distinct from the special meaning of the term in Freud). To my knowledge there was no other way to handle the matter. I quote from the Abstract, to suggest the operations of the scheme as a whole:

> Section I, "The Two Ancestral Terms," aims to indicate the internal logic of the terms that follow from the union of "repression" and the "unconscious," in the special meaning assigned by Freud to these terms. Section II, "Contributory Rules," lists major principles that guide the terministic developments discussed in Section I. Section III, "Varieties of Unconscious," deals with ambiguities in the term, "Unconscious," that necessarily arise when Freudianism is extended beyond its clinical function and becomes a "philosophy of life" in general.

As things look now, I may get a chance to do some speculating on prblms f trmnlgy at Havvud in April. (Parsons has asked me to join in a two-hour session at a seminar, and to address a Graduate Colloquium—enterprises in which I have participated twice before. The Drew seminar ends April 24th. And I'm doing three days—mostly on Wm. Shakespeare and Poetics—at Kearney, Nebraska, in May. Then, you-know: finish the godam Poetics.)

Meanwhile, all hail to the protraction of Smile Week, and may it bring the Rueckerts vast prosperity.

Holla!

Sincerely,

K.B.

Bobbs-Merrill sent me an advance of $500 bayries for their paper-back edition of *P&C*—so I assume that Erving Goffman did or is doing the Introducsh. But today I recd. royalty statements from Prentice-Hall, sans mention of any further sums from Meridian paperbacks. So I 'gin wonder whether the Grammarhetorica Motivorum has been slumping into innocuous desuetude. "In one volume: two great book on a philosophy of language and human conduct"—and now gone down the drain? If you want to test that newly plastered smile of yours, try it out on Heidegger's *Introduction to Metaphysics,* Anchor, 95 cents. It has some good spots. But on the whole it is so irritatingly misterioso-bulldozo, and so long-windedly so, I wanna smash something.

K.B.

[Libbie Burke]

Andover

April 15, 1964

. . . Spring is bursting out all over the place here now. KB has had the Chickadees eating out of his hand all winter, and they even follow him around when he takes his walk in the afternoon. And nag at him while he's doing his outside chores. He loves it . . .

R.D. 2, Andover, NJ - 07821

May 23, 1964

Dear B&B,

Sorry Indeed to hear that nothing came of the Rochester and Penn State leads. I'm as uninformed as ever about both, aside from remarks of Bill's.

I continue behind in everything. But I have a slight sense of relief today, since I mailed off the galleys to the two Burkables that Indiana U. Press is publishing. And now, at odd moments, I fuss about the galleys to the Hermes bookofverse.

We saw Wescott at the Academy-Institute festivities the other day, and he was as self-effacing as ever. Bill certainly picked two shrinking violets to write about.

Recd. a note from Hugh Duncan. If he agreed with Bill's notion that there was some oddity in their meeting, his letter gave no hint of it.

The battle to keep the field mowed is on. And so far, praise God, the putt-putt has been behaving.

I have agreed to take a job next fall at Santa Barbara, unless they would be willing to postpone it until the same time the year following.

Tonight, it's almost like midsummer, except for the profuse fragrance of lilac about the house, and azalea on the edge of the woods. And through the moonlight there vibrate as many batrachian noises as insect undulations in the autumn. Anything like winter? Yes, though the temperature was in the nineties today, I still haven't replaced two of the storm windows with screens.

And now, I'm so sleepy, the only way I can be sure to keep awake is to get ready for bed.

Yours for resignation, catharsis, transcendence, and transfiguration,

Sincerely,

K.B.

And/or

8/22/64

Dear Bill,

Having just finished the morning's self-slaughter (and on another typewriter yet), I herewith k-nock off a k-vickie.

You're absolutely right about the Nembies. I know it well, e'en though no one would cast me for a movie star. The goodwife's admonitions come from my telling her about what I had found out firsthand. (Her job is to be my ///// conscience—apparently I stutter at the word—when I have transcended such lowly burdens. Our agreement is that, though I may revile her at the time, I thank her the next day.)

E'en so, I think you had it coming to you. And all the more binnuz we necessarily know how to discount such exercises.

The really important thing is your second paragraph about the unpurloined letter. I do indeed hope that that godam accident is not ultimately formative. I mean: You may or may not have decided that you want the job—but I do hope that the issue is not settled by a mere mussiness in the mails.

As for the wolume, I have no objection to "execute" as a pun. So please erase "no pun intended." And I'd *love* to have Black Max included in the book. Also, Shitney Hook. If they wanna do some more dirt, I'm all for it. I'm not at all interested in the principle of *nil nisi bonum de mortuis*. The list of friends I'll suggest later, after you have given me your tentative list. I'm interested, first of all, in the stinkeroos, whom I'd love to risk trying to kick in the ass.

Incidentally, in the summer issue of Sewanee, Joseph Frank, while reviewing my RR, pauses to give your book a side-swipe of praise (but only, apparently, because he can use it as a way of saying that I said what you say I said). The ploy suggests the possibility that your best chance of getting reviewed is if someone finds a trick way of using you against me. And since Frank is an exceptionally decent reviewer, you now know *ab intra* what's up. It's an Iron Law of Reviewing that the reviewer must win. Hence, keeping that in mind, pray watch what this friendly man does with quotation marks around the word "real" (which in his hedgings he contrives to let look like *my* word, though it is *his*).

But dooty calls. —So many interruptions have turned up in the meantime, I doan quite no what to say. So, for the moment, I don't too iggerly want to decide whether things are "in spite of" or "because of." I'll take a chawnst. For whether or not you say "Long live Burke" or "To hell with Burke," Burke is most interested in the fatal fact that he will live exactly as long as he will live. And his only decent reason, for trying to live as long as possible, centers in his admittedly burdensome observations as regards the ironies of the differences between its nature as a sheer flow of water and its nature as water "playing" in a piece of real estate. I reserve the rights mussily to quote.

Meanwhile, flourish,

Next day. I guess the ellipsis in the last sentences arose thus: Talk of dying brought up thoughts of the still drastically dwindling pond. And from there I got to my never-ending worry about the transforming of nature into real estate.

If you want to go real blotto, finish off a day of whiskey with a drink of pernod. The goodwife tells me I ate my supper like an animal. I am not boasting.

(And all the while, I keep batting myself down, batting away at this idiotic article, which would doubtless have been a damned sight better if I had simply tossed it off in the first place. I refer to a piece on "Dramatism" I'm doing for an Encyclopaedia, trying simultaneously to get me in and keep me out, to write officialese and not write officialese, to be cumbersome and sylphilee. Wadda woild!)

K.B.

325—1 Moreton Bay Lane
Goleta, Calif. - 93017
Oct. 2, 1964

Dear Bill,

Itshay. Along with your letter came one from Howard Nemerov beginning thus: "In keeping with me present policy of giving up, I just wrote to TLS and gave up me on Rueckert and you. Regrets, or rueckerts, but there just isn't anything I can manage right about now."

Wadda woild! It's an acute case of PSYCHOLOGY—but hell, so are we all. A few months ago, Nemerov wrote a two-hundred page autobiographical item which didn't turn out very well. So he's glum, moody, sulky, depressed—and since he's kind to his dog, I guess he has to take it out on us. Tough titty. But so it goes …

The comment by Ransom was a hit-and-run reference in connection with some comments of his on a poem of his. Here, by the way, is a statement he once sent to Ed Darling (of Beacon Press):

> Kenneth Burke's *The Rhetoric of Religion* is a grand book, beautiful in its exposition, and extraordinarily knowing and authoritative. I keep picking it up to browse in for pure pleasure. The dialogue at the end is of Platonic quality. There have not been many philosophical structures wearing so well the graces of literature.

I am sure that you'll find the other reference (which is about the same as this, though even briefer!) in a number of *Kenyon* about a year ago. Incidentally, I wonder whether you happened to see Joseph Frank's review in the recent *Sewanee*. Friendly, but he ends by building an objection around a position that I don't hold. Since he couldn't find a quotation to substantiate it, he makes up one of his own, and puts *his* word in quotation marks. I sent in a good-natured letter pointing out the misrepresentations—but I haven't yet heard from Lytle.

I do hope your deal with Rochester comes through. Incidentally, I am puzzled about your reference to Hazard Adams as editor of the *Centennial Review*. I thought Herb Weisinger is the editor. At least, he's the guy that I have always negotiated with. (I recently reviewed Weisinger's new book, a collection of essays for the *New Leader*, though to my knowledge my bleat hasn't yet appeared. I sent it in a week or so before we started our treck West.)

Once we got fifty miles or so beyond Chicago, the madness of the turnpikes and freeways began to abate, and so did the knot of pain in my forehead. We enjoyed at least eighty percent of the going from then on—and our young mare held up admirably, even at 70 miles per hour across the desert in the heat of the day. (I took few books, but enough notes to make up at least eight volumes.) In particular, we liked the canyon in Zion national Park, where we rented a cabin.

This is going to be quite a handsome campus when it gets finished. But now it's in the throes of being slung together. So there are oases of impressive blgs. with beautifully landscaped surroundings, but btw. them are broad expanses of weeds and nude dirt. Presumably some of this will be seeded during the rainy season. Shorty and I have got in several walks on the beach, where there is usually quite a number of sturdy fellows riding surf boards. (That sentence didn't come out right, but you get the idea.)

I have had four sessions of my seminar. Things seem to be going well, though not a single student from the social sciences signed up. All English majors. One pulled out, though I don't know why. In a curriculum vitae I asked each member of the class to write, he testified that he is a nudist, was iluminated by mescaline, likes to fart in the bathtub, likes to dispute, and distrusts systems. I presume his distrust of systems was the motive for his withdrawal. In a note returning his paper, I assured him that systems necessarily arise in the attempt to dispute intelligently. And I added: Think of me the next time you self-express, or communicate, or consummate in the bathtub."

So far, only the most fleeting of contact with any member of the faculty. But in the attempt to write up my notes on "Kubla Khan" I have been pounding away at all available times. (Last night, disgusted with the boredom of lying awake, I got up about one o'clock, and worked until 5:30 in the morning—at which time, having towards the end worked up a semi-snootful of Old Grand Dad, I slept until 10:30, with my trusty red bandanna on my eyes. The damned article is taking some unexpected turns. But the prime irony is in the fact that I'm supposed to be doing a comment of about twelve hundred words for us in an anthology; I have circa nine thousand, and am still going.)

A chap at the U. of Texas has written, asking me to take part in a symposium on Formalist Criticism next February. It looks as though the time would be just right for me, as we planned to stay in the South for a while on the way back home. (Things end here circa the end of January, and we don't want to be back at Andover until about the beginning of April.) However, they might not take to my proposal for a talk on the principles *and limits* of Formalist Criticism. Wellek is apparently to be among the Symposiasts, also Frye and Vivas.

We're subletting a mollycoddled place in a Development called New Horizons, populated entirely (except for us) by oldsters who have retired. It makes me ask the self uneasily how long I can hold out yet. I have never seen a cemetery with a greater profusion of well-kept flower beds. But everything is done by hired hands, so the poor old men can't even putter around. Yet there is a swimming pool, and the lawns are so arranged that there is a kind of golf course, except that there are no long drives possible. There are several of these developments hereabouts, the houses selling for about twenty-five thousand dollars. And though many are still unoccupied, the grounds around them are kept in perfect condition.

Best luck.

Sincerely,
K.B.

325—1 Moreton Bay Lane
Goleta, Calif. - 93017
November 30, 1964

Dear B&B,

Holla! We're delighted to learn of Bill's reprieve. I'm sure that the Rochester sichaysh will be all to the good. And it's surprising how few enemies one really *has* to make. There are some. But it's like prize-fighting: Usually even the guys that pummel hell out of each other professionally can get along famously when not in the ring. True, this sorta thing can be carried too far, but not by the likes of us. (In the case of Wescott, for instance, in view of your different ages, nsech, I think you could have afforded to send him a slightly whimpering petition before taking the last step. I was greatly impressed by a note in a pamphlet they give out at Yellowstone. It said that tame bears are much more dangerous than wild ones. For wild bears completely avoid people, whereas tame bears walk among them without fear. Thus, you might happen to get between a cub and its mother—and so much the worse for you! Not being an expert Aesop, I can't point that up as well as I'd like to. But it suggests the general drift.)

I recd. four hunnert bayries advance for the Suhrkamp Verlag translation of PLF, with another hunnert due when the translation is finished. They're now inspecting C-S and ATH; but there's been no mention of GM.

This week I finish my public talks at UCSB. (I am scheduled to give talks at three other divisions: Davis, Riverside, and L.A.) To the best of my knowledge, my seminar (after reduction to eight students) has been doing very well. (At least, I look forward to each session iggerly—and it's hard to believe that I could be blunt enough to have such an attitude if the Studententum loathed me.) Your reference to PLF reminds me of a sichaysh I encountered a year or so at Amherst, where they had me up for the better part of a week asseverating with that book as text. I encountered resistances like this: 'But you don't approach things as literature. For instance, one of the pieces that we were required to read was your talk on proverbs.' Whereupon I: 'What?! Proverbs not literature?! And if you want to rule them out because they may have begun among illiterates, the same is true of ballads, and maybe even epics like Beowulf and The Iliad.' But as regards my competing with Frye and Richards, please do ask 'em to take a look at my essay on Poe's essay on writing 'The Raven.' It's reprinted in one of the two paperback burkables, which are now in print, and copies of which I owe you and will in time summon the resourcefulness to send you. (Indiana U. Press, edited by Hyman: *Perspectives by Incongruity* and *Terms for Order.*)

Meanwhile, I must look up the Feidelson review. I once reviewed a book of his (as you will discover by consulting W.H. Rueckert, p. 236). And my memory is that I reviewed it with considerable admiraysh. So, things 'gin make sense. I know Genet only via reviews and a movie. But I'll try to catch up with the flower-girl, at first hand, e'en though the hand is made to stink like the finger the aging Yeats wrote about. (I mislead. Yeats suggests that Joseph must have liked the smell, though the thought is somewhat outside the bounds of orthodox Mariolatry.)

In any case, bejeez, it's good to see you happy. Swing into it—and the more power to youenz both.

Sincerely,
K.B.

University of California, Santa Barbara
English, 1/11/65

Dear Bill,

Hell! I should be working my head off, preparing for a talk I'm slated to give on the 31st (four days after my term here expires). And tomorrow I get my students' final papers. But I'm in a slump.

Strange, some people beef about my style. Yet others as discerning as John Crowe Ransom have even complimented me. Wadda woild! Too bad about Simon. I rather favor his criticism.

We were at the Center (for Advanced Study, etc., Stanford) over the holidays. There I met Brown, Crews, and Luciano Gallino (who gave me a copy of his article). One of my students who knows Italian offered to read it for me. But apparently he has some philosophic angles which she wasn't up to. So I remain a little vague (except for one stinking quote from Richard Chase, which is in English, and which Lucky the Chick seems, as far as I can see through my fog of Latin and French, to be citing without wholesomely strong denial, by a damned sight). I don't know about the Rooshians and East Germans (the test, I should think, wd. be how they could take *Attitudes Toward History*). But the Poles send me *Polish Perspectives* (on their own initiative), and the recently deceased president of Bennington told me that, when he was in Jugoslavia, he encountered specialists there who knew me and asked about me.

The galleys of the poems are in Babylonian captivity. You don't need to say so publicly, but I have made a dismaying discovery. For reasons best adapted to her finaglings, it would seem that Mrs. Hermes is happier with a book sewed up in Absolute Potentiality than with it published. I don't wholly understand these things. And I couldn't unless I were a real-estate promoter in California. But on the basis of my studies in the metaphysics of Idealism, I'd suggest that the sichaysh is probably something like this: As long as a book is sewed up in Absolute Potentiality, it might be capitalized at God only knows what; but as soon as it is reduced to the strict materiality of publication, the range of evaluating for purposes of accountancy becomes quite debunkingly restricted. I speak only on the basis of my studies in German metaphysics.

It is too bad about Mrs. Nichols. When I was at L.A. recently (where, honest to God, I gave two quite effective talks, one right after the other, the second in answer to a request sprung on me at the last moment), I was told that she is coming to give a course on Brk and Rchrds there. But her slant is so strong on the Rhetoric (I think the course is to be given in the Speech Dept.) I guess that she honestly doesn't want to have interferences from the other dimensions. She sees it thus, and God bless her, e'en though it haint the whole story. (Incidentally, I have not heard from her since God only knows when. On taking over the editorship of the Q. Jrn. of Sp., she asked me for a contribyoosh. I wrote saying that I'd give her a batch of pages that considerations of space had caused me to drop from the original edition of the Grammatica Motivorum. But she dint answerve. And this makes sense inasmuch as her essential interest is in Rhetoric. It haint a matter of your picking fights. It's a matter of a different angle. Her angle is right for her purposes. Yours is right for a different purpose. And so it goes.

It would be fun if you turned up down there, in re formalist criticism. (Incidentally, I think they tried to get Frye; but he must have been involved elsewhere.) As for us Oldsters: You forget that we're still young at heart (except for cardiac symptoms, and other such negligible considerations). And bejeez, I wish I could be a flyonthewall at the Northwestern speech association you mention. Ennihow, I trust you and Duncan will tell me how badly I got mussed up.

I know Yates. (I met him once when we were both holding forth at Wisconsin.) He slashes around, lively-like. I liked him. And I think his lines are fun. And I can make sense of every one, if I have to (though, as I see it, he sometimes adds extra suffering by introducing syntactic inversions not sanctioned by traditional Poetic License). No. I can't figger dun dopes dunce treading and 'Ammann.'

Seminar, I think, went pretty well. Formula: 'As a lion, he was mousified; but as a mouse he was tremenj.' I shall have survived unless it turns out that, in my various exhaustians, etc., some damned canker had a chance to get a foothold (establish a beachhead), with corresponding results to show up later.

Going back over again: No, no bibliography. Projected title for the poems: *Introduction to What* (title taken from the introductory poem). Another title I'm thinking of is: *The Orphan's Cheek* (in keeping with the Spanish proverb, 'The barber learns on the orphan's cheek'). Two of my Oldster poems ended the year in the Dec. issue of *Poetry* (incl. the one on the chickadees, that gave us delusions of grand by eating out of our hands).

Incidentally, I still owe the Rueckerts that godam book (the two burkable combined in one volume). Everything has been mussy. but copies are on the way now. So I'll be getting that off soon. (Incidentally, start boning up on the second part of Gayties Faust; for apparently the Sewanee Rev. is to present my presentation. Formula: Nobody would dare take on that job but a great Goethe scholar or a barger-inner-onner like De Burp. I was asked to give a talk on that text. I was perfectly aware that I had been asked only because the scholars had begged out. And having done Fowst One, I was all set to agree. And I did. But I never dared offer it anywheres. Then, on sweetly objecting to Joseph Frank's review of RR, in *Sewanee,* I bethought me: Why not? So, along with my demurrings anent Frank's story, I sent a copy of this bundle. And lo! there is a God. For Lytle will take it, though he wants some emendations or omissions (I'm still not clear on this point, and now await further advices).

And I gotta good thing going on 'Kubla Khan.' (It helps me finish up with a hitherto unfinished job.)

In the meantime, it's good to see how buzzy-wuzzy you now are. That Rochester angle has perked you up unmistakable. You're out of whatever previously weighed down upon you. Your letter, as read btw. the lines, says you're striking sparks, and feel accordingly.

Gott segne B & B. Holla!

Sincerely,
K.B.

University of California, Santa Barbara
Inglese, 1/16/65

Dear Bill,

At last, the book is on the way.

And I suddenly bethought me. I did assign a reading list, but not a large one. Aristotle's Poetics and Rhetoric, Coleridge Biog. Lit., Thomson Aeschylus and Athens, Marianne Moore Predilections, Wm. Rckrt, Passage to India (for Indexing and final paper), various items by De Burp, the Brooks-Wimsatt history, with other items that turned up along the way (Longinus, Young Goodman Brown, Joyce's The Dead). Also, from the start, Yvor's Winters' none too sweet-tempered essay that takes off from my principles of form. I also called the class's attention to the paperbacks: Poetry: Form and Structure, edited by Francis Murphy; Aesthetics Today, edited by Morris Philipson; Aspects of Poetry, edited by Mark Linenthal; Computers, The Machines We Think With, by D. S. Halacy, Jr. My notes are in such hellacious shape, I am giving this from memory.

But this is Behind in Everything speaking. So I desist.

Holla!

K.B.

Ongroot, bejeez
2/4/65
(at present, in Tucson)

Dear Bill,

Help! Help!

Have started to work in earnest on my Grand Texas Deposition. And have been punishing myself with super-insomnia while, on the side, I race through Brooks on Faulkner.

Of a sud., I realize that maybe you can help me tremenj. Namely, to wit, viz: If you happen to have easily available a letter I once sent you anent *Intruder in the Dust.* In ptikla I was struck by the fact that Brooks wholly ignores the 'pity and shame' formula—and I think that, by citing it, with attendant observations, I can show fairly readily how, in his present book at least, Formalist Criticism has just about gone down the drain.

I'll try to pick up another copy of the book at a local store. And shall probably locate the passage sans too much effort. But I think I might use the whole bleat. (My notes in connection with the girl whom I dragged through *Light in August* are out of the question, doubtless being filed with that year's flotsa and jetsa—what Nemerov calls 'teachersht'—anent my class at Bennington, and now lying at four degrees above zero in NJ.)

Ennihow, if you could oblige, by either mailing me the letter or a copy, or bringing it along with you in case you decide to join the fray, I'd be most grateful. I may not be able to use it in the talk itself, but would have it for the discussion period that follows. Hopefully, salivatingly, I avow: please send c/o Prof. Wm. J. Handy, Chairman, Committee on Formalist Criticism, U. of Texas, Austin, Texas, 78712. (Incidentally, I expect to arrive at Forty Acres Club, Feb. 10th.)

The stop-off at UCLA seems to have turned out quite well (though I was vastly worried in advance, owing to acute Reorganization Trouble—and the brilliant, temperamental fellow who was to work with me went dizzy at the last moment, with some kind of inner-ear infection),

Whiled away one night with a sixty-cent dictionary reading Luciano Gallino's essay, greatly aided also by the fact that his quotes are left in English. So far as I can gather, he never read a single word of such stuff as I have published along Poetics lines. I wrote him some bulletins and gave him some offprints—but necessarily I have not heard from him, though he could have reached me within a week after receiving my first offerings. We'll see. But I has me doots.

Meanwhile, oof! as insomniac as God and/or the Devil.

Sincerely,
K.B.

And/or
4/13/65

Dear Bill,

At last, back at headquarters, after more hitherings and thitherings than it's worth shaking a stick at, I find awaiting me a most welcome of thine (of the tenth inst.).

Jeez, it's good to hear therefrom.

As for your alarms and excursions:

I see no reason why Frye should not take over. He is just about where I was in P&C, when I tried to make the "poetic metaphor" do the whole job. Obviously, such an error flatters the dept., and that's that.

Wherever we overlap, you're the most competent to tell us who is overlapping whom. In other words, when did I say it, and when did he? (Some of the overlap, of course, has to do with guys like Aristotle and Plato, who are obviously indebted to both of us.)

The Kirk angle is entrancing because he did his Ph.D. on me—and he has got me engagements to yipe in areas as far apart as Florida and Nebraska. I like him a lot. We had some delightful sessions with a bottle at odd hours of the night—and it's quite possible that, at some stage in the developments, something he said elicited the goodfellowship kind of response from me he seems to have in mind. Maybe yes, maybe no. But in any case, your letter reminds me that I forgot it—so I'm writing him to ask what the hell it could have been. Maybe it was all to the good. Who knows? If it was, I'll certainly add the twist, and give him credit.

And in my capacity as one who taught in a girls' school for many years, I do hope that the girl who had been living inside your book was pretty. But I am puzzled as to why, somewhere along the line, they didn't let Frye and me confront each other. Books be damned. Please let it be known that I am ready to confront any of these superior farts.

The Cowleys are likely to be with us about June 7-9. If your travels would not bring you into close conflict with those dates, keep us in mind. And God bless you for loathing our shitty policies in our dirty war in Vietnam. Gott segne B und B.

Yes, thanks; I got the stuffo at Austin. And I thought that the record (to be published in the Texas Quarterly) would speak for itself. But a great silence has fallen upon the entire enterprise, so that I have not had a chance to see one single sparkilla of the record. And it follows that, as of this writing, I doan no from nothn. Naturally, since I subscribe to Kafka's notion that bureaucracy is God, I keep thinking up all kinds of fancy ways in which my asservations could get distorted. Over thirty years ago, I learned to fear that machinery. I keep remembering uneasily that, when I gave a taped interview there a couple of years ago, they agreed that I would see a transcript before publication. But SOMETHING WENT WRONG—and I am credited with speaking of 'a great big movie' when I referred to 'a Grade B movie.' So I grow fearsome.

Meanwhile, love to B & B,

K.B.

R.D. 2, Andover, NJ - 07821
Sept. 2, 1965

Dear B&B,

In looking for Bill's letter, I found a lot of other things I haven't been able to find. But I have ruefully decided that I won't find his letter until I'm looking for something else.

Meanwhile, I remember that you're back at the river. And if you feel like voyaging hither before school starts, by all means Yes.

At present our only engagement is for the seventh-eighth. Last weekend we were in Connecticut—and as usual I nearly killed myself.

Prepare to see me looking like the wrath of God—and constantly reiterating my firm conviction that if all the shit in the world were put in one pile, it would not even remotely add up to our policy in Vietnam.

Our phone: 201-347-3249. Our address, as always: New Appalachia. But at least, the drought seems moderately broken.

Don't miss the luscious story in today's NY Times. Another grand instance of

C orruption
I volving
A merica

Meanwhile, I have been in quite a slump. Having several things to do, I let each one interfere with the others. However, I have signed a contract for the reissuance of TBL (U. of Cal. Press); and I revised the "arguments" which I intend to put at the heads of the chapters—also I wrote what I think is a good, short new preface. But I still have to fill out the dope for publicity, nsech. The books of essays must now be finished for the press. (I don't intend to revise them, but I do have a notion of adding comments designed to point up the continuity among them. If I can finish this job in the next few weeks, I could then settle on the Poetics. I have turned down exactly six offers to teach, the hardest to reject being Hawaii—but I have sworn to do nothing along those lines next year except for an occasional lecture or conference.) The Hermes sichaysh has been morbid, but may soon take a turn for the better (at least to the extent of my being able to do something elsewhere with the batch of poems which have been bottled up in galleys).

At intervals, such waves of pure Disgust come over me, I'm beginning to wonder whether it involves some ailment (physiological) not yet made wholly manifest. Or does it have to do simply with being sixty-eight? "A two-party system of government is one in which either party may, if possible, be rottener than the other." "Das Leben ist ein Grobian,/Und grosser Ekel greift mich an." "There's no hope for literature until the paper runs out." "Listen,/ All you Shrewdies,/ Buy Consolidated Overkill." And so on, including, "There's things around my heart not done by love."

Holla!

K.B.

R.D. 2, Andover, NJ - 07821
September 15, 1965

Dear Bill,

Here's hoping that my saturnine, non-saturnalian mood didn't freeze you into silence. And that—on the contrary—you are zestfully Forging Ahead.

Recently Armin Paul Frank and his wife were here. They are a pleasant young couple—and I guess they sufficiently readjusted themselves to the joltings (or whatever) that inevitably occur when one meets in poison someone whom otherwise one had but known on the page. At least, all *seemed* to be going along quite smoothly. Their bibliography of De Burp's publications is most impressively enterprising (even unto lil mags like *Sansculotte* and *Slate*). Deutsche Grünlichkeit. Also they are katholisch, as they delicately let me know after I had been ardently displaying my Dictionary of Heresies, Sects, and Schisms. It all happened because among the exhibits is one on Arminius.

I just heard from Andrew Lytle that *Sewanee* looks with favor upon my Emerson essay (on the earlier and longer of his two essays entitled "Nature"). And I have just seen a dispiriting review (in *Poetry*) of the Hyman-edited volumes. The only other major piece of news is that there's something dead somewhere behind the walls upstairs. But it begins to grow less assertive than it was.

What happened to your plans? We await advices. And what is your address to be in Rochester? I'm expecting to receive a couple of offprints which I'd like to send you.

All the copy is in for my novel (which the U. of Cal. Press plans to reissue in the Spring). I am now not too successfully goading myself to finish the editorial work for the collection of essays. Whether through courage, stupidity, or disease, I have turned down no less than seven offers to teach under various conditions this coming year. However, I have transformed a couple of them into talks-and-conferences (postponed until next Spring). I think we'll linger here until some time in December, and then amble aimlessly South.

Meanwhile, I have just found your letter, and I discover that you do not speak of trekking hither at this season. Also, I say jeez thanks for the kind words anent my verbalizings. And the account of your various installationings sounds most imposingly aimful. May you not end by hating the place!

Holla! Let joy be unconfined.

Sincerely,
K.B.

nil VII VIII II I … 11/26/65

Dear Bill,

Many thanks for thine of the 20th inst.

This is a kvickie, in a jam, to say that my main essay on boydy-think is in *The Psychoanalytic Review,* Fall 1963. (There's where the stuffo on Aeschylus and Wagner nestles.)

I didn't see the essay on Wilson.

I do indeed look forward to your elucubrations on Wescott. I'll take 'em with me southwards (we plan to leave circa Dec. 12th), and will write you from the other end of the line.

It looks as though we did contrive to keep the valley "Residential"— and that's enough for the time bean.

It looks as though the new edition of the novel is to appear next March. The books of essays promptly next autumn. (I'm now in a jam trying to finish the editorial work, while also taking time out for three yiping sessions, one at Syracuse next week.)

Brown's a brilliant writer. But I think he has a naively Utopian strain. He would make *too* much of body-think, o'erlooking the tremenjous incentive to the excape goat that pops up right at the start, in the ease with which language lends itself to *substitution* (the substituting of one term for another, as even in processes so "rational" as mathematics). It's so easy, so "natural," to say: "It's *his* fault, not *mine.*"

Don't say "ad homin*u*m," or we're lost. (From Augustine I learned the wise injunction: Never try to smite an enemy with bad grammar on *your* part.)

The Fraser review broke my heart simply because it was so *wasteful.* I'd rather be ferociously attacked than so pissantly malaproposed. It's a crime against our forests.

Chase was close up with the stinks of the Phartisan Review. That's a good first rough approximate for Chase, where I am concerned.

After having heroically turned down seven jobs for this year, I'm being sorely tempted to take one for next year, since I have already succeeded in cutting it down to half-time. But I may be saved by the final decision as to the mazumatics of the case. I'd rather rot for nothing than kill myself for not enough. (Here you get a glimpse of true Burpian heroics.)

As for Vietnam, please consult the Cumaean sybil (I'll try again: sibyl). ((???????or some such??

Holla!

KB

And *please:* Don't miss my item on "Kubla Khan," due to appear any minute in one of the Pocketbooks, *Our Hundred Masterworks,* or some such title. Oscar Williams started the project; and after his death it was taken over by a friendly fellow name Flayderman.

The new *Southern Review* evidently treated your boikbook somewhat—but I don't have a copy of that issue. (Incidentally, they are publishing an article of mine on Diana Barnas's *Nighthood,* the distillation of several years' discussion in the classroom.)

Address after Feb 1:
c/o Schellhase
R. 1 Box 342
Englewood, Florida 33533
January 25, 1966

Dear Bill,

Holla! I have done my homework—and herewith salute your Opus No. 2.

One gets a strong sense of your thoroughness. At times I feel that you are a bit tough on the guy. But you make amends elsewhere.

I must confess that when I read *The Apple of the Eye,* I was tremendously impressed. I was working on *The Dial,* but was home with the flu. I remember returning to the office and telling Alyse Gregory, in a mixture of admiration, envy, and dejection, "That is the book I wanted to write." I haven't seen it since. And maybe, if I have time when I get back home, I'll try it again. But your severities make me wonder whether there was something in the times that added to the book's lustre then, but that your comparative youth puts you outside of. In any case, I was surprised by your reservations, though I won't deny that you may be right.

I sorta wish you had quoted more. Often you do by asseveration what might have been accomplished by citation. And in a book of that sort, it seems to me that it profits by maximum interlarding of excerpts, particularly a constant smattering of brief ones.

Be that as it may, you authoritatively establish it that you didn't skimp on the job. One feels that one is getting an expert survey. But I believe that many of your references to character-problems and the like could have been handled more diplomatically by using Wescott's own words at all or nearly all such spots. Also, I think you could have increased the percentage of sheer description, with fewer statements of evaluation. (Incidentally, somewhat lawlessly, your several references to when the hawk "bates" got me to wondering what expert in the story might be the Master Bater—but that just comes of having a doity mind.)

All told, it's a solid performance, and should net you another commission from somewhere. Best luck!

Me meanwhile, I have sent in the copy for the book of essays and am now hurrying through some odds and ends, hoping thereafter to work only on the Poetics Ms. At the moment, ten P.M. after a very busy day with the qwerty uiop, I am flat as stale beer.

. . .

Next morn. Light rain falling o'er the bay outside my window. Six hours' sleep on two 1 1/2 gr. Nembies, "potentiated" by one aspirin. Not a bad percentage, for me. I was thinking: If you do another job like the Wescott book, you might consider a frequent use of the sheer *general outline* method, for peddling plots. As per Arst. Poetics xvii. I think there are many good results to be got by the procedure. "Boy meets girl" rather than "John meets Mary," nsech. It should also help show any differences (if there are such) when a character by the same name is used in different works. And I wonder why you dint do more "indexing." For instance: If "hawk" in the great story, how about "hawk" incipiently and retrospectively in passing contexts elsewhere? And why not little catalogues, illustrating by explicit quotations exactly how many major attributes the term possesses, as a term in W's ptikla nomenclature? And why not attempts at a cluster of terms that variously "imply" one another in W's work as a whole or in some one ptikla work? In brief, why not more accentuation of Methodismus?

But heck, you did enough!

And now, to the grind. Schechner, of *Tulane Drama Review,* had asked me for something (in a letter dated Dec. 22.). I found it yestiddy, scattered among my scatterings, and started an apologetic letter saying I had nothing to offer. Then, of a sud. I remembered some stuffo I had done on Ionesco's *Victims of Duty*—and bejeez, not only had I brought it with me among my mob of MSS, but I was able to find it within five minutes. So I did some last-minute reshaping for the particular purpose of the gazette, and hope to get it off today. Hence, though it looks as though staged, my letter to him changes in the middle, and what began by saying "No soap" ends by saying "I'll have it at you within a few days." It involves questions of form (as regards differences btw. classical criteria, like Arst. on Sophocles nsech, and typical modernique goings-on). At the moment, the fair copy is being hammered out by the aesthesiat-culinariat-secretariat dept. in the adjoining room.

Best De Burpian wishes to all the family.

Sincerely,

K.B.

R. 1. Box 342
Englewood, Florida 33533
March 11, 1966

Dear B&B,

Where was we?

How goes it with the Wescott enterprise? Any reviews? Any admirations? Any altercations?

Things are moving towards a close here. I'm scheduled to leave by plane for Kansas City on the 20th. Shorty starts back with Old Dobbin the next day. Perhaps Butchie will fly down to drive back with her. I'm to be bandied about among various departments of both U. of Kansas and U. of Mo., mainly the latter. And to fly back to NYC on the 27th.

I got into a damfool haggle with McLuhan (me and his books; I have had no direct correspondence, though I have sent some yipes to a friend of his), and doubtless I wasted much time. Point was: In an item I did for a Symposium at the U. of Mo., I mentioned him somewhat. Then, just before sending off my piece, I noted that he was among those invited to attend. So I decided that I had better muster *all* my evidence, just in case he was there and a first-class brawl developed. The whole business became hilarious, because there is such a large area of overlap between things he says and things I have said, yet I contend that the differences are TREMENJ. The only ideal way to proceed would be for me to take up his book paragraph by paragraph and say why I think his statement should be modified a little or a lot. I almost did that, for myself. Then I started trying to find the argumentative shortcuts. And all told, the jumping back and forth between the exhaustive-pedestrian and the sloganized quickies ("with his notion of 'communicative media,' you couldn't tell the difference between a wheel and a rondo") has taken untold years off my life. I must have been slated to live into my nineties; for otherwise I'd now be dead already, instead of damned insomniacally half-dead.

Have agreed to various academic enterprises of varying duration and scope. And may take on an especially enticing one, though at the moment there's too great a discrepancy between its rewards as kudos and its sheerly mazumatic seasoning.

Mainly, this note was written to say: I think it would be nice if Bill got in touch with Dr. J. S. Watson, at 6 Sibley Place, with the idea of a meeting. I did not make this suggestion until I got an indication from

Watson that he liked the idea, though maybe his wife would thereupon take the lead, since she is more enterprising as regards the machinery of public relations. He is the JSW to whom I dedicated one book, and the W. C. Blum to whom I dedicated another. And I think that, the Rueckerts being thereabouts ... etc.

Meanwhile, as I'm sure you know already, each night we pray (so far unsuccessfully) that God give Johnson guidance.

Yours in Christ, and
Vietnam,
K.B.

R.D. 2, Andover, NJ - 07821
May 3, 1966

Dear B&B, Ink,

Speaking of birthdays, the second Burkeboy is 27 years old as of this May 3rd. And in two days I reach the distinguished age of soixante-neuf. Also, I recently received a copy of the Suhrkamp Verlag's incipient whirlwind seller, *Dichtung als symbolische Handlung* (or rather, a translation of the first part, up through *Wahlkampf in Psychoanalysien,* though I wonder what the hell the Germans will make of "Hobo-i-ugha dumbella," which is left sans explanatory footnote.) But it's a pretty lil wolume, and under a noble imprint. Meanwhile, Shorty has got the machinery to going, and young JFBR will be receiving his appointed pewter mug ere long.

Except for the dates around June 18th (when I am slated to get knighted at Bennington), we expect to be here steady, and glad to see the Back-erts. So, spick, and it/thou shall be spoken unto.

Yes, Little Boy Brown is an enlivener, by a damn sight, though I think his Apocalypse racket is bullshide. I can think of nothing more fun than seeing him, Marshall McLuhan, and Albert Ellis all thrashing around in the same circle of litry hell. And for a grant of five hunnert dollars I'd contract to put them there. But he did help a weighty conference levitate. Meanwhile, wd. say: a three-grand raise is somethinx real. I could live on the mere difference btw. Before and After.

If you ever do get around to getting that "damn (affectionately) thing assembled" (and jeez, don't know what you mean!), I wonder if you considered the Sat. Rev. piece on BkMom. I ran into it the other day when looking for something else, and I said to the morbid Selph: "My Gawd, what we wasted! It," with Marianne Moore's, and the one in *The Nation*, by Ciardi. (Did you see my bleatlets in *Poetry* for March?

Meanwhile, my novel goes on both not be republished and AD-VANCING INEXORABLY toward the appointed day. E'en as I write, the presses are presumably grinding, like god-mills. Obviously, were you as up and coming as you ought to be, you'd have written Carey McWilliams, asking to do a review on it for his gazette. But what can I do, if you choose rather to sit around there and rot at a pissant rate of three thousand dollars a year, when you might have made as much as 25 bay-ries, just for a sneeze? How can I learn you?

Yes, I *know* Berryman. Indeed, I knew him personally, before I knew you. He transcended one of the most beautiful Irish girls conceivable (I'd call her a coleen, if I knew how to spell it—and Dick Blackmur used to caress her legs in public, while praising their form, to establish a sheerly *esthetic* position on this sumjick.) But Berryman had to move on. Denise Levertov asked me to review the book from which you are appar-ently quoting, but I was pressed by other obligations. However, I don't think that the lines you quote are as good as you presumably do.

Next morning. What a ginny note! But postim is due. Holla!

K.B.

R.D. 2, Andover, NJ - 07821
July 6, 1966

Dear BillR,

An outfit at the U. of Minnesota prevailed on me to fill out an "in-terest inventory." On the basis of my answers (which I slapped down in a sort of alcoholic rage) the sibylline computer, out of its high-speed digital fog, prophesies these as my top rated vocations, in this order: psychologist, librarian, biologist, minister, psychiatrist, social worker, mathematician, musician performer. I score low as a YMCA secretary, and tearfully low as: purchasing agent, sales manager, policeman, and banker (alas!).

We were sorry to hear of Theron's troubles (due possibly not to aller-gies but to the need of building up a new psychic economy that would comfortably include the newcomer, a difficulty that even a papa can confront, say I, remembering my expeeeriences along them lines). But hoffentlich all is eased by now, unless you are getting slain by such mean weather as is incumbent upon us hereabouts. And we were glad to learn from Betty that all goes swimmingly with lil Tetragrammaton. I told the Franks that you hoped to see them—and let's hope that some sort of arrangement can transpire. We expect them to stop by here in early August. If at any time you all feel venturesome, spick.

The Rockefeller Foundation gave me a grant to the ends of Self-Expression nsech. On the basis of it, I cancelled my agreement to teach at Michigan State next spring, but didn't have the nerve thus belatedly to ask that I be freed from my engagement this autumn at Central Washington State College. (One seminar, though they had offered me a year's assignment full-time. I'm off'n that kind of athaletics for good. But I do enjoy part-time one-termers, each at a different theatre.) I am also hanging on to a one-seminar, one-term deal with Havvud, the following autumn.

Delighted to learn that you're doing the two boik items for the Nation. Q: Does this mean that you are doing them both in one review (which could mean that you are to pontificate circa next December)? Q: Has the new edition of the novel yet reached you? (I recd. one copy by airmail about two weeks ago, but no further ones have arrived. You were on the list for copies from the publisher.)

Galleys have started rolling in, for the collection of essays (due for publication next November). Since I already had three articles to finish, and I invariably kept shifting to whichever one I wasn't working on, these new inroads, plus the ferocious weather, have kept me in a decidedly dirty-dishes-in-the-kitchen-sink state of mind. Howe'er, after an ailment that caused me to cancel engagements at Indiana and Wisconsin, I am scheduled to do a three-day stint at Binghamton, NY next week. We'll probably be leaving here quite early in September, as we're planning to drive West (though none too eagerly, for I never forget that driving is a nuisance and a menace).

My letters to Bill Williams are wherever he put them. (Possibly some at Yale, some in the ashcan.) I'd not be averse to their publication, but there'd be all this other machinery involved. (There is a passage about sleeping that I seemed to remember. But I may be wrong. At least, I was not consulted about its use.)

Ab urbe condita (which is Arabic for "under separate cover") I am sending you a reprint of the Symposium (anent First Writers Congress) in recent no. of American Scholar. Please read it at least enough to see that I worked off my dirty quatrain on the Partisan Review. (It had been spoiling for years, and clogging me with silence.) The Symposium was at least accurately named. We did drink together. And the story of my woes should at least serve as a minor contribution to the comedy of politics. To your present administration is being entrusted the job of turning politics into a tragic farce. Which reminds me of the current Humphrey joke. Johnson turns to him and says, "Did you fart?" Whereupon Humphrey eagerly, "No. Did you want me to?")

Did I tell you? I am now transfigured, with an honorary D. Litt. from benny Bonnington, and a most beautiful hood to keep, and to remind me that I led the Recessional, followed by all them lovely, angelic-looking girls. I was touched to learn that you are still tinkering with the thought of Operation Boikwoik II. I wonder: Are you including those two great stinkers, Max Black and Shitney Hook? Or is that a state secret? (I poisonally, of course, think it would be fun.)

But I must fare forth and pump some aqua pura.

Holla! to all!
K.B.

R.D. 2, Andover, NJ - 07821
July 12, 1966

Dear Bill,

Despite the furious heat and my tangle of unfinished bizz, I decided that I simply must put my papers into some semblance of order (my study being still cluttered with random piles of stuff, on bed, chairs, table, floor, not yet sorted after our trip last winter—and now I'll soon be starting another one).

This morning I sent off 87 galleys of the essay book (a lot more still to come), and galleys for a long essay on "Formalist Criticism: Its Principles and Limits," to appear in next issue of the Texas Quarterly. And now I'm trying to decide what to take with me, for my three days at Binghamton.

Josephson's address is: R.D., Sherman, Conn. 06784. Kirk's is: 804 E. 34 St., Kearney, Nebraska 68847.

Anent Va. Holland, I feel thus: As regards the portion of my Cause with which she can identify herself, she has been a doughty warrior. Naturally, I do wish that you could bring yourself to include her, even though you felt moved to disagree with what you included. Above all, if you would exclude her purely on the basis of your personal battles with her (whatever they were I never quite understood), I think you and I should join together in praying to our Father that He give you the grace to transcend such motives. If, on the other hand, you can find no whole article of hers which fits your Design, could you propose to include some portion? But in the last analysis, though I would grieve is she were smacked down with silence, the decisions are yours.

The other day I received a letter from Cowley, saying among other things: "Did you know that a prof at Rochester ... is doing an anthology *For Kenneth Burke,* for your 70th birthday?" I gather that he does not know of your book on Boik, or does not associate you with it. Wadda woild!

Was much interested to learn of your older boys' wrestling with the Reality Principle. (Down with the Idealism of the W.C., that primal cultural lie that attains its ultimate fruition in plans for fighting dirty wars with clean bombs.) And I do hope that Lil Tetragrammaton's trouble is soon arrested.

Meanwhile, best luck to one and all.

Sincerely,

K.B.

In answering your inquiry about my letters to Bill Wms., I should have given you Floss's address: 9 Ridge Road, Rutherford, New Jersey. She'd probably be a better bet than Thirlwall; for though he'd know where the letters are, he'd have no rights—and he's on bad terms with Floss. (He wanted to do a biography of Bill, but she wouldn't give him permission to quote even a comma.)

Oof! Twice today, when I took a drink, I got a sudden twinge in my back, to the right. Circa the kidneys? Is this the Next Phase? Bah!

I'm glad to hear of the move towards Watson via Segal. —As for the godam novel, I don't know what the heck. I received one copy via airmail a couple of weeks ago—but nary an inkling since.

K.B.

R.D. 2, Andover, NJ - 07821

August 25, 1966

Dear BillR,

We were glad to hear from Betty, but sorry to learn that lil Tetragrammaton picked up a local bug. Here's hoping that all is now total health.

Meanwhile, I've got somethinx on my minifany. I've just finished my article "On Stress, Its Seeking." It's now being typed, and will probably run to about 36-38 pp.

If you're free to look at it, I'd be vastly interested in knowing what you think of it. Howe'er, I'd certainly not want to send it until you had finished and shipped off your review (which should be written sans the burden of your having suffered these comments). Roughly, it divides into a section on the novel, viewed internally (description of its form, contents, method), and a section viewing it psychologically and socio-logically (its relation to me, and to the times when it was conceived and finished).

Thinking back on this unwieldy item, I could easily be persuaded to believe either that it is quite good or that it is lousy (though probably, like everything else, it's somewhere in between such morbid extremes). In any case, at the very least, it's somewhat difrunt from what it might have been. It neither weeps nor boasts, and in a few spots even becomes a bit frisky.

Meanwhile-within-meanwhile, jeez, the agony of this Permissions business, nsech. I should have made a full-throated, heart-felt speech to you, in recognition of the damned nuisances you have apparently been suffering, anent the Burpian Septuagenary. Greater agape hath no man.

I received a belated note from Arminius, en route West. They appar-ently went through a couple of weeks of high-powered deadline-meet-ing immediately after they left here, but are now fancy-free. And their schedule is now so altered that we may be meeting again in Ellensburg. 'Twas indeed a delight to see that the Franks and Rueckerts got along so merrily.

Signed contract and sent off new preface for new unabridged edi-tion of PLF (LSU Press). Due for publication circa next April. Now in a muddle because, just as I started one bit of negotiating anent the poems, another possibility turned up. So I'm caught double-dealing again, my only excuse being that I am crying my condition from the housetops. Also, I'm trying to line up a book for the College Speech Departments (Knopf) before we close up here. Negotiations went through the prepa-ratory martini stage yestiddy, so I can't remember now whether we ten-tatively lined up the material seven ways or thirteen, but things should certainly sift out somehow.

Holla! our best to all.

Sincerely,
K.B.

07821 - 9/9/66

Dear Bill,

Bulletin, Bulletin, Bulletin!

Don't miss review on Dahlberg and the Aphoristic, by one Frank MacShane, in Sept. 12th issue of *Nation.*

Incidentally, the tenor of the piece leads me to weaken somewhat in my resolve, and quote betimes one paragraph from my article "On Stress, Its Seeking" (done for the Washington D.C. Bureau of Social Science Research, Inc.):

Before turning directly to the socio-psychology of our present concerns, perhaps I should mention one further point as regards the sheerly literary aspect of the book. At the time when I was taking preparatory notes, I was also doing much research in studies to do with the mature and etiology of drug addiction. As a result, I became interested in the notion that the "case history" could be readily adapted for purely poetic purposes. The form made for a kind of vignette plus a strongly aphoristic aspect. Since the narrative is so designed that the plot gradually emerges from a sententious context (though the aphorisms are "in character," hence not to be taken as strictly identical with the views of the author), I discovered that the "case history," taken as a *form*, blends well with the aphoristic; a reader hardly notices when one leaves off and the other takes over. This relationship is of great assistance to the effect I mention in my preface to the first edition: "Lamentation, rejoicing, beseechment, admonition, sayings, and invective—these seemed to me central matters, while a plot in which they might occur seemed peripheral, little more than a pretext, justifiable not as a 'good story,' * but only insofar as it could bring these six characteristics to the fore."

Meanwhile, I'm still in the agonies of Permissions-Gathering, plus the vexations of packing. Did I say? We plan to leave here circa the fifteenth. Our address at the other end is to be: Central Washington State College, Box #78, Ellensburg, Washington 98926.

In haste, holla!

K.B.

*heck! I think it *is* (or *becomes*) a good story.

Central Washington State College
Box #78
Ellensburg, Washington 98926
9/28/66

Dear Bill,

This moving around keeps one fragmenteder as hell. Already I'm dizzy with a whole new batch of unfinishednesses.

Afore I forgets: Try Munson at the Hotel Wellington, 7th Avenue and 55th St., NYC 10019. That's the only address I have for him this side of Limbo.

Anyhow, we had four wonderf days, gorgeous weather, and with not many Americans around, at Glacier National Park. (The organization was still intact, but the rash of visitors was over for the season.)

Herewith my thesis on TBL. Did I tell you? Denis Donoghue wrote the NY Review of Books, avowing as to how they should get the book done in their pages. And they told him that a chap from Cornell (whom he considers quite competent) has been given the job. So far, to my knowledge, the reception has been deafening.

They've fixed me up with a handsome, spacious office here, so I guess I'll have to go and be seen regularly sitting in it. (I prefer to work at the apartment, and to be on campus only when absolutely necessary—but I fear that such doings would be frowned upon. Just now, I'm trying to whip my first public lecture into shape. The seminar, I think, will pretty much take care of itself, though I have a full two-hours of verbalizing planned, in case nothing gets to going of itself.)

Many thanks for the book about the setting of omens. I'll read a bit of it each night in bed, before going to insomnia. And I'll report later. The beginning is quite frisky-like. I was interested to note that the author teaches philosophy rather than some branch of straight lit. That in itself should add a twist.

I also include a copy of an item I had in the Tulane Drama Review, a copy of which I don't think I gave you of which.

Our best Burpian greetings to thee and thine outfit.

Sincerely,
K.B.

Residence Address
University Village, Apt. 22
E. Illinois Street
Ellensburg, Washington 98926
October 7, 1966

Dear Bill,

Of a sudden I got an idea. That was ten minutes ago. Now I'm not so sure it is any good. Point is: I was asked (some months back) to comment on a paper by Norman Brown, at meeting of M.L.A., Dec. 28th. I didn't definitively agree, though I said I'd attend and comment if I happened to be nearby at that time. (They're paying my expenses, but only a hunnert bayries for the performance; but I'd hate like hell to go that far at that time for even considerably more.)

It occurred to me that maybe you intend to attend the meetings, and that, if you did, you'd be willing to sing my song for me. If you yea-said, I'd suggest the idea to my chairman and see what he thought about it.

But lo! there's a bit of a hitch. Though my paper on Brown (now perhaps too long, being 12 pages, hence in need of cutting) is quite respectful (natch), it flatly begs to differ. Brown is working the sex-racket for all it's worth and then some. And when confronting his "poetry is sexuality" slogan, I bring up all the reserves to push through my doughty claims that even a hot love-poem (say Sappho's sapphics) is not reducible to said equation. In sum, says I, though a poem might get the girl, it can't produce a baby (or, less delicately put, it can't knock her up).

Then it occurred to me that, even if you do plan to attend the meetings, you might not want to sing my song for me, as it might be embarrassing to your relations with Brown. In any case, I have to write my Chairman soon. So if you do have any bright thoughts on this sumjick, I'd be grateful for a line or two anent same.

Meanwhile, throughout my many trials, I have jerked my way happily through two-thirds of the Omensetter saga. It is, indeed, a fresh breeze (it is fresh and breezy), and every now and then it strikes home (strikes gold). ((Mixed metaphor?)) But (((to mix the metaphor a bit further))) I find that it inclines to the logorhoeic side. Or, at the risk of still more mixing in the interests of literal accuracy, might we say that it needs not so much cutting as wiping? But be that as it may, I'm grateful indeed to the B&B outfit for giving me a copy (thus calling the book to my attention)—and I expect things to get still better as they pull towards the close. (On that, more anon.)

I had my first seminar last evening. Am scheduled to give my first public talk ("We Are What? - Uneasy Thoughts on Automotive Man") next Tuesday. Taking notes for my three public talks while we were crossing the continent, I used this "moving" experience as a basis for my thoughts and sentiments. It looks as though I may have hit upon a good rhetorical device. For whenever things tend to slow up, I give a glimpse of us going, going, going—and what Amurrican can tell the difference btw. motion and action? So I dare hope that, by this snide trickery, I can meet Demosthenes' formula for the good orator: "Action, action, and action."

Holla!

K.B.

As regards the bleat I sent you: I now think that my memory tricked me, and that the eyes (?) obsession *did* follow TBL, not P&C.

University Village, Apt. 22
E. Illinois Street
Ellensburg, Washington 98926
10/20/66

Dear Bill,

First: Yes, by all means, let's drop my sudden alcoholic notion about the MLA entanglement. I'll just write My Leader, asking him what he wants to do, if anything. (At the moment, for instance, I'm sure that my first draft is too long, since there are to be several comments. And such. But in any case, I think it would be absurd for me to travel so extensively for so brief a bleat.) So, erase that from the record. (And in writing him, I'll not mention thee.)

But damn it, Bill, I do think you were wrong to get so involved in the departmental contretemps as you apparently did. Jezoos, Bill. When you run into a sichaysh like that, let it ride, e'en if they're all set to hire the worst thing known to man. That's a time to roll with the punch. And you make a come-back later, when conditions are favorable. And by all means, be careful that you don't gradually re-enact all over again the role that you loathed in Illinois. Forget about giving me advice. Let me give you some (along the lines of a letter I wrote you when you shook clear of Illinois and started singing to me about the wonders of Rochester).

As for my sichaysh here: I purposely cut the job to the proportions that I wanted, with corresponding cuts in salary. And *I'm* the guy that's in danger of using me until I'm used up. As with every place, there are all sorts of pressures going on. And there's always the possibility that something can go radically wrong. But, so far, I'm being treated damned well. But I say so without the slightest doubt that, if at any time conditions are such that a witness is needed who saw me in bed with Stalin, the witness will be forthcoming. Or with Mussolini, or whomever. But one hopes that such dire finaglings won't be necessary. And the chances are good that they won't, e'en though I always fall somewhat out of line.

You say that you wrote to "John Crow Ransom." Unless your orthographic operations as regards his middle name were a fanciful way of disporting in good clean fun, dunt be sooprized if you don't hear from him. He hasn't acknowledged some things of mine either. But I have good reasons to know that illwill is not involved. (Why? Because a man who is a former student and ardent loyalist of his, phoned me recently, to tell me that JCR had been with him for a week, and that they had talked over all sorts of things, and that JCR had done a most effective job there, and that I could get five hunnert bayries for a one-night stand, repeating the very talk which I had given in Texas, on the very program the publication of which had been held up by Ransom's delays.) And so it goes …

Meanwhile, I wonders if you saw the October 20th issue of *The New York Review of Books,* incl. the paragraphs anent TBL and De Burp. (All I know otherwise is that N. J. Osborn is to do the essays for Hudson, and apparently will throw in, through sheer superabundance, like the Creator, considerations anent TBL.)

May thy homelife continue happily—and may your operations eventually break clear, like going West of Bismarck, across the prairies so that our 560-mile trip that day was pure relaxation.

Holla!

K.B.

University Village, Apt. 22
E. Illinois Street
Ellensburg, Washington 98926
11/6/66

Dear Bill,

My salutes to the New-Born, Roll-With-the-Punch Rueckert. Obviously in a few years you'll own the place. And you'll have written the book, since it will be full of all the scraps your resigned silence caused you to sublimate.

And I'm happy to learn that you uncorked the review for *the Nation*. (Incidentally, about the time you receive this note, I shall be flitting off to the Stress Congress, which is held on Nov. 11-12. My paper, by the way, is to be discussed by David Brion Davis, Dept. of History, Cornell. His own offering is: "Stress-Seeking and the Self-Made Man in American Literature, 1894-1914." Among other things he talks about works by Stephen Crane, Owen Wister, Frank Norris, Dreiser, and Jack London. I was given the job of commenting on the paper on international law, by one R. A. Falk, in Center of International Studies, Princeton U. I tried to peddle some of my stuff on the "Dialectic of Constitutions" in GM, and I already mailed my observations to Falk, who will take them I wonder how. Jerome Frank took a shine to my Grammar, and wrote me about it. And a guy at the U. of Chicago swiped quite a bit of it sans giving me credit. But legalists generally don't take kindly to my theory of the Constitution's clutter of "sovereign wishes.")

By all means, if you feel moved to adjudicate anent L as SA, please do. The book is not out yet, but is due to appear some time this month. A few days ago I heard that it was just about ready for binding. I should think that you could work from the galleys, and that you would receive the copy from *The Nation* when they get it—also possibly one from the Press. I dunno what their plans for complimentary copies are.

Finished my comments on Brown. They are to be read by the Chairman, Eli Sobel who seemed quite happy to take over the job (so don't tell him of my original notion). Incidentally, the piece has turned out to be a bit mean in spots. Shorty is now typing it, and maybe I'll tone down a couple of places before mailing the pages to Sobel. But in any case, it's all love and kisses, as compared with John Simon's hilariously vicious review of Brown's recent book, in the current *Hudson*. (But maybe Sobel won't be so happy with the job, in case he happens to love Brown, as some people unaccountably do. I think that Brown, like McLuhan, has invented a brilliant kind of quackery.)

Meanwhile, best luck to one and all. And Shorty salivatingly awaits the missive from Betty.

Holla!

K.B.

[Libbie Burke]

Ellensburg, WA

November 11, 1966

. . . KB is in Washington D.C. at a conference on, guess what, STRESS SEEKING. That should be a natural for him. And he was actually very excited about it, and eager to be there. All the papers that came in were really interesting, on war, mountain climbers, Amer. literature (pioneer stress seeking type thing of Jack London, not bad at all—Stephen Crane, etc.) . . .

. . . People are most congenial, but we are not doing much socializing (always think of McNamara when I use a word like that) because KB is so busy—and really busy—he is turning out much good stuff. He spends two weeks on a job that most people would knock off in an afternoon, but when it comes through, he has really gotten to the center of it. So there's no use pushing him—that's the way it's gotta be . . .

. . . Received the complete page proofs of the new book today. And it looks pretty good. KB had a bad time with Djuna Barnes, who wanted to prevent the publishers from including his article on Nightwood. As it now stands, it looks like a real literary scandal, for instead of keeping them from publishing it, all she did was to refuse permission to quote— so that when you come to certain places in the article there is a space with a note saying Miss Barnes would not give permission to quote— and it looks as if she were ashamed of the sections from her book, instead of that she was against KB's interpretation of the book. She said she would not give permission because this would imply she approved of the article. Which is of course not the case—as all other authors and publishers gave permission for quotes without even seeing the article. I don't share KB's admiration for this book; I think it is most unpleasantly dirty—so I can't understand why she should object to anything anybody said about it. That dirty old man in a woman's nightgown in bed talking about blood and/or excrement, etc. really alienates (if I may use a well-worn word) me. So now, in her old age, she wants to get insulted at someone analyzing the terminology of that book. She says it is not a novel about homosexual love, but about faithful and faithless love!!!

Returning to the book. Aside from Djuna, it really pleases me as it covers so much ground. And I am so pleased that the Univ. of C. Press wanted to put all of it together, even the long Negative business from the Journal of Speech—which you can take or leave. I.e. the table of contents looks good . . .

. . .We are looking forward to seeing Bill's review of TBL in the Nation. Still my favorite of all of KB's books. And I still have trouble reading certain passages of it . . .

. . .11/12 KB phoned last night to say he was having an absolutely wonderful time with the Stress-seeking people. The man (Davis, History, Cornell) assigned to comment on KB's article (on TBL) did a most interesting job, he says . . .

[Libbie Burke]

Ellensburg, WA
December 13, 1966

. . . Also delighted with Bill's review of TBL. Very fine! Would make only one change—that in speaking of the new book: Language as Symbolic Action, would have noted that it contains all the ideas and methods which will appear in the Symbolic—explicitly stated and exhibited in action. But I have no objection to Bill's opting for the publication of the Symbolic! God knows. And my only objection to this new book is its size—it is three books in one. This does not bother KB at all, or the U. of C. Press—they feel that libraries will have to have it. Maybe some day a Stanley Hyman can put out chunks of it in paperbacks . . .

(Ellensburg, Wash)
Abiturus
12/17/66

Dear Bill,

Sorry to hear that you got trampled on and pushed around. I always thought *The Nation* let authors see proofs.

Actually, Carey McWms. sent me a copy of the review. And I assure you that, however infuriating it was to you, it seemed to go along fine.

I started to write you, saying *Thanks Indeed*—then got side-tracked by last minute events here.

But I know how infuriating that can be. When I was at Santa Barbara, the Herald Tribune *Book Week* botched a review of mine, and I damn near had a stroke. (They turned it around—and as a result, sentences that applied to one book looked nonsensically as though another book was being referred to—and they dropped a really interesting quotation.)

Meanwhile, I'm most grateful though I certainly commiserate with you in your vexation. I guess Miss English wanted to assert her Yglesia.

The Academy telegraphed a request for pictures, but I guess none were forthcoming. (Also, they offered to pay transportation costs for both Shorty & me, if we'd come to the occasion—but it fell on the day when final papers were due here.)

We're now in the midst of packing (Hope to clear out on the morning of the 19th.) I'll let you know where we are when I know. But here's an address where things will be left for me until I turn up there:

c/o Robert Y. Zachary, Editor
The University of California Press
60 College Library
Los Angeles, California 98926

Meanwhile, don't fret too much about the review. True, when an editor tinkers with one's style it's like cutting off one's balls. So maybe Miss English is suffering from the kind of envy Freud attributes to girls young and old.

Ever the aging compromiser, I says thank God you got the message through at all. (To my knowledge, this is only the second review the book has received so far, the possible one or two of the quotations may mention it.) Anyhow, the main thing is: How about helping found an ABJ movement? ("Anybody But Johnson.")

Let joy be unconfined,

K.B.

It turns out that I'll probably be at the MLA meeting; or rather, I'll be at the Norman Brown one, and shall possibly stay over for one day.

(Ellensburg, Wash)
12/18/66

Dear Bill,

Further puzzling development?

All mail sent to Andover is being forwarded to Butchie's. After I sent off my letter to you yesterday I talked with him by phone.

He said the Yglesia lady urgently wanted an article of mine on McLuhan. Carey McWilliams had sent back such an article a couple of months ago—and now it has appeared in the book (a copy of which should have beset you by now, or should soon be besetting you).

What all this may or may not have to do with your revision and the attendant contretemps, I can't know.

Ennihow, I do hope we can have some time togidda at the MLA doings. Since so many of the family are thereabouts and Butchie expects to be in town, I expect a joyous reunion of some sort. Also, here, a major joyousness. Unk (Michael) has got official notice of his discharge. And Butchie's age, plus his science specialty, leaves him pretty safe. But a coupla of the grandsons are in danger.

Today's *Seattle Times* features on page 1 an article reprinted from *Washington Post*:

U.S. SPENDS $322,000 TO KILL ONE VIETNAM ENEMY

My *Anybody But Johnson* movement can use that—but suppose I have to vote for Nixon!!!

Meanwhile, remember, the present criminal policy is *middle-of-the-road*. Jeez, what kind of road are we on?!

In haste,

K.B.

Statler Hilton
MLA
Dec. 27, 1966

Dear Bill,

Damn it, I was so godam fuzzy (not having got to sleep until 6:30), I forget what arrangements we made. But it goes sans to say, I very much wanna seeyuh. If the feeling is mutual, would'st please keep calling me (in Room 1521)? Or, if all that fails, please turn up this evening at my daughter's house on Horatio street, circa 8 P.M. It's in the Village. See phone book under Eleanor Leacock.

Con amore,

Ignatz De Burp

La Jolla Shores Hotel
Years End 66

Dear Bill,

Sorry I didn't see you again. And I hope that our subsequent grievous separation was due to *your choice* and not to *my errors*. (I'm a bit vague on some details, as there was considerable improving of arrangements, from moment to moment.)

I cleared out the next morning, circa six o'clock—an it would have taken even a meaner man than Ignatz de Burp to awaken you by saying good-bye at that hour.

Within a few days, I hope, we'll know where we're going to sojourn hereabouts. I'll let you know,—but meanwhile we remain incommunicad except for this hit-and-run kind of facility.

When you receive this, think of the De Burps as having been (at this particular writing) in their hostelry, and solemnly planning to celebrate the New Year in their room, entirely sans alky, except whatever perchance remains in the blood stream after a potent pre-prandial participation in Old Grand Dad (and long live sparagmos - sparagmos?)

Our joint Burpian love to all—

Sincerely,
K.B.

Postcard
Tecate, Calif.
1/4/67

Dear Bill,

This is a kvickie to say that our address, until probably the middle of March, is: Box 231, Tecate, California 92080. ... I'm sorry I didn't get another chance to see you at the MLA doings. (I checked out the next morning at six A.M., and I knew you'd never forgive me if I called you at that hour.) But I do wish you had come down to Hap's, as I'd like you to have met Henry Sams (head of English Dept. at Penn State). ... Do tell me how everything went, and I'll depose later anent our wanderings and present establishment. (And don't forget to show me the evidence anent the mayhem in connection with the review.) ... Meanwhile, best Burpian greetings to all.

Sincerely, in haste,
K.B.

Box 231
Tecate, Calif. 92080
Jan. 10, 1967

Dear Bill,

Damn it all. We're most sorry to hear of the affliction. But praise God and/or the Nature of Things that your world has moved non-calamitously on. You certainly have paid more than your share to the prosperity of Amurrican Medicine. (I speak as an ex-Christian Scientist who believes only in detestation and alcohol as basic ways of keeping alive—plus, let's admit it, a primitively pious sense of gratitude for wondrous natural moments, like the skyline here at sundown, and attachment to friends.)

If Quentin is like me, you might try going easy on concentrated foods. At first they pep me up, then I start getting rashes, pimples, bellyaches, and the like. Conceivably they could also affect the glands. (Obviously, that's unprofessional medicology—but it's at least something to check on. Even cod liver oil, after a short time, gets me to blossoming like a fertile meadow in spring. Ditto a few pieces of chocolate. And two ascorbic acid tablets can turn my gullet into molten lead.)

Our first days here were hectic with ailments (trick ailments, possibly related to the intestinal bugs that tend to lurk in such areas). But we've just abut recovered now, and the factory has resumed operations. I do wish you could see this place we stumbled upon. In the middle of a near-desert, it's most moderniquely accoutered, and with w.w. carpets so thick, I tend to waver a bit, and to blame the effect on alky. But they build up so heavy a charge of static electricity, I'm constantly electrocuting myself on doorknobs. The sunsets on these stark mountains are solemn and severe. The slopes are marked by nothing but chaparral (orthog?), sage, cactus, and boulders that look as though they were put there by design, like stonehenges. Everything lives on the edge of disaster, and in that respect it flatters me into loving it as an honorifically stylized portrait of mine own present moods. (Maybe I said all this. I doan no what I said—and my earlier notes were sans record.) Plus radio and TV—and beauteous water. And jeez, I nearly forgot! Also a bar.

Don't worry about having called Butchie Unk (Anthony Michael). They enjoy being mistaken for each other.

I'm glad you liked the MLA show. But I must say, poisonally: Never was I proved more Christlike than in my resolve not to haggle with the dirty deal in *Love's Body* (full of shameless stunts that undid by sheer non-mention a tremenjous amt. of distinctions I have spent about 35 years trying to get straight). But I'll discuss that in an artikkel elsewhere, at least glancingly. Gawd, what reaction, in the name of the apocalyptic! (My venomous delight was Fiedler's claque that didn't click. It looked like a sure thing, since the show was over the audience would necessarily be rising to leave. Yet when his schemers rose to give the impression of an ovation for his ecstatic bullshit, the assembled multitude resolutely remained sitting on their multitudinous asses. That sorta thing makes life worth living.)

Our fond Burpian greetings to the now, let us hope, happily recovered Dorsals.

Holla!

K.B.

[Postcard]

Tecate, Calif.
1/14/67

Dear Bill,

In my letter, I forgot to say that Osborn, who is reviewing the books for Hudson, informs me he has received *L as SA*. I assume that you should have ditto. Or have plans been changed owing to your differences with the Editricks?

Holla!

K.B.

(Osborn, whose own name is "Neal," wants to read our hero's name as "Nihilist," who's to say? But I troubles.)

Box 231
Tecate, Calif. 92080
2/10/67

Dear Bill,

How goes it avec the Dorsals? All ailments have subsided, I hope.

Meanwhile, here our stay continues exceptionally pleasant—and nearly every afternoon we tramp for about two hours o'er these big semi-arid bulges that make for vistas everywhere.

Minor triumphs, too. The godam book of essays has already sold a thousand copies, though not a word about it has yet appeared in print. And come April, the Brandeis U. Creative Arts Awards Commission is giving me a grant of One Grand.

What e'er happened anent you, the book, and The Nation? Did your disgruntlement add up to a severing of relations, or has all that been forgotten? I did a review of *Love's Body* for them. (Much in the spirit of the thing I did for the MLA session. I.e., a gently remonstrance by an one who, after only one drink, shouted himself horse around the house. Brown wrote me a letter, thanking me for my "generosity" in re the MLA comments. But a personal letter, I felt, called for a different kind of expression—so I yiped considerably, though it's not the paper, but the book, that makes me so furious. By sheer obliviscence the baystard does all he can to undo every basic distinction about the nature of language I have been trying to make clear for the last 35 years. I imagine my answer means the end of any possible good relations twixt us, unless the tone of my review, in contrast with the tone of my letter, mollifies him.)

Meanwhile, damn the luck, I'm beginning to goid my lirns for a different battle, namely against the guys who claim that "transformational grammar" nsech is the gateway into a "New Rhetoric," or "the" New Rhetoric. I'm to give a talk this summer at Marquette—and I think I'll use, for the basis of my talk, the various items in the recently published paperback, *New Rhetorics,* edited by Martin Steinmann, Jr., Scribners. (In any case, you might want to take a look at it.) Also, on the side, I'm suffering *Universals of Language,* edited by Joseph H. Greenberg, an M.I.T. Press paperback.

Incidentally, today I got a letter from Denis Donoghue, saying among other thing: "Someone told me there's a gathering of essays to be published soon in honour of KB's next birthday. As your most devoted, faithful, longstanding (6feet6inches in my socks) reader I want to know about this." Anything to tell him? His address is: Department of English, University College, Dublin 2, Ireland. He's their Professor of Modern English and American Literature, spells his first name with one 'n,' and claims to be the first (and only?) person to assign TBL and deliver a classroom lecture on same. I hand on these here data just in case ... (I know that he has been tinkering with some stuff anent TBL, and he took a shine to that "stress-seeking" bizz I did on it. Incidentally, the whole batch of Stress papers is to appear in an Anchor paperback, though I know not when.)

If you happen to read the *New Rhetorics* wolume, I'd be much interested in hearing what you think of it. It is by no means the kind of brilliant quackery you get in *Love's Body* or *Understanding Media*. Indeed, it strikes me as having some sound pedagogy in it, as compared with Brown and McLues. As I see the sichaysh, the troubles arise only when they try to make linguistics look as though it could solve more of the problems than is actually the case. My simile is: Using linguistics to solve the problems of Rhetoric is like trying to pack twenty people into one telephone booth. So I'm trying to figure out a talk that will give the guys their dues, along with my reservations. Also, at least one of the guys whom I must push against is also to be among the speakers at this conference.

(Incidentally, the book ends on the stuff about U speech and non-U speech. Among other things, I learn that whereas Non-U says "home" U says "house." So, ever the climber, and seeking earnestly to perfect myself in the ways of U-speech, I go about my business singing, "Be it ever so humble, there's no place like house.")

Ennihow, we must always keep reminding ourselves: The real issue is Vietnam; and it is perhaps the filthiest chapter in the whole history of imperialism, for never has hypocrisy been more brazen.

Love, love, love,
K.B.

Box 231
Tecate, California 92080
2/20/67

Dear Bill,

Your elation is both understandable and infectious. If only I could get Burke off *my* chest so definitively!

And I'm morethanhappy to learn that, e'en after so much suffering, you can still speak friendly-like about the possibility of deposing anent LSA.

More about other matters eventually. Meanwhile, here's what I have on my mindifany:

I have been asked to name a possible candidate for some bounty. Only one nomination is allowed. And I'd like to name you.

It's the same Organizaysh that granted me Ten Grand. I hesitated to tell you about it for two reasons. First, they may throw out my nomination; second, even if they accept it, they may reject your answer to their inquiry.

On the other hand, I think our best policy would be for me to tell you, and for you to tell me a few things about your plans for the Next Phase. (Nothing much. Just enough so that I'd have a talking point when sending in your name.)

If you agree to my nominating you, we should hurriedly see to it that everything gets presented in as persuasive a way as possible. So you should send me a few sentences quickly (including your age!)—and I'll slap out my statement pronto.

I had to do a lot of soul-searching, in making my decision. But fortunately all the other guys whom I thought of have had windfalls of one sort or another.

The only damned trouble is: We may bestir ourselves in vain. Yet it's not too much of a hardship, except the part about raising expectations. Perhaps I should merely have sent in your name without writing you. But I thought that, by telling you, I might get a better sales talk for my letter.

But in any case, please answer me in one way or another soon. For I should not delay my answer.

(Incidentally, I had a deal with Michigan State, but they let me cancel it when I got my Rockefeller Grant, on which I am now theoretically living, though it's supposed to be administered through Bennington, and Bennington has so far dug up not one pfennig. Howe'er, that's the least of my worries.)

Love to all the Dorsals.

Sincerely,
K.B.

I've seen one review of my book. Zestfully on my side EXCEPT, though it quotes me admiringly, the quotations are garbled almost beyond recognition. Wadda woild!

[Libbie Burke]

Tecate, CA
February 22, 1967

. . . I am of course tremendously interested in your KB book & how it turns out.

I am having trouble with my arms—general weakness. I should see a dr. but you know my distrust of same & I do not want to be treated for the wrong thing. Will try to find some reliable specialist when we get back home . . .

. . . Brown* wrote KB a very nice note; figures they should accept the fact that there is no solution to their literary quarrel but there should be friendship nevertheless. KB's complete frankness in writing him all about his resistances—even vehemently, as he did—was in the long run good. KB *has* to make the direct approach, which is honest and works out best in the long run (I hope!). God knows, you have certainly been exposed to it! I think he would have welcomed a counter-blast from Brown—but that kind of exchange could go on forever. How he loves a good literary *battle* . . .

*Merle Brown

Tecate nsech 2/26/67

Dear Bill,

If my sales talk succeeds, I'll show you how I did it. Otherwise, except for the files, it's btw. me and my God.

True, your involvement in my behalf added another angle. But things like that can be given a twist—and if the twist works, it's better than if the problem hadn't turned up at all.

Ennihow, I have put in jeopardy the reputation of us both. And all I ask is that, for a while, you speak not about the whole bizz.

If you get an inquiry, I think it might be well for us to consult anent same. But if you feel otherwise, I'd like to make one basic suggest. Thus:

In talking about your future plans, add this angle: Instead of simply listing your various prospective enterprises, say rather that you have taken notes on all such possibilities, and that you now see a further step whereby they might all be variously incorporated in a single project along the lines of so-and-so.

Hope for nothing (for it's not good to let oneself salivate along them lines). But if the lightning benignly strikes—but begad, our metaphors are getting us into trouble.

In any case, I dug out an attempt of mine in the way of Didactic Poetry. (I'm trying definitively to put the whole bizz together fairly soon.) Maybe you're among them baystards that would call the expression a contradiction in terms, though your idealizing of Brown's racket wouldn't seem to fit such a policy. My mean claim is that there is one heck of a lot of difference between didactic verse and fragmentary criticism that hopes to be exonerated as a kind of poetry for all the obligations it has failed to meet as criticism. My Gawd! the pile of subsidies that went into Brown's Body, and thence down the drain! (Though system is equated with death in his set-up. I dare attempt as systematic a review as I could, making clear the triperoo that he slaps around, in the Body-Book. And if you can find one sentence out of place, then learn me, boy, learn me. You were indeed right in saying that you hadn't finished the book!

And also, now that my blurb is on its way, I militantly invite you to teach me how any self-respecting pedagogue can use that fuzzy book of Frye's as a text. I saluted it originally as a kind of conceptual fun. But I never for one moment thought that anybody as astute as you could put kids to work on it. Jeez, learn me, boy, learn me! And I pray, give me some examples of how *you* use it, in *your* work.

But, be all such things as they may, I know that I'm a grouchy old man, and I discount accordingly. So, though I may fuss and fume, the whole godam family is for you, and that's that.

And may you flourish and flourish, in every respect this side of the population explosion.

Sincerely,
K.B.

Tecate nsech, 3/10/67

Dear Bill,

Heck, I realize it. Since I tried to be nice to you, we have to be mean to each other. But I daresay we'll survive the ordeal.

In the meantime, I'm glad to learn roundabout that you would include Dr. Watson's piece anent BkMom. To this benign info he adds: "Wonder if he will also have the one from the Satdy Review on the same subject. It was remarkable." Then he goes on to say that he is happy to be included (and indeed I very much am that he is.)

Things are moving towards a close here, me frenn. As you well know, if I can just hold out until May 5th, from then on in, or from then on out, everything is velvet except the doctor bills. And they give signs of picking up, not now on my score alas! but in re my sweetest Other, who has turned up with a trick symptom that would seem to have been building up for a long time.

But we're out to track it down. And along with our collaborations in these studies, we're shrewd. Thus, though we necessarily respect the high-paying machinery of diagnosis modernique-wise, we don't feel obliged to believe anything, even if it costs a lot. But it is true that my darling Snooze has a vexing symptom; and it must be tracked down (though she loathes me when I hopefully aver that it is from out the psyche, which I'll grant is a filthy field, but which in our realm would be so easy to patch up, binnuz I wouldn't even mind if she failed to kill me, unless the error kept me awake all night).

No, I'm being mussy. The undeniable fact is that *Osborn was here.* And if I can survive (at least in this stage of the game) I can just about survive anything.

But I 'gin fear I must be nasty. You start letting down the bars because you want to let the kids in. [a line is drawn from the two preceding "you's" and he writes in, "I mean one, we"] Then where the hell are you? What is your value, even to the kids, if in that area you have already gone easy on a mutt, and now you would plead for a student whom you would rate much higher?

I started out, treating that damfool with respect. But by God, before the day was over (and my much-better half had set up a heavenly garlic-laden meal), I decided (on 87 counts out of a possible 89) that he is a dumb bunny. On the other two counts, I assured him that I loves him.

I feel sure that he knows I'm an honest man and that he knows how to add. And the odds speak for their selves. The godam sichaysh is almost beyond belief. If he decides that your position is such-and-such, and you go and show by a specific passage in the text that it's not your position, the guy blunts off like a clam (except that a clam knows its business—and I greatly respect a clam, and some day, I hope, I'll be allowed to clam up for good, and not hang on for ever being tortured by a Gawd that loves not only me but great saviors like the current administration than which nothing ever more persuasively stank to high heaven).

Jeez, I realize all the more what luck I had in being allowed to have such friends as theeart. Please always count me in.

> Signed,
> Ignatz de Burp—or, in old Latin, our
> olufrom Burpius Ignatius—and may
> God have merry o in soulsifary.

Good Sign—In my files, "Rueckert" comes just after "Rockefeller Foundation." Long live Sibyllinity and its dealership.

[Libbie Burke]

> Tecate, CA
> March 13, 1967

. . .They have given me all kinds of diagnoses—I've been through the mill. They don't really know what is the cause of my trouble but I have come to the conclusion myself that it is due to tension and I am taking steps to un-tense and I expect to get results. They did do me the good of telling me what it was NOT which has helped me a lot. Not arthritis, not Parkinson's disease, not brain tumor, etc. etc. The program is rest, good food, and concentration on relaxing those tense muscles, *all* the time. I think I have been mistreating myself, attacking what I thought was a budding arthritic condition.

We continue to think this place is wonderful. All the spring flowers are beginning to bloom. We walk miles every afternoon. KB is getting such good work done (except for the *Symbolic*!!)

We expect to take it easy on the trip home and rather look forward to it.

KB has come up with a good new slogan: We the U.S. *demand* an *honorable* peace in order to end this *dishonorable* war . . .

Abiturus from Tecate
3/29/67

Dear Bill,

For a few days we'll necessarily be incommunicado. But do, on the other end of the line, tell us how all goes with Quentin. I am doubly sensitive to such worries now. For Shorty has a mean symptom, too. And we gotta locate that, and battle accordingly. We have been busy at this end of the line, but we'll fight towards greater precisions when we return to greet the spring in And/or.

Meanwhile, if Frye gives you any solace, then (to cop a pun I ran across somewheres along my journeys, amongst the studentry), frye Burke rather than burke Frye.

Send the verses. I think I know what you mean. I just signed up with the U. of Cal. Press to do my collected items, BkMom plus my later bleats. Cordelia may get the one-two from Goneril and Regan—and maybe it'd have been shrewder of me to sign up outside the academic press, in keeping with a chance I had to go along with the Eighth Street Bookshop, in NYC. But ennihow, here's how it is. And I'm at least temporarily in, binnuz the book is spreading delightfully from the academic grassroots—so maybe I'm going to be your next President. What job would you like in the cabinet? Just speak, and it's yours. (But frankly, I had planned to retain Secretary of State Rusk, since I can't think of a lower organism who is so dedicated and respectable. But if you don't mind being embarrassed in a big way, we could certainly set you up as Top Liar on our side in the United Nations, though you'd have a tough deal trying to do a worse job than Goldberg in the fantasy area.) Yet you might tell me where I should go and consult a single ideal analysis of a single text, poeticswise. Obviously, I'm green with envy. But I've met him, and he's a mouse. And by inspecting my texts, you can find that, at the very least, I'm *mice*, scattering in all directions when a foot is stamped.

But in the meantime, the point is this: Think of writing your article two ways. Think of addressing it to me (a specification that can later be dropped), and think of letting others sit in (a specification that might lead to publication). And relackus accordingly. And if you can learn me, it will certainly go to show something about old, new, wine, and bottles.

Hell, Bill, my bleat anent Brown is in the March 27th issue of *The Nation*. I think I made a basic statement anent McLues in LSA, though some of his advocates disprove me by simply saying (sans quotation) that he has been saying something else. As for Frye, if you need him as badly as all that, obviously we gotta get you psychoanalyzed—and where can the money come from? But you must grant: He couldn't have wasted that hundred thousand given to McLues via Fordham. But McLues is competent to waste it. So consider both Frye and Burke down the drain. Neither can turn up the ideal amt. of busy-work required to keep the machinery going at sufficiently high and pointless speed.

I love I love I love, and let joy be unconfined,

Sincerely,

K.B.

[Libbie Burke]

Andover
April 28, 1967

...The Columbia Univ. Neurological people (best in the country) corroborated the San Diego diagnosis—and don't know any more about its cause or cure. But KB and I are working on it. He is my "healer"— modern medicine having failed us as usual in a crisis—we return to ancient lore—with massage, vitamins, and just good care. As a male nurse and masseur he is a gem.

He is at present re-writing a review of Kermode for N.Y. Review of Books, but it has reached such length, there is a likelihood they won't want to give that much space to it. And he can't see how it cd be cut as he has so much to say. . . .]

. . .Good review of LSA in Chicago Literary Review, March issue, with priceless cartoon of KB as Spider!! Title of review: "Won't you come into my parlor?" . . .

07821 - 5/5/67

Dear Bill,

Delighted to learn that all goes well with Quentin.

Shorty's ailment has slowed down, thanks in part we think to my new-found prowess as a male massoos. (I have now proved that my years pounding the piano were not in vain, as I play unheard melodies along the spinal column.)

The Duke episode was by impulse. I received a letter from Beacon, asking me what to do with some stuffo they had. Having just recd. an inquiry from Duffey, I said: Send to Dook. Other outfits nearer home have inquired. Most things I don't want to release now—and if they get lost, to hell with them.

As for Myron Simon's inquiry, things is thus: I know that Bob Zachary has hankerings after both the stories, and a paperback edition of C-S. But it all takes time. However, he's on my side. And I'm sure that, if other offers turned up meanwhile, he'd say Take. There are no obstacles whate'er in the way of a C-S paperback. The sichaysh as regards the short stories is diaphanous, thus: Originally, all we did (Albert and Charles Boni and my morbid Selph) was to exchange letters (theirs one page, mine one paragraph) attesting to publication and royalty rates. There wasn't even a time limit. I recently found their letter, and then promptly misplaced it. It was the most lackadaisical contract ever made. The ambiguities arose mainly, I think, from the fact that, *Black Oxen* then being a best seller, they thought they might get some movie outfit to buy *White Oxen*. Immediately after our exchange of letters, Albert Boni phoned me asking, "How about fifty-fifty?" I said Sure. But apparently the Hollywooden thinkeroos opined that wasn't one box office in the whole project. A few months later, the Boni Boys informed me that the book had been remaindered. And that was that. (Incidentally, I have also come upon a few juvenilia which I think vaguely of adding to any such project, appendix-wise.) I like your notion much.

In a letter from Allen Tate recently, I learned that he had been asked to pass on the Septuaginary Ms., and had okayed same.

The Kermode job has just about undone me. In sending my review, I freely granted that the editor maybe ought to haggle with me. So he did. In trying to answer his inquiries, I got still more entangled (plus the need to repeddle, for his readers, my stuffo on the "temporizing of essence" done in GM and RR). Much that I approached via beginnings,

Kermode approaches via endings—and binnuz both approaches are legitimate, I got entangled in trying to deal with many of our differences non-invidiously, though also avowing that his use of an "apocalyptic" model needed my further stress upon the distinction btw. *temporal* and *logical* kinds of sequence. An incidental problem here was that when, in my earlier version, I spoke of terms as "terminal," ye editor thought I was merely riding a pun—and I fussed and fumed considerably trying to make it apparent that I wasn't. With the house still full of unsorted bundles (its turmoil a perfect portrait of La Belle Dame Bedlam), I wrote and rewrote—and it's cwazy how much time I wasted in false starts, probably to no avail. Never was I less unfutile.

Last week I got One Grand from Brandeis. But I had to sing for my supper by making an address which, since I couldn't prevent myself from introducing some hit-and run remarks on Vietnam, split the audience into friends and enemas. The outfit, which gave nine awards (all the other grantees being allowed to receive in silence if they so desired, though two who didn't turn up sent in brief thank-you statements to be read for them) provided food and liquor for about four hundred freeloaders. And it was rewarded by getting a story of exactly two inches in the next day's NYT. It must have broken the editors' hearts to mention me at all—but they compromised by making no mention of my address.

Thanks tearfully for thine aid. Just think, after tomorrow, all will be velvet, since I'll have got my threescore and ten. That they can never take from me.) And I did indeed await thy avowals anent LSA, e'en though you are shortening my life by finding things "good and usable in Frye." Jeez, isn't Vietnam enough for me to suffer in matters of public policy? And atop all that, I'm restive with a kind of verse-thing that goes on and on (built around the role of driving as a Wandering Scholar who takes notes ong root)—and for which I have the couthless title, "Tossing on a Flood-Tide of Sinkership: A Fragment." It's a muddle of sensation and ideation.

But, dooty calls. Best luck!

Sincerely,

K.B.

Recently, in a phone call anent other matters, Hildagard Watson said that she was reading admiringly Rueckert anent Dramatismus and such.

[Postcard from Andover]

June 27, 1967

Dear Bill: Glad to get your letter. Shall write later. At the mment, I'm trying to finish a paper for some sessions at Marquette in July. But this anent Isidor S: He wrote at least two books. (At least that's the number of his I have.) *Doctor Transit,* a novelistic fantasy, 1925, signed simply I.S. *From the Kingdom of Necessity,* an autobiographical novel, 1935, signed by full name. In the 64-65 Manhattan Telephone Directory, I find an address, 890 E. 6 St. That's probably the guy. If not, I can probably locate him through Cowley. ... But it is a groan, adding such extra info. Oof! ... Incidentally, if you happen to be near the London TLS for June 8th, take a peep at Denis Donoghue's piece on Cowley and me. ... More soon. We're in a considerable tangle, including alas! Shorty's vexing symptoms. /Heck, just slap out some quickie ¶'s on LSA and call it a day! K.B.

Residence address:
Harvard University
Adams House I - 12
Cambridge, Mass. 02138
9/29/67

Dear B&B,
How.
Shorty's symptom remain vexing, but we keep fightint back. Mostly with massage, which is no cure, but a good remedy. Also, a weekly injection of Vitamin B-12.
I am essentially non-existent, but professional obligations keep me letting on that I give a bit of a hoot what I'M saying.
In any case, we're most pleasantly and conveniently housed.
Father Daniel Fogarty, S.J. Saint Mary's University, Halifax, N.S., Canada. I was on a show with him a few weeks ago at Marquette U. A very pleasant fellow.
Va. Holland is mit Jesu. She was an understudy of Marie Hochmuth Nichols, who could prombly tell you want you wanna know, in case you're on writing terms.

I thought I had sent you a letter about reviews. But godamt, I find no evidence of it. LSA got a rather amusing, longish treatment in Chicago Review (I believe March issue—everything is hopelessly lost here). Stanley Hyman blurbed it zestfully in *The New Leader*. The Times Litry Supplement of June 8 gave me quite a sendoff, referring to all my books. ("Twas done by Denis Donoghue, whose piece on TBL has just appeared in *Encounter*, and who can smack it out vivacious bejeez.) Several others, of small size and various complexions also. And oh yes, one other long one: By Geoffrey Hartman, in *Book-Week* (since its shift to Washington). He builds me up as "the wild man of Amrcn criticism," which might sell me to hippies except that hippies don't buy books. Generally friendly in tone, but I don't quite recognize myself. The Chicago one has a big spider in a web, with my face on the spider.

Osborn, who had advance galleys of both books, continues to do nothing. Ditto Rueckert (but he's the one guy in the world I can't cuss, in view of his other mighty annoyances).

A few weeks ago, in my impotent old man's fury anent our foreign policy, I frothed in a letter to Armin Frank, who has not said anything in reply.

I really shouldn't be teaching now, I am in such a tangle. But the show must go on—so I dare hope I'll squeak through somehow. Should I raise a beard? What does it do for you? I have a tremendous compulsion to do *something*. The other night I dreamed that the house master (who has been the soul of friendliness) was horrified by a poem of mine, and insisted that we clear out immediately.

This was after my first teaching session. The room was packed with window-shoppers, but I came away feeling that I had scared off all potential customers. There is an introductory period here, when the students come around to sniff you—so I don't know. Matters are still further complicated by the fact that I do not have the slightest notion of my audience. If they are a soc. sci. group, I'd present things one way, but I'd do so differently if they have filtered in from English nsech. So, the first session, I felt as though I were standing on a street corner, talking loudly to myself. Having for weeks kept trying to decide on a beginning, I ended—yes, you guessed it—by talking about the problem of beginnings, approached via some comments on Frank Kermode's *The Sense of an Ending*. Dot's I'm. And I started out things perfectly by failing to get in time the notice of the first all-important meeting for newcomers.

Ennihow, best luck to yall—and, as Johnson and Nixon say, let joy be unconfined.

Sincerely,

K.B.

Just recd. a 270-page MS, "Ad Bellum Purificandum: The Rhetorical Uses of Kenneth Burke," by Charles Lowell Martin, Dept. of Speech and Dramatic Arts, Clarion State College, Clarion, Pa. Seven Chapters, thus: The Burkean Critic, The Symbol-Using Animal, Rhetoric and the Purification of War, The Rhetoric Cluster, The Form Cluster, The Pentad and Ratios, Indexical Analysis, Bibliography, Notes. I haven't had a chance to read it, but the stress seems to be on the analysis of texts from the standpoint of Speech departments. But, to the grind.

William James Hall 1250

Cambridge, Massachusetts 02138

House of Adam I - 12

11/4/67

Dear B&B,

Being a good-natured Mean Man, I takes it for granted that Bill's Ucs must hate me like pisen, as my Cs undeniably does (along with its devious or deviant self-love).

But I do feel that, binnuz Arminius is doing the chronology job in a big way (and beats me all hollow whene'er I try to catch him up), 'twoud be an act of supererogation for *both* of youenz guys to unfold all them other details. Also, ironically enough, the resources are more available in a lil town in NJ than in Widener Libry. Why not just do the job as it is in *Whosis,* and be freed for more self-expressive matters? What more is neskessary? But cd. say: I got my one-n-only degree, as Litt. D., an honorary bizz, from Bennington in 1966. But watch us grow. The visitings are all o'er the lot, a haze, like remembering a novel you read in adolescence.

I'm glad to hear more of Edward Anthony Watson's thesis. I haven't seen it, owing to the conditions that beset us. But if you see him, please do tell him I meant it when I said I hoped we might meet here sometime this wint. As for the German angle, here's the story: I know just about nothing in re Von Hofmannsthal except for the things I translated (on commission) for *The Dial.* Only in recent years have I been trying to catch up in re Heidegger. (In my opinion, he'd be ideal if he but rounded things out by arriving head-on at "logology.") Nietzsche began being a part of my Bible as early as at high school. But not until I read Beda Allemann's "Metaphor and Antimetaphor" (in *Interpretation: The Poetry of Meaning*, edited by S. Hopper and D. Miller, Harbinger Book, 1967) did I learn of that essay, though my whole approach to Nietzsche in P&C is obviously in that spirit.

As for my plans, me frenn, please at this time dunt esk. I'd love to come thither, at some time or other. But at the moment I'm psychically immobilized. I'm so estopped, I shouldn't be here in the first place. But I am here: and perforce I goes along. And, come the 20th, I'm to risk a public reading of my worses, publication of which has been delayed until come January. Roughly, it looks to me as though the job you mention shd. amt. to circa one grand. But I wouldn't take it now, because your firm would get cheated, what with me being so immobilized. I'll tell you when I think I'm worth it. I'd give a public talk, and some relatively intimate sessions—and I think a good time could be had by all.

Meanwhile, we battle against Shorty's symptom, and I go on battling against Incumbency Everywhere (via insomnia)—and I read *The Nation* week after week in sorrow, binnuz they won't publish Wm. Backert on Ignatz de Burp.

Holla!
K.B.

[Libbie Burke]

Harvard
November 14, 1967

. . .I'm sorry to let you down on the biographical data but Armin Frank did a most thoro job, cornering KB at Andover where facts cd be checked in the files and at a time when KB could really work at it, remembering and being reminded. It was good to have this done, once but I am not too keen on repeating all these dates and listings (other than Who's Who—honors, publications—things to do with the teaching and writing activities). The dates and places of all teaching jobs wd make an interesting list. I'm not sure Armin covered these but my guess is he did. I haven't been able to type for ages and am beginning to have trouble writing . . .

. . . The U of C press is continuing their good work of keeping Burke in print. Poems old and new out in Dec. (Jan 1968 dateline); reprinting of White Oxen proceeding; also Counter-statement paperback; TBL in paper—etc. After all the difficulties we have had with publishers this situation is wonderful. Lang. As Symb. Action has sold even without reviews. (What is your blocking on your review? Why doesn't Betty just sneak it and send it in? You did such a beaut on TBL. KB is going to do a poetry reading next week—for English Club—small audience—this should be fun . . .

. . . We haven't made definite plans for when we get thru here in Jan. Our new addition at Andover is so beautifully convenient we may hole in there instead of going South. There are various members of my family in that area who wd take care of me while KB goes off on some short speaking engagements he has accepted in Feb. and later in the Spring and summer . . .

[Libbie Burke]

Harvard
November 15, 1967

. . . As for me I spend all day every day working at trying to keep myself alive and going & I often wonder for what purpose since I am of no help to anybody. Being a lady of leisure is surely not to my liking. KB is an angel of care and patience. He has great battles with the dishes; he doesn't wash them, he fights them! We try to keep all this kind of labor to a minimum with simple meals & paper plates. We are getting the one big wholesome meal from the dining hall every evening—designed to take care of a working growing college-age male.

The wing we added on at Andover is not only useful, but beautiful. All the numerous family were around off & on all summer with much pleasant activity—some problems, but not too bad.

I think KB's spirits will pick up here when his seminar gets well started & he has people to haggle with. At present everything is sort of hanging—large attendance at first class, to sample it; he had no idea who which how many wd be his permanent students . . .

William James Hall 1250
Cambridge, Massachusetts 02138
House of Adam I - 12
11/15/67

Dear Bill,

Yes, let's let the Twayne thus meet, ptikly since it saves us all much toil.

As for the local situation: Yes, damn it, Shorty has a lousy symptom. It's called progressive muscular atrophy—and it's the biggest reason of all for me to hate the very word "Pr*gr*ss." There is a bitter irony (isn't irony always bitter?) in the fact that, just as we were all set to enjoy a somewhat mellow old age, with enough jobs on the side to keep me from being too psychologically and/or financially morbid, this damned thing turned up. It's a gradual failure of the voluntary muscles, due to some godam thing (still unknown, but probably a virus) that attacks the nerves. There are some procedures by which one hopes to slow the process down; and we go through those. But as yet there is no known cure. So we don't have anything to which the two of us can look forward—and bejeez it does stump me, except for a crazy spell now and then when I get stewed, and of course I get hell for that (and rightly, I guess, since the likelihood is that I'm just seizing upon a noble reason to get stewed whereas I'd have got stewed anyhow). We'll probably work out something. But it's not easy for a septuagenarian to become a different kind of seed, with his seventies requiring a new logic of development (this old Bark teaching himself new tricks). Until something like this turns up, one never realizes how much one had taken for granted, and had planned accordingly. And whereas the issue is in its essence Shorty, the conditions of production keep turning things back to me, with a corresponding sense of humiliation for my underlying self-engrossment. In any case, fortunately, there's always the thought of Mine Enemies to keep me wanting to Do Something. But certain belated improvisings are in order.

The thing on Bill Wms. is bitterly ironic, too. For many years while Bill was alive, we both wanted me to do that essay. But I couldn't finish it until the poor duffer himself was finished. It *should* be good. For all it does is put together cullings from his humanity, and every word of it is meant.

You shouldn't be as tough as you apparently are, on Poe. Go back and try him from Baudelaire's angle. And please read chapter two of Burke's LSA, though the author's godam Ucs made him get the title of Poe's essay wrong. And it haint easy to some of the jingles. And the structure of ratiocination to which Poe clung, in many of his stories, was in its way heroic.

Last night, here in Adams house, I read my longish Wandering Scholar poem, "Tossing on Floodtides of Sinkership." (I forget whether I ever showed it to you. Among other things, it breathes hatred for the Johnson outfit's filthy war in Vietnam.) It went over well. But I had used up all my Nembutals, and lay burningly awake until six o'clock this morning. Next Monday, the 20th, I'm to give a public reading of my poesies in general. Also, the computers tell us, it's the day when our two hundred millionth fellow-citizen is to be born. I'll let you know whether the kid lives and I get by.

This evening, towards sundown, a profusion of snow befell us. A wild snow-storm in a city, at night, is a wonder. Of a sudden I felt again the snow-ecstasy that underlies (or overlies?) my "Book of Yul" and "In Quest of Olympus." I swore that I'd go out on the streets and yell. But instead I wrote a letter to Cowley, for I remembered a snow-storm when we had raged from bar to bar in NYC, in the late teens or early twenties. And then bejeez I fell asleep, and in two hours sopped up slumber enough to keep me going for who knows how long.

Meanwhile, our friendliest greetings to B&B, until the next time.

Sincerely,

K.B.

Domus adamica I - 12

Cambridge, Mass. 02138

1/13/68

Dear B&B,

Sorry to hear that the other Burke is no more. And that all is in disarray about Bill's book *De Burpio.*

Speaking of disarray: My poems were supposed to be published in Nov. or Dec., with a 1968 dateline. But since Christmas a Great Silence has descended (even after that joyous advt. in the PMLA orga). My editor-friend won't even write or phone telling me whether the troubles are personal or organizational. (Naturally, I 'gin worrying lest the Goneril-

Regan faction may have got activated—for some of the items are mildly doity, and some take political cracks.)

An American lady in Paris sent me a dissertation she did (in French) on the Structuralists. I haven't read it yet. But at a glance I got the impression that she thought they had been pretty much anticipated by our domestic brands of criticism. (She has been partial in different way to Erikson and De Burp.) A student in the audience (a large class in the Education Dept.) that I was vociferating among recently seemed to think that the movement has a strongly *epistemological* slant—and thus, by my tests, would seem to favor the scientistic over the dramatistic. I still hold that not *truth* but *verisimilitude* is the test of poetic appeal (though often truth aids greatly to this end). I.e., poetry is not (at least not immediately) a matter of *knowledge*, but of appeal to *belief*.

Incidentally, if I could raise the money, I wonder if Bill would be willing to get psychoanalyzed, so that we can find out why the hell he won't finish that review? Is it possible that he has a Phartisan-Review complex (probably caused by the traumatic experience of working so long and hard on *De Burpio*)? Or is the project by now outlawed? I fear to suggest that it could be reactivated by reference to the *Collected Poems*! If he could just use the time that he now no longer needs devote to the other Burke (who, I hadn't realized, was such a rival), maybe …

I enclose some versifyings done recently. The rhymed ones are explainable thus: One of my students was working on Pope, so I saturated myself with heroic couplets. And I got so damned much tied to jingles, my notes for Flowerishes didn't feel right any more. So, although I didn't do rhyming couplets, I did try translating some of my notes into rhymes. And I enclose several herewith. The two I have checked, I sorta hope I might peddle to the NY Rev. of Bks. The free verse poems ("A Count-In" and "A Juxtaposition") I have sent knocking at Rago's door.

Shorty has gone out with a girl-friend, and I don't know where she put Bill's letter. So I can't check to see whether I am egregiously overlooking something. As for the sichaysh here: After a bad start, things are picking up considerably. And I fully expect that we shall leave in a glow of goodwill. I'd question whether I earned my keep. But be that as it may, to speak feudally, we're in a most pleasant and comfortable keep.

We'll promebly leave a few days afore the end of the month. Back to And/or. For Shorty's damnably irreversible symptom leads her to veto a quickie trip south. Irony is all. We had it all set up. An elderly couple that got along fine. And the conditions whereby the old gent could have made enough to let us roam about in a mild way. But irony is all. IN ANY CASE, we go on pressing against the irreversibility—and that's that.

Naturally, I'd be much interested in seeing a copy of Bill's paper anent the Structuralists. Also, that'll help me when reading the Sorbon dissertation of the Amurrican lady in Paris.

Our fondest to yall.

Sincerely,
K.B.

P.S. Watson wrote me recently, saying that he had ordered your book on Wescott.

PPS: I forget whether I told you. I'm to be holding forth at Brockport, May 2-4. I'm on a program with McKeon. He chose Rhetoric, and wants me to do Poetics. But, binnuz the fields overlap, I have asked him to say (on the basis of my *Language as Symbolic Action* volume) just how much of the territry he wanted to claim—and he won't vouchsafe me even one little mumblin' word.

Post-PPS: After the charmingly effective job that Denis Donoghue did on me in the Times Litry Supplement, I now can't get a word outa him. Jeez, what happens?! The only thing I can figger out is that I once wrote him an alcoholically relaxed letter, and maybe it didn't turn out right. He had gone to a hospital, and I tried to be cheery—but that's a tough job. I doan no from nothin. All I say is: Just don't write me from a hospital, unless you're willing to forgive my bungling attempts at good cheer. Or, better than that, please keep out of hospitals, those spreaders of infections.

K.B.

[Poems attached to above letter]

Statements of Attitude

When God (or so the story goes)
decided to be gone,
Theology arose
to help men linger on
by working out the dogmas for a Church
to cling to when things left them in the lurch.

* * *

Unknown to Joseph, Jim had done him dirt—
and hence by compensation
kept constantly alert
for Joe's retaliation.
Thus all that Joseph did while blindly dreaming
Jim saw as sure-fire evidence of scheming

* * *

"The coward dies a thousand deaths,
the hero dies but one."
Whereat my heart leaps up with joy.
Old boy, you are not quite undone,
not totally bereft;
you have some dozen left.

The while the war goes on
the estimates of experts vary
how much we pay Saigon
to let us be its mercenary.

* * *

Major Lobotomy

Should dirty wars abroad need doing, yet
through decency he might prove hesitant?
Sever the strands that make him feel regret,
and pick what's left to be Our President.

* * *

"Caint you gut a feesh?" she said—
and she had the most lovely hair
I have seen in all my life.

> Kenneth Burke,
> Adams House I-12
> Cambridge, Mass. 02138

With what the Mafia's racketeering earns
It's buying into regular concerns.
Here is the ideal counterfeit:
The Mafia has gone legit.
And who commands the art
to tell the two apart?

* * *

He was so frank in saying how he felt,
They thought his purpose must be something else.

. . . .

A Juxtaposition

Like all empires
ours covers so much ground
it ends up treading on its own toes.

Between high treble
(a shriek turned songful)
and bass
(the profound modifying of a groan)

make of me a harpsichord
that I could not
so much as raise my voice
above a tinkle.

> K.B.

Needless to say, I feel this way only sometimes!

A Count-In

One. Here's how it goes
here's how with poetry and poetics:
We are beset by some great hope or hopelessness,
or something as though sudden.
Growing from out the state of nature
and the nature of the state,
it makes us sick.
It is a special mode of sufferance
that sums up somehow our trick ways.
It is the osmosis of a psychosis.
I mean:
It is the makings of a poem.

Two. Or posit some rare twisted bitch.
You wouldn't have her
if handed to you on a platter.
But put her in a poem
and begad
you're both made.

Three. A friend writes:
"These are my burdens—
my wife's illness;
what Seneca might call
my incurable (insanabilis) old age;
my nation entangled in the filthiest of wars
while I am asked to be
none other than Proud Patriot."
I answerved:
"I grant it's hard to take,
but you have there
the makings of a poem."

Four. Tell me what these fools believe,
what they believe in.

Tell me what they fear or hanker after.
Work up indecencies blamed on the enemy.
And there you've got
the makings of a poem.

Five. Ingratiating-like,
Mr. Everyman confides:
"I have something I wanted to ask you—
and I wonder
could you help me
remember what it was?"

Six. The Mirror, in admonishment:
"Don't look.
The face you see
might be your own."

Kenneth Burke

[On the back of a copy of a letter from Erica Freiberg.]

Domus adamica I-12
1/14/68

Looking for the lady's essay, I found that, for some reason not wholly clear to me, I had xeroxed her letter. So I enclose (herewith over) a copy.

And, now that I'm at it, I'm not sure that I included these further sunshine thoughts:

With what the Mafia's racketeering earns
it's buying into regular concerns.
Here is the ideal counterfeit:
The Mafia has gone legit.
And who commands the art
to tell the two apart?

* * *

By murder he came in—and history squints:
It's murder murder murder ever since.

* * *

Twenty-seven billion bucks a year
for senseless slaughter—that sounds mighty dear.
And then, to cap such elegance, we're told
the policy is "middle of the road."
By tests like that a napalm bomb seems mild
that slowly cooks a woman and her child.

* * *

For this year's hacks and cheats
the way to climb
is sloganize on "crime
in the streets,"
and thus get in
by reviling sin,
inducing anesthesia
about our crimes in Asia.

But what a hell of a way to make a living! Oof!

K.B.

Domus adamica
1/16/68

Dear Bill,

Just back from a Chomsky talk. On "Creativity and Linguistics." By mistake I picked a chair in the room that happened to be next to his. (I had talked in the same room some weeks before, and had spoken from a different corner of the room—and I unthinkingly assumed that he would do the same. He wasn't in the room when I came in and took a seat. Indeed, everything was still unsettled.) But on finding myself so close, I refrained from entering the discussion—and as a result, I nearly blew my top with bottled-up disgruntlement. The answers to his talk were partly in my stuff on perspective by incongruity in P&C, and partly in things like my "Definition of Man" and "Terministic Screens."

It was tough, me lad. So I gotta write to someone, or bust.

Well, maybe I'll get my chance tomorrow evening, when I'm to be a guest at Eliot House. I'll make myself an obnoxious bellyacher, while everybody observes a polite embarrassed silence. Or no, maybe if I get the beef out of me now, I can by that time be back in my "make of me a harpsichord" mood, the perfick genkman.

When I talked to him a bit afterwards, his answers were shamelessly evasive. Imagine, horsing around for over an hour, without even the slightest hint of a single sample! When I offered samples, and showed why they mussed up things he had said (on Levi-Strauss, for instance), he dissolved into dodges.

As things look now, we'll be leaving here about the 27th.

Next morn. It wasn't so bad. Two nembies (three grains) did the job. (Kazin once made it impossible for me to sleep on four, when I attended a talk of his at Princeton (six grains, which nears the risky area, I guess, though not with so much adrenalin flowing.)

After the expeeerience I had with Richard Ohmann at Marquette, and now this, I'm getting it gradually clear just what linguistics can't do. And I can make clear the distinction btw. a Philosophy of Language and the mere use of linguistics in the wrong place. Imagine an hour's talk on "creativity" in language, without one single mention of metaphor! Primarily, I guess, the trouble starts from Chomsky's overstress upon grammar, or more specifically his ptikla kind of grammar. At Marquette I showed why Ohmann's attempt to define styles in terms of transformational grammar couldn't do the job.

Incidentally, be on look-out for *Poetry Therapy*, edited by J. J. Leedy, Lippincott. It's due out soon. Shd. at least be interesting as a classroom conversation piece. When I was at Tecate, they asked me for a piece. I sent in a partly minority report (in keeping with my thesis that it's idiotic unction simply to treat "creativity" as a categorical good. "Creativity" can also be damned dangerous, as per much in the contemporary physical sciences). At first the Lippincott editor wrote weeping. He said it didn't fit the pattern. Then they changed their mind, on the basis of a reader's report (a copy of which they sent me). Everything was so last-minute, we did our final negotiating by phone. Then long silence from them until a couple of weeks ago. Not even answers to my simple inquiries as to date of publication. But recently I received New Year's greeting saying that book wd. soon be out. It might be interesting at least to look at.

Yours for the esthetic secularization of theology (bah!),

K.B.

William James Hall
Cambridge, Massachusetts 02138
1/30/68

Dear BillR,

First and foremost: I thought your verses had a real zinggg. A few changes occurred to me; and I'll give them, though you'll probably hate me like pisen for this invasion of your privacy.

The last line of third stanza, possibly change "cry" to "outcry."?

Changes fifth and sixth stanzas, to read thus:

> The tablets are risen
> are sawing my legs
> are tearing my guts
> undoing my seeds
>
> the words are the laws
> are killing

And by all means throw out that suffocating last line.

There's still a bit of a problem about tablets sawing.

The lady's MS turned out not to be what I said it was. It's a thesis on the poetry of Yves Bonnefoy. Ingenious study of the dialectic underlying it. She's the only person I know who ever paid attention to my summary of the dialectic underlying Eliot's *Quartets* (RM 324).

I didn't know anything about the French Structuralists *before* reading your paper on "Kenneth Burke and Structuralism." But *after* finishing it I know still less. I think you cheated, and made amends by somewhat promiscuously slinging around that blessed Mesopotamian word "transformation." Self-portrait of an exceptionally bright young man who got buggered by Nobbie Brown. The Brownian movement is perhaps worse than even the McLues ailment. True, the talk had a certain swing, and that was to the good—but at too great a cost.

You write, "I will not publish another review in *The Nation*." Jeez, I tremble. Is this your ferocious decision prior to reviewing LSA? Or is it in connection with fresh battles you and Mrs. Yglesias have been having? Incidentally, the NY Rev. of Bks took my "Statements of Attitude" items. The others I didn't try.

Oof! I feel lousy. Do I begin to be flooey? Be happy.

There's a big series (under the general heading of Philosophy, I think) going on at Brockport. Our session is the next to last. The outfit puts us up while we're there. (Any word of your book?)

K.B.

God willing and Deo Volente, we leave Saturday morning.

[Undated postcard]

Dear Bill,

Big day. Butchie and Unk took one load out to And/or. Tomorrow we finish the job. Hence, back at the old stand, beginning the 18th.

Meanwhile, things have started moving. Having been asked to talk at the U. of Pittsburgh Dept. of English next September, I suggested a postmortem on the Rueckert florilegium of pros and cons and cons and cons. And it's a deal. So I'll so set up the project that your Mighty Fortress is the text.

I forget. Did I tell you? The Nation has taken my "Eye-Crossing" item—and apparently plans to publish it quite soon. I doan no how it will fare with eye-readers. But I feel pretty confident about it, as regards *hearers*. (I speak from confrontation.)

Holla!

K.B.

Heresome
2/8/68

Dear BillR,

Truce, truce!

All I meant was: I also wanted something along the same lines, but better! as, than, the thing on "Levi-Strauss, the father of structuralism," in the maganazazine section of last Sunday's NYT.

I had no kick about thy comments anent my sickly Selph, but I wanted to know more about the bad guys. (Incidentally, I have been tinkering a bit with Lévi-Strauss, in ptikla his stuff on totemism. I read him this way: Each tribe has its particulars, but they all embody the same universals. However (and I wasn't sure whether this would be his however or merely mine), though the same universals would apply universally, they do so with a difference because the particulars set up conditions local to particular particulars. Or am I getting giddy?

Basically, of course, the whole haggle about "history" centers in my ponderings on the ambiguous relation btw. logical sequence and temporal sequence. And kinship systems are particularly beloved by anthropologists because (as I sees it) a kinship system is at the very center of such an ambiguity. For not only does a father make a son; he can do so only because his son makes him a father.

Meanwhile, I was glad to receive a note from your Wesleyan friend, Wheatley, attesting to his admiring reception of your asseverations (to the pace of which I already paid tribute, and rightly, though I must warn young men against the dangers of the Brownian movement).

And guess what! Yes, you guessed it:

Here I am, preparing a talk on *King Lear,* for delivery next week in Va. And I'm out to contend that the play's appeal does not reside essentially in its message to oldsters, though oldsters can read such meanings into it (for they are certainly there). But, by Gawd, I never said it as neatly as that enniwares in the whole artikkel. So I'll steal it, right now, in broad nightlight.

Meanwhile, I'm gettn gradually clearer as to just how that things goes on at Brockport. And as soon as I get it all as clear as can be, I'll tell you all. For it would be wonderf if thou and some of thy men and/or ladies helped out by coming in.

And if ever you do feel like telling me how radical your fight with the *Nation* lady might be, please divulge accordingly. Please!

Our modernized best to thee and thine,

K.B.

& da capo - 07821
2/11/68

Dear BillR,

Just finished revising my bleat ("*King Lear*—Its Form and Psychosis") for my part in the jawing job Stanley Human has arranged for several of us this coming week, at Washington and Lee, In Va. (Also, of course, I'm to participate in commenting on the other papers. I believe there are four in all. Each of us is to speak about some play of Will's, after his fashion. Others that I know to be spoken for are *Othello* and *Hamlet*.)

I'm still working the *vaticinium post eventum* side of the street, valiantly and daringly prophesying just how the tragedy should turn out (and surprise! why it turned out exactly as it did). But like all professional pitchmen, I have added an angle to my recent slant (the *Coriolanus* piece, for instance). I have avowed that the dead center from which the play is generated (and at which, in a beauteous form, which arrive when exactly halfway through the piece, with corresponding reversal of direction) is its extra-dramatic or non-dramatic (none other than the Paradox of Substance itself, with the first strategic step into drama taking place when the playwright opts to individuate this universal quandary in a cycle of terms implicit in the idea of abdication).

Owing to our acute stenographic problem, I shall be speaking from a twistedly revised copy of my original draft. But maybe when at the school, I can get an opportunity to have the talk y-xeroxed—and if I do, I'll try one on you. Ptikly now that, for a season, you are at leisure, I dare think that you might feel inclined to sit down and haggle avec, anent the item—and I'd most certainly appreciate news of your response. (Incidentally, won't you *please* gratify my morbidly curious Selph at least to the extent of telling me as explicitly as can be, whether you have done the review for *The Nation*, or have definitively decided that you will not submit anything to them? Haint a author allowed to ask such questions of a guy who, at one stage along the way, zealously announced his intention to tell the world about what he called a "Burkefeast," and presumably without any reference to Nigel, or Alkaseltzer, or other remedies for an upset stomach?)

But all these are minor matters. The main thing concerns your references to a possible visit. Bill, I can't think of anyones we rather see than youenz. But you simply do not realize the extent of Shorty's troubles. It is only by ingenious, imaginative finaglings of her own, for instance, that she can raise her arms even high enough to eat. And even under those conditions, I must do much ministering. I do all the cooking, marketing, house-cleaning, laundering (I refer to the major laundromat jobs, when members of my family take over—and often they come out from town and relieve us by preparing a meal and cleaning up afterwards). Remembering how skilled she was at all her doings, you simply can't conceive of how crippled she is, as regards the kinds of operation involved in our being hosts. It is conceivable that, come the milder season, we could work out a feasible scheme. But certainly not during the wintry austerities when, for instance, we perforce keep the whole upstairs blocked off. But will you still be fancy-free, come blossom time?

And not least among my hopes for such a modus vivendi is the fact that I'd dearly love to discuss with you your recent developments. We might even tape our deliberations, to check on ourselves afterwards. Naturally, I still stoutly contend that (so far as criticism is concerned) the proper step is out of mythology into logology. And it haint no mere "preparation" for some farthandles working on a shoestring, or is that a metaphoric mix? True, in a sense, everything is a "preparation" for something else, as Hegel was a preparation for Marx, and our installation of plumbing was a preparation for our current plumbing troubles. If you wanna call me a "preparation," I'd gladly fight like fury, and get every godam word down on the record. I'm not "preparing" for a bunch of shoestring-operating farthandles; I'm *finishing* something.

If you would thus belatedly situate the Next Phase in historiographic models, please know: Though I'd gladly read history all the day long, and though I wish I knew more history but in *philosophic* problems (with their corresponding reflection in terms of *personal* relationships). History is a valuable step along the way. But, *as written,* it is no ultimate grounding, nor can it be. For it necessarily retreats behind the limitations of language, plus accidents whereby some records survive and some don't. Use it? Yes. But use it as a *grounding?* Oof! Once again I beg you to go get psychoanalyzed, and to ask your doctor that he help you find out why you refuse even to recognize what Poor Ole Honorary Rejected Father (Kink Leer) Burke has been talkink about.

Wadda woild! But frankilee, I do wish that we could work out a design, say im wunderschönen Monat Mai, or thereabouts, whereby we could joyously confront all such issues togidda, plus having it all down, so that we could verify for sure just where we were. For, until I get my stroke, or some such, I refuse to be symbolically slain by being piously (query) honored as a "preparation." I'm in there, flailing around, boy. And I'm not renouncing my throne (query!!!) until somethinks better than them presumably pissant Structuralists turns up.

In the meantime, I eskyuh. You mentioned several books. Please either give me a usable bibliography, or lend me your copies. In either one way or the other, I will humbly sit down and read the texts you advocate. (I exclude Hall's *The Silent Language*. Hugh Duncan sent me a copy, and I was reading it in a state of considerable rapport, when my copy disappeared. I think I know who took it, but such unverified suspicions make *me* feel even worse than *he* ought to.) I owe that commitment to us both. I will sit down and eat out of their hands (even unto washing their feet?). And whether I eventually vomit remains still to be seen.

For a conclusion, shifting into a different dimension, I would say: Several of my jingling jobs, *like* the ones I sent you, but particularly different, have been accepted by the NY Rev. of Books. And I happily learn that *Poetry* has taken two of my recent elucubrations. And the thought occurs to me that you might try that piece of your on *Poetry.* And though Henry Rago clearly judges for himself, I wish you'd try those bright lines of yours, either with or sans my suggestions, or both.

Yes,
K.B.

You say that words are coming out your finger tips. Then let 'em come!

Pesthaven 07821
2/21/68

Dear BillR,

Bug-laden. But today my fever has shifted to the minus side. Our sessions in Va. turned out to be quite zestful (three days of orating, conferring, and partying). But I guess they made me more susceptible to the flu germs that are everywhere on the look-out for friendly asylum this year. So, since Sunday, I have been burning as brightly as a Blakean tiger, e'en while doing the housemaiding and nursemaiding and janitoring for the two of us.

I did (at Washington and Lee) a piece on *Lear* that I consider the next step (methodologically) beyond the kind of thing I tried on *Coriolanus.* I trailed things back to a jumping-off place *outside* of drama, then reversed, and did my successive prophesyings after the event. The main effort (quixotic? desperate?) was built around the thesis that the play should not be "generated" from the thesis of old age, but from the "paradox of substance." Exactly how this postulate befits my gray and thinning locks, I must perforce leave it for others to decide.

More on all that anon. Meanwhile, I write you anent another matter:

Bob Zachary (my L.A. friend on the U. of Cal. Press) phoned me the good news that the whole edition of LasSA has been sold out, and they intend to issue a paperback edition, along with a second hard-cover printing. Various people have spotted misprints, plus a few errata less forgivable. And I wondered if you happened to have noted any, which you might care to contribute. For now would be the time! Any such info would be gratefully recd.

Also, praise God, the U. of Cal. Press definitely wants to take over Grammarhetorica Motivorum. And a lawyer-frenn in NYC, after some sporadic negotiating, writes that things look good—hence I may get shut of Pr*nt*c*-H*ll. It may cost me a few hunnert bayries—but the Press will give me as much as five of such without charging them against my future royalties.

Since writing you, I have read the paper of Dick McKeon's on which I am to comment at Brockport. Wow! It races through permutations and combinations of possible philosophizings in 31 pages, every sentence of which is like this: "The subject-matter of the arts of knowing can not be modes of knowing and their judgmental consequences considered in themselves, unexpressed in language and unembodied in action; and they can not be applied to the data of experience or the facts of existence objectively segregated from subjective presumptions and associations." As you can see, silly ole Kink Leer is going to have his hands full, since it would be equally hazardous to abdicate and not to abdicate. Jeez, my methodologic polysyllables are baby-talk, the billing and cooing of young love.

Meanwhile, may all the Backerts be infinitely more healthy than I today can even imagine—and may your recently expected output now be outputting plenteously.

Holla!
K.B.

Parturition 07821
3/18/68

Dear BillR,

Thanks. I saw the advt. for the 5/5-foot Shelf of Books. First a University Press limbers up—and now McCarthy. Maybe things are moving after all. But I don't think you should use the over-relaxed paragraph on Brown, McL, et all.

Why don't you persuade the U. of Minn. Press to wait just a little longer, and get the book out for my eightieth birthday? They could get a Spiritualist Medium to include some comments by me.

Felicitations on your riotous productivititity. Smack it out!

I suppose the Assembled Poesies have caught up with you. I wonder what the general treatmentifany will be. As you know, I always keep myself prepared for the worst (which is, of course, the Quietus).

Incidentally, as an aftermath of my talk at Washington and Lee, Shenandoah wants me to give them same. Good luck on yours.

Things go along as usual here. I'll let you know about our viability later, when the weather mellows.

Me, meanwhile—I'm quite inefficiently trying to finish up my papers for Brockport.

Holla!
K.B.

Hastyville 07821
4/28/68

Dear Bill,

Glad to get thine of the 26th.

Yes, 'twould be fun to have a get-togidda of some sort. If you must *choose* btw. Thursday and Friday, I'd rather that you picked Friday.

On Thursday I make but a brief Response to Dick McKeon's paper. (The paper is expert, but quite difficult. The conditions for the Response would not permit of any line-for-line discussion. My job was to attempt a kind of *summarized* attitude.)

On Friday (since McKeon's key term was "communication") I peddle my proposal for a supplementary term, "consummation." But when I next proceed to characterize it as the "entelechial" principle, McKeon will surely have some noteworthy things to say. Will he, for instance, accuse me of but "platonizing Aristotle"?

I had hoped that by now I'd have reprints of my article on "Dramatism" in the recently published *International Encyclopedia of the Social Sciences.* But in any case, the recent publication of that helped me dodge the business of peddling de whole woiks over again. I contrived, rather, to fit my talk into the panel, and thus to stress only the details that bore most directly on McKeon's paper. So, in effect, even my own paper is a Response to McKeon's. (There's nothn in it that won't have known already. The fun will be to see what McKeon does at me. He fights fair, but he's as competent as they make 'em. We have haggled for many years—and often have been in agreement, too.)

Incidentally, it occurs to me: As things now stand, I am slated to arrive in Rochester on Wednesday, May first, 7:25 PM. (United, flight 715 from Buffalo.) Someone from Brockport will meet me at the airport. But if you were free that evening, and wanted to replace the Brockport guy, there's the best possibility for us to have a talk ongtra noo. Unless it's completely convenient, think no more on't. But if such an arrangement should seem feasible, you should get in touch with Prof. Joseph Gilbert, Assistant Director, International Philosophy Year, and tell him that you'd take over. You'd also have to learn exactly where I am to be housed at Brockport, and such matters as key to the room, etc.

It all sounds so unwieldy, maybe we'd better expunge it from the record. But I thought of it, just in case. And, depending upon the location of the airport, we might even think of a quick saying-hello to the Watsons. All this occurred to me after two swigs that I shouldn't have allowed myself this morning. So mebbe (doubtless) it's all cockeyed nonsense.

But time presses. Letter can get mailed if I stop now.

Holla!

K.B.

Ad Interim 07821

5/16/68

Dear Bill,

'Twas good to see youenz, and all set up so pleasantly. And thanks greatly for voyaging to the field of battle, whither I whenced.

I see by the papers that, soon thereafter, I dint clear out of Illinois any too soon. Even as it was, there were already disturbances around St. Louis that required me to go from Bloomington (Ill.) to Chicago by limousine, or otherwise miss my plane from Chicago to Newark.

Me meanwhile—already I dare hope that my physiologically outraged body is responding to the decencies of exercise. My bugle has surrendered some of its sniffling hegemony—and I 'gin feel I can push back the symptoms of arthritis that already had picked a place where to set in.

And I learn by the local paper (front page story, along with the auto accidents and political battles: "Rutgers Will Honor Byram/Author and Literary Critic") that I'm to be knighted along with U Thant, Udall, the "conservative economist" Milton Friedman, and several others, making a dozen in all. Among my novels are not only *Towards a Better Life,* but also *White Oxen,* and *Counter-Statement.* But actually, the mistakes are at an exceptional minimum—and I was doubly delighted when I learned that Butchie and Unk were also to figure, as graduates of the local highschool and Harvard. And when I went to see my local doc, who for a small fee helps me chase my migratory symptom, the previous patient (whom I didn't know from Adam but could have clearly distinguished from Eve) greeted me by name and said that he had seen the local divulging. Think of me on the 29th.

I'm glad that you met the Watsons, and got a glimpse of their exceptionalness. And I hope that further contacts will follow.

Also, as the Bard says, "Here I am, Fighting Dandelions," even while I am advancing some retrospective observations for the prospective volume of stories.

In any case, by God, may we all flourish (flowerish even). And for tonight you couldn't scare me with a man-eating tiger. For my weapon is now loaded with a new cartridge-belt of 1 1/5 gr. Nembies. So, as The Bard says, "Nothing to fear but lack of fear itself." (I'd like to meet that bastard some day, if only I can avoid meeting him head on.)

And let's look forward to our working out a viability when you are in Connecticut this summer.

Yes,

K.B.

07821
7/22/68

Dear B&B,

News, for once, not from the Bellyache Dept.

Prentice-Hall has given me definitive assurance that the rights to the Grammar and Rhetoric From Motives revert totally to me. And that means a U. of Cal. Press paperback edition.

The paperback edition of Language as Sin-Ballix Action is now on the market.

A Japanese outfit wants to translate Phil. of Litry Frm. A Woppalian firm wants to do the Grammar and Rhetoric.

Mack Rosenthal gave the Poesies a frisky column in The Satiddy Review, June 22. And Denis Donoghue's piece on Boikwoiks in general has appeared in recent NY Rev. of Bks. Very friendly, but I wish he hadn't had to cover so much ground.

The short stories are to appear in August.

Last night I slept without nembies. But unfortunately, I had half a snootful—so anything further I said on this subject would belong in the Bellyache Dept.

Poets, both old and young, expert emoters,/ skillful in all the ways to be poetic,/ what would you think of such astute promoters/ as do the job with verbalized confetti,/ after the style of Ginsberg, Kerouac, and Ferlinghetti?

Mine enemies (to whom all due respect/ in this odd world of crazies and absurds),/ mine enemies, however incorrect,/ mine enemies, unlike the wild storm-birds,/ creep mouselike through the kitchen where they tellingly leave turds.

Let angels sing, let cannon roar, let loose/ what all might shout or trumpet forth or screech./ Let all the world in riot grow profuse/ with all that clangs and blares and resonates./ For now the shitty times are past: I'm shut of Prentice-Aitch.

(Time off, to get the mail. Royalty statement from Random House. For last half year, sales of Vintage PLF went up 55%.)

But damn it all, the family ailments continue irreversible. But at least, Shorty presses valiantly against her oppressor—and is in good spirits.

Zealously,
K.B.

Nixonheld 07821
8/8/68

Dear BillR,

Legalities has got me so godam scairt, I sent this first to Bob Zachary (I mean the Permissions item) and got it back, and here it is.

The Hermetic bizz isn't quite settled yet. But I recently recd. an encouraging telegram.

I may have blow-horned a bit too soon about the Pee-Aitch bizz. At least, I haven't yet recd. the documentary finalities, though my lawyer-frenn assures me the thing is sewed up otherwise.

I was delite to learn as to how the tome is going, but glum all over again to learn about the San-Laurentian smells.

As for Maine: I went back to a place that had been a veritable dream to me some 46 years ago (cf. my poem, "Here are the Facts," and many related details, for instance, "In Quest of Olympus")—and I was horrified at the slaughter. Where there had been a stand of stately trees by the lakeshore, now there was nothing but skinny shoots all jumbled like weeds. And I will spare you all the rest, though praise God the lake itself was still there, though I didn't inquire to learn whether and how much it had been poisoned. (The roadsides were all horrendously poisoned. Some chemical company put over a big deal.)

It's a mad night, a Nixon night, and a full moon—and I'm full of gut aches and heart aches; and all but five or six of my teeth are at the dentist's (the son of a bitch, he keeps me chewing on my gums).

I've done a lot more quinquains in that same stanza-form I unveiled to you in my earlier letter. Somewhere, in various stages of repair or disrepair, twixt 40 and 50. It's my occupational therapy, cheaper than getting psychoanalysed, and more masculine than knitting. In some ways it's a fairly exacting form, since bat-cat-fat-sat kinds of rhyme are automatically ruled out. It goes through quite a range. Here's one:

> Where are we? How profound might be man's dream?
> How buried can a living person be
> within his psyche's self-enclosed regime
> of trance-entangled cumbrance and debris—
> three levels deep (of sex, religion, and technology)?

Psst. There are three ways to do those quinquains. And I've done a batch, all three. And here's a bet you'll go along with suchlike minstrelsy.

In meantime, flourish, thou and thine. And whatever the hell turns out next, if it's to the good, let's be towards that, e'en though an oldster couldn't consider even as much as a billion dollars much of a good.

And as I write, it turns into a Prickson, collectively in favor of Dick Nixon.

K.B.

Holiday Inn of Stony Brook
Tuesday, October 28th or
Thereabout 1968

Dear B&B,

Please forgive long silence. Things have been in one hell of a mess with us. Shorty was in the hospital. Is now out. But has graduated to a wheel chair. We are living in the city. Our address is: Standish Harbor View Hotel, 169 Columbia Heights, Brooklyn Heights, N.Y. 11201. Shorty's troubles made the change advisable.

I am at Stony Brook for a few days, trying to recoup some of our losses. (Actually, finances have not been a strain. The Institute gave me a thousand dollars to help pay expenses—and much of Shorty's costs are borne by Medicare.)

We were delighted to get the safflower oil—and brought it to town with us. Many thanks.

Here's hoping that all goes well with youenz, and your careers. (With us, Careen is still speeding to replace Career. We have gone from "geared to production" to "steered by infirmity.")

Best luck,

K.B.

[Libbie Burke; dictated, handwritten.]

Brooklyn Heights, NY
October 30, 1968

... Yes, the safflower oil came a long time ago and we have been using it right along. As we believe in it we are most grateful. I have not written sooner because this is the first time I have had someone patient and thoughtful enough to write this letter for me. I gave up writing quite awhile ago.

But I am going to be able to make my X's on my absentee ballot for Dick Gregory and Thompson (a McCarthy and peace guy)—very unusual for New Jersey. Trying to get all our New York friends and relatives to vote for O'Dwyer.

I am a shut-in here with the most fabulous view of all lower Manhattan & NY Bay and can watch the boats go by all day. I have had 2 trips (via thoughtful family and wheel chair) all around this wonderful neighborhood with all of its old beautiful houses.

KB is spending this week at Stony Brook and my sister Virginia is taking care of me ...

> Standish Harbor View Hotel
> 169 Columbia Heights
> Brooklyn Heights, NY 11201
> December 23, 1968

Dear B&B,

We're delighted to get Bill's deposition of 12/17, with the charming picture of the younguns. Also, whereas for some time the Old Folks had Bill's picture turned to the wall, we have turned it around again—and it looks much more Christmasy that way.

He speaks of breaking silence as though it were something like breaking wind.

As for the stories, my formula is: Some antedate, and some simply date. If I ever does the Memories job, I might do somethinx more with a bit here and there. And I stoutly contend that several are pretty damned good intrinsically, over and above their sheerly diaristic relevance to my Morbid Selphness.

But essentially, more and more, every day in every way, I WANT OUT. So, I'm looking for a grant that would enable me to die while bathing in the Ganges. For I have been told that, if it all works out that way, and I pay the priesthood their honest graft, there'll be no danger of my being reborn.

Being a man of principle, I am in principle TIRED. I'm even losing my interest in refuting an opponent. And when that's gone,

(time off, to make up for fact that the Home Aid lady dint turn up, so I perforce 'gan dishwashing frantically, towards eating lunch)

and when that's gone (the Service having turned up), —well, I don't know.

It looks as though Big Shot done us dirt, me frenns. Just when the Old Folks were ready to be mellow for a few years, Big Shot remembered that "irony is all," and decreed accordingly.

Hell, no. 'Tis a skientifick fack, there's still a will-to-fight-back. Though too old to love truth, I can still hate error. (If I remember correctly, The Bard said something like that somewhere.) Except that I don't really hate an opponent, since I know that, if anyone *can* make me want to hang on a while longer, it's an attack (*if, at the same time, there's an opportunity for rebuttal,* as only too often there haint; and there is nothing more terrifying than The Quietus, dearest of all to all kinds of bureaucracies, however petty or overarching; the very thought of The Quietus nearly stops my heart—which is how I got from "heart" to "cardiac" in the first place).

But as I always love to say at this time of year, Noël, Noël, Know-Well. And never the twain shall meet.

Ovelay!

K.B.

Standish Harbor View Hotel
169 Columbia Heights
Brooklyn Heights, NY 11201
February 26, 1969

Dear B&B,

Wow! I find it was as far back at the 19th ult., when BillR sent me his gracious letter. And so frennly, it just about shut me up. And I was most touched of all by the fact that, just when youenz should be nauseated ad nauseam by the need to go on being worried by the galaxies (orthog?), the guy attested to feeling zestful even.

I'm scairt. I'd better hurry up and say, I meant galleys, but through a bit of prepsychedelic relaxation (alky to you).

Incidentally, this is my Better Half's birthday. And we look iggerly forward to May fifth when, e'en though I make as many millions as a big non-tax-paying oil company, I'll be able to collect my stipend from the govt. For come 72, my lads and lassies, from then on I am IN A DIF-FERENT BRACKET. And if only through sheer hatred, I'll try to hang on long enough to get back at least a fragment of what I had to pay in, in behalf of Vietnam and all such shitty enterprises.

As for the black problem: Heck, one of my daughters is now married to a black man whom I like a lot—but jeez, do we yipe back and forth, when we gets with dwinks?

It's amusing, in a way (after a fashion). For when we become too noisy, the other members of the fambly make us pipe down. So we whisper for a while. And then, lo! we're shouting away like crazy. Yet, not in a mean way, only in a decible way. For I really do believe that, whatever our embarrassments back and forth, as the felluh sez:

> Reverse the order. This must get put over.
> Down with the current scheme of arrogance.
> Those living as it were in times of clover
> must face the need to modify their plans,
> Whitey must share with black men what we took from
> Indians.

Or did I divulge that already? And in any case, they was a black friend who claimed as to how he was nourished on ATH. And he picked off a big govt. job, e'en to the extent of buying a yacht. So far as I am concerned, ever the liberal, I think that some of the loveliest creatures on this earth are some of the high yallers, plus touch of Chinee or such. And I caint be budged.

But it remains good that Hickel raises our hackles—or did I already spring that one? (Boy! it's tough not to have a secrtry.)

But flourish all, e'en to the extent of flowerishing.

Holla!
K.B.

Stan Dish 3/26/69

Dear Bill,

Wow! I see you have meanness enough to spare. Welcome, brother, welcome to the Guild.

We like your twist anent the Upward Way and Downward Way. Why not try to peddle it? Did you ever try Tennessee Poetry Journal? My *Tractatus de Strabismo,* by Ignatius Panallerge Bruxistes, has been rejected by Poetry; and if it gets ditto by Hudson, I may try it at the Tennessee outfit. Incidentally, however it *reads*, I have tried it with audiences in Kentucky, Wisconsin, Iowa, and Indiana, while a friend has tried it in California—and I can promise you that, as *done aloud,* it WORKS. why not try it on your class, without divulging the author, until afterwards? Henry Sams tried it thus at Penn State—and he has sent me xeroxed copies of the students' comments—and (sooprize!) I found them vastly entertaining. I prepares 'em for a few spots (for instance, the meaning and etymology of "boustrophedon," or my trick with "behemoth" owing to the accident of its being pronounceable on two different syllables, or the info that the "Olympian leper" is De Gourmont—and I don't even risk their missing what I did with Scylla and Charybdis. Also, I pause to explain my pride in the line, "Or are our, are our what?" since it can't be pronounced without growling. (You stinker, you should have found that out for yourself.) And I tells em how I translated the opening line of the Divine Comedy, in distinguishing btw. "nell mezzo" and my oldsterism. (Some of Henry S's kids thought I was a youngster acting old.)

You'd be amuse at this one: Last week I did a three-day stint in Iowa City (at the appropriate uniworsity). Smacked and banged there morning, afternoon, eve, and night, under various auspices, including the Grim Reaper's. My final host in public was a gent who is doing a pamphlet on me for the Minnesota series of such. Relaxing, I got into a shouting match. I clean forgot it, for it jes seemed to me the norm. But the next morn I learned that there had been a great flutter among the departments. So maybe, in three minutes, I ended one heck of a lot of good work.... I then moved on to Terre Haute, where *all* went well (at Indiana State U.). Then home, to a job in a local Presbyterian Church, me and Edward (Silent Language) Hall—again all sweetness and light (though in the meantime, somewhere along the line, I have lost my glasses). Though I've aged a lot since last week, I cleared seventeen hunnert above expenses. And if I survive the many deals in April and early May, I'll have earned quite a bit of taxes to help support the filthiest war in all human (inhuman) history.

Meanwhile, our ultimate sorrows here continue inexorably. When I am away for a few days, I dodge the realizations for a time. When I return, I return to a suffering wife. No other home-coming is conceivable. I fuss and flutter, while on the road—but the brutal truth is that I face nothing but bleakness. The few mellow years before the end are to be denied us. The Old Folks have been robbed by the nature of things. We had learned so well how to live together, and then Irony Prevailed. Me frenn, it's tough titty.

Meanwhile, may youenz flourish,

K.B.

Standish, etc. 4/17/69

Dear Bill,

You were cruel beyond imagination. Here come THE EVIDENCE, and I am in such a hell of a jam that I can but glance at it. (My entangled sichaysh, until May 9th, is totally morbid.)

But I have shopped around, particularly sampling your valiant Last Words at the end of the articles.

And I am profuse in admiration and gratitude. And Shorty was surprised and delighted, in re your gracious dedication. Even within our gloom, there are these joyousnesses.

And all hail to Jordan's birthday, too.

Next week, I'm to be in Madison and Chicago. I'll take the tome along avec, and commune with it at night, in rooms with my "many-mirrored other." And you'll hear from me further, somewhere along the way.

(Don't tell Adams—but I never knew of "plodge." I just plodded along with "plod." But it was a helpful sentiment to start out with—it was that!)

I might tell you about many other things. But not now. Let this be but an absolute THANK YOU, ME FRENN, ME FRENNS, THANK YOU.

It all adds up to such consideration as I would not even give myself, me being sick of same.

You have lots of things I never saw. (Both the Self-Love and Self-Hate Departments are much less well-informed on such matters than should be—also, I have a superb forgettery.) At first glance, the only thing I know about that seems missed is Wayne Booth's review of RR (in *Modern Age.*). I think of that since I'm going to be a program with him next week, in Chicago.

Meanwhile, know that the Old Folks plan to leave here circa the middle of May (returning then to And/or). We are in sorry shape, though I may do a quickie trip (less than a week) to southern France, in mid-June. (My expenses are paid if I give, in exchange, a 30-minute oration—in English—on a certain trick aspect of "creativity.")

. . .

Should say also: I thought (we thought) your Preface set things up quite nicely (to take care of the con element). The con against an old pro. I think that Allensby Titti was right: It's better to put in bits here and there, as things develop. And once again I want to thank you for the lovely gesture towards Shorty. It pleased her greatly—and Gott segne every every bit of such scheming as that.

More later, God willens and Deo volente,

Con amore,

K.B.

Stand ish 5/1/69

Dear Bill,

Holla! The finished book (with the blockbusting price) reached me in time for a May-day march. So I've been parading about the room.

"Tis a stupendous job. And we decided that the placing of my mug was probably the way to do it.

I'm still cruelly caught by the pressure of ad interim obligations, but every once in a while I swoop down on one item or another. My one puzzle is why Wayne Booth's review of RR got omitted at least from the Bibliography. And I wish to heck you had seen my reply to Joseph Frank's *flatly wrong* statement of my position (on p. 405). And I think you let that bright mutt, De Mott, push you around much more than need be. (Somewhere in my correspondence files, I believe, I have a record of my answer to him.)

But everywhere I look, I see signs of your great energy and scrupulosity. The Old Folks are basically grateful to the Backerts all.

This afternoon, the Franks are due (and thence, for dinner, which I'll import from a local Chinese jernt). So maybe I'll hold this until after our session, binnuz somethingx else may turn up.

Meanwhile, uneasily I goid my lerns for a 5-9 (fifth-to-ninth) job next week at Dartmouth. The twist is that, whereas I had been invited circa a month ago, the Revolution has busted loose there. The man who invited me is a former student (at Indiana) who has since become a Dean, and now doesn't quite know what hit him. He phoned in bewilderment, and seems minded to enlist me in the fray. I told him both to reserve me a room and find me a rail. I'm wondering how my role as a drop-out FIFTY YEARS AGO relates me to the current wave of sit-ins. I also ran into some angles at Chicago recently, since I was on a program with Wayne Booth (who had become a Dean, and is now unhappy at finding himself in the role of an Establishmentarian sinner, for reasons that he can't fershtay). Things are made more poignant by the fact that one of my prime exhibits now involves further development of my notions anent "The Rhetorical Situation," which gets entangled with the problems of Confrontation.

Great heroic moment: Returning home, I found a letter containing Four (4) contracts: for GM, RM, RR, and the Devices, which I doubt you ever saw, though some samples are in the article reprinted in the *New Rhetorics* volume, edited by Martin Steinmann, Jr. (Scribner).

5/5/69

Godam the luck. I found the reverse (or is it the obverse?) just when I was being initiated into the age at which I don't have to fear even making a billion dollars. For come 72 (if one can come), the Govt. pays a bit to every hanger-on, no matter how much he gathers up on his own. That much, at least, can't be spent on Slaughter Abroad.

But I thought I had written you, and sent the letter off. Now I doan no where I am.

Arminius seemed so disgrunt at not having recd. a copy (and doubting whether he would), I gave him my unbound unsewed (unsewn?) proofs.

Many happy returns of the day, dear frenns. And as soon as I can settle down for a spell, I'll try to write you along page-by-page lines. And we'll hope to see youenz all, back there at And/or. For though the Old Folks find less and less inducement to salivate towards the future, there is the mellowness of friends plus descendants plus acreage (I'm not sure as regards the ideal order of that series). Peeeriod.

True, one's flags flag now and then—and don't we all? In any case, beneath all such expurriments there *is* (not *lies*!) the reality of shipspassinginthenight (in broad daylight). There is that reality. And if the world (the universe—uniworse?) is as infinite as they sometimes say it is, then it necessarily follows (follows?) that we have thrashed all these things out, again and again, infinitely often—so it stands to reason that we might somehow feel intimate.

Meanwhile, I don't dare tell you of my back-broken symptoms today, lest you grow over-shrewd. And all I wanna say (or did I already say it? I caint check under these conditions) is: You have been devoted to this job. Vexing though it necessarily was, you did it. In brief, you allowed my particular morality-of-production to tie in with yours. I doan no. Maybe in the long run, you'll decide that you were cheated. I hope not—for I think I have been fairly honest (though not as honest as I wish I could be).

With love, and (without salivation) still hoping somehow,

Sincerely and lovingly,

K.B.

I have packed my bags early, so that I might already be set up to fare forth. (1) Every detail must be just right. (2) Nawthn matters.

And again, thanks for all that blockbusting work, though the block-busting price might serve to keep it a secret.

K.B.

[The following appears on a separate sheet.]

A Sure Solution for the Problem of Armaments

To begin with, let us take it for granted that the military-industrial complex wants its profits to be as great as the economy can possibly afford, and as its lobbies in Washington (in league with the Pentagon) can induce Congress to support by federal taxation.

Second, since we are now in the Age of the Computer, when decisions are being made, insofar as possible we should always bear in mind the role that the computer might play, if properly consulted.

For instance, computers could tell us how much more a given military project will cost than its promoters say it will. They can tell us the extent and nature of the personnel that the project will require, the amounts that would be allocated for subcontracting, advertising, entertainment, influence-peddling, and the like. Also, there would be the proper allowance for legal advice. For it stands to reason that adequate measures must be found whereby, the greater the profits from the undertaking, the proportionately greater number of loopholes for tax-evasion must be set up. It is taken for granted that only those in the poorest paying jobs will be taxed adequately.

So far, I grant, I have been but reviewing the stand ways in which many corporations derive income from federal subsidies. *But here is the great improvement:*

Instead of asking the munitions-makers to carry out all these operations that are so wasteful of our substance, I propose that we merely *give them the money,* without requiring that the clutter up the world with their unwholesome products. By this simple arrangement, the economy would be left free to develop its productive resources in useful ways. And the ever-mounting threat of the ever-accelerating arms race would wither away.

[Libbie Burke; postcard postmarked Brooklyn, NY, May 9, 1969, dictated.]

It's a beautiful book.*

> Love,
> Libbie

[*Critical Responses to Kenneth Burke,* which was dedicated to Libbie Burke.]

> Back at the Old Stand 5/21/69
> 97821

Dear Bill,

Market tip:

Sell all your General Motors stock, and put your money in the June 2nd issue of The Nation.

My galleys were bristling with typos, but I think we caught 'em all. Only two items omitted (X and XI). I regret the loss of X because, at least as read aloud, it allows for a notable contrast in pace, before racing again.

Today, total anguish: I must sit down in earnest to write my piece for the trip to St. Paul de Vence, but meanwhile the dandelions are again trying to sneak up on me. Divided mind.

Best luck. As a title for my Pittsburgh talk next September, how about "Critical Responses to Critical Responses"? And thereby we might also get some of the assembled multitude to look through the book, in preparation for hagglings of their own.

In frantic haste,

K.B.

I still haven't had time to do more but shop around in The Book.

5/26/69

Dear B&B—

Libbie is no longer with us. She got free sometime 5/25 A.M.

She was so greatly pleased about the dedication of the book—and her last afternoon here, she was surrounded by the family, all of us in a good mood. I kissed her goodnight (and we said goodnight with total love, as we didn't every night). And she went to sleep, and never woke up.

And she is still so necessary to me, I'll quasi-commune with her. There were few oldsters who were so close.

K.B.

Here are some sentimental lines I wrote many years ago:

Oh, call me not
by the call of a bird
lest I, left alone,
go into the woods
and hear that bird call.

R.D. 2,
Andover, NJ 07821
6/9/69

Dear Betty,

Thanks for your words about Libbie. There was nothing to do but watch the inexorable advance of the symptoms. Yet she was sharp and participant up to the very end.

I forget whether I told you in my note: I have a chance to attend a conference in southern France—and I'm grabbing at it. I have extended the trip into a three-week arrangement, planning to look about a bit.

I expect to be back about July 3rd (I'm leaving this Friday). Maybe some kind of trek hither might be worked out, after my return?

Harry Slochower was here the other day. When he saw The Book he said that Bill should get a copy sent to *The American Imago* (which Harry edits).

I am in such a tangle, I still haven't had a chance to do more than shop around. It really is a jam when one doesn't have time to read about oneself. But some good fan-communications have come in about the poem (*Nation*, June 2nd), plus some generous words about my criticism—and believe me, I could sop up one hell of a lot along those lines these days.

I hope all goes well with all the Backerts—and, Deo volente, I'll send you some words from somewhere along my moody, moony journey,

Avec Liebe,
K.B.

26 June 69

Dear B&B,

Am in Paris airport, waiting for plane to London. The battle to find a room here, at *any* price, wore me down after two days. I spent most of my time in offices, and well-filled places that looked like dentists' waiting rooms. So I gave up, and stood in the middle at a public square singing "God Bless America."

Am off to England and Ireland, where friends (I hope) will put me on to somewhere or other.

Did you see Merle Brown's pamphlet on my sickly self? I wrote briefly, saying he should be ashamed of himself for the oldest trick in the deck, namely: a pile of rhetorical devices, all in the name of "No Rhetoric."

Incidentally, our Uncle (Sam) gave me a grant of seven grand. But before I mastered the Metro system here, I feared I'd spend it all on taxis.

Flourish!

K.B.

I plan to return on the Irish line, July 3.

R.D. 2,
Andover, NJ 07821
July 22, 1969

Dear Frenns B&B,

How are things going?

I have been back for circa three weeks. Am often lonesome, though surrounded by family. (I do greatly suffer from a one-man ailment which if have named "Libbielosigkeit.") For a while I felt as low as could be. But I sometimes have hopes (even when sans alky) that I might get to work in a somewhat sustained fashion.

The place is falling apart. But at least the roof doesn't leak. So, if youenz feel like voyaging hither some time, and are willing to help with the meals, etc., we should start negotiations.

How goes it with all your plans? Have you heard so much as a peep about the *Cr*t*c*l R*sp*ns*s?* Did your publisher at least unload a few copies on the libraries? In connection with the Award of Seven Grand I got from our Uncle (Samuel), I at least received a friendly congratulatory note from the Director of your Press, Mr. John Ervin, Jr. And he didn't seem bitter about over-investment.

I was understandably irritated by Merle Brown's pamphlet. (I get so weary of that age-old trick; namely: Rhetoric in the name of "No Rhetoric.")

Since my "Eye-Crossing" poem (which appeared in the June 2nd issue of *The Nation*), I have published nothing but a quasi-John Donne sixteen lines in the July 5th numero of ye olde *New Republic*. Also, I have sent in my review of the Hart Crane biography (which I found quite poignant in places, though the details sometimes make one impatient). Released the *Lear* thing to *Shenandoah* months ago, but have seen no proofs.

I am now trying to do a merely editorial job (which I hope to clear up within a coupla weeks).

And then I may settle down to clearing away the Poetics bizz. (I have taken on a few quickie performances for next wint; but I shall probably have turned down the longest one—two weeks—by asking for more than The Company is likely to agree on.) As for pedagogic assignments of any duration, I have definitively sworn off, unless some unforeseen financial obligations besrt me.

Every once in a while now, I dip into the CR—and I am touched anew by all that toil I caused youenz.

Suddenly, vast crisis: I had to meet a train, and couldn't find my glasses. Had to round up the one of the grandsons who is the professional finder. Now the schedule is all awry. After all, we can't all be in the Moon Trip business.

Rejoice,
K.B.

Paraphernalia, NJ 07821
8/6/69

Dear Bill,

At least, it's good to know where you are. That's more than I know about myself.

Recently, to round things out with a vengeance, I have been revisiting my early translation of Mann's *Death in Venice*. It had some mistakes, which have been caught by one who knows more German than I ever will. But he gratuitously adds some other changes, many of which irritate. Also, alas! I see many other places that I now myself would translate differently. But jeez, I could spend the rest of my life revising that one text. So I hope to hurry on.

Did I say "hurry on"?! Jeez, sometimes I sit here, stopped by one word, for as much as two hours. How, for instance, can one translate *Psychagog* to the best advantage? I had originally said "lure." Lowe-Porter says "Summoner." The Liddell and Scott Greek dictionary notes that the primary form of the verb means "lead departed souls to the nether world." Mann uses the word just before Aschenbach dies. (He calls the boy a "psychagogue" who is as though beckoning to Aschenbach.) I have already stagnated more than two hours on that one, things being further complicated by the fact that the text has a passage referring to the *Phaedrus*, and in the *Phaedrus* itself rhetoric is defined as an art of *psychagogia*.

Wadda woid!

As for that NR poem: I don't quite know either. I saw a way whereby modern medicine made literally possible the kind of neo-Platonic conceits that John Donne tinkered with. I began by thinking of myself as the two people (my sober, plodding half and my impatient alky half). And I was tinkering with thoughts of my own willed suicide, though without any such current conflict. (Possibly they were left over from my tangles many years ago.) Then I transformed the sichaysh. So what the heck? Thoughts of death, in many forms, were in the Burke household. (And they still are.)

Incidentally, if you can get any mazuma for an utterance by me among you, I'd prefer that it be in '70. I've booked up jes about as much as I wanna do, this autumnality. Last year I went wild, trying to make money. For I thought that Libbie would end up in some stages that would be both wretched and expensive. But there's now no more pressure along those lines. And besides the Seven Grand that our Uncle (Samuel) gave me, each month now he gives me 161 bayries, which I can regularly add to my other bits of income. (Though not in any spectacular way, even my books bring me sums. And there are no obligations · o'erhanging me but mine own self-sickness.)

Watch for the Aug. 28 issue of the NR, which will probably have my review of the Hart Crane biography. I considers it a review-plus, because it fits into my Scheme of Things in general. (What a sense of folding-back, of this-is-where-I-came-in, I go to bed with, and lie awake with, and get up with …)

　　　　　　　　　　　Rejoice, all ye, rejoice,
　　　　　　　　　　　K.B.

You ask who might review the book. It's not unlikely that I shall be severely left alone. However, I shall use it myself, in connection with a talk I'm scheduled to give, on things in the twenties.

　　　　　　　　　　　Verlorenberg 8/15/69

Dear B&B,

Yestiddy was a Great Day. I recd. copy of a stinko hatchet job (using the stories as a pretext), in recent Kenyon.

Now that gloom is ever lurking, to jump out and grab me, I was much more effectively bopped than a professional fighter of my long experience with shitasses should ever allow himself to be. I drank everything in the house. But fortunately, supplies were low—so, today, I felt sufficiently cleansed, and sans the murderous hang-over that would otherwise have impinged upon me.

If opportunity offers, don't miss my review of the Hart Crane (Unterecker) biography, in last New Republic. I think it gets a good mixture of methodology and moodiness.

Have finished going over the Mann translation (of Death in Venice), which had some mistakes, though it has always beat out Lowe-Porter's anyhow. Henceforth it will be better. And I shall be $750.00 less poor. (Doubtless the German scholar who ferreted out my weaknesses got considerably more, though often I had to retranslate his translations, towards the lines as I felt them. Maybe there'll still be some haggles; but on the whole, I think that the thing as it now stands will stay put.)

Jeez, every here and there I wanted to redo my own version. And I did sling in several such moments. But I decided that I'd live in other ways rather than spending the rest of my rapidly dwindling remainder re-revising my revisions of that masterpiece (which I still consider it to be, though it sometimes gets wery wordy in any language, as don't we all?).

Hell, I could tell you about many more problems than those having to do with these damfools who believe in moon-probes as the solution of human stinkerdom. But there's been a lotta rain down hereabouts, so "the pond is plenteous" (as The Bard says)—and I'm gwan down and get wet.

Rejoice!

K.B.

Worer Binich 9/4/69

Dear Bill,

Felicitations on your royalty drag. But I can tell you how to get more. Just live to be 72—and from then on your Uncle (Samuel) will give you $161.00 a month. (Yet I must admit, living to be 72 is quite a price to pay for such a sumlet.)

I think your meadow-lines have good making. Mainly they need but trimming. But I was puzzled about the ending. "Squandered" seeds sound sorta onanistic. I could readily work a scheme whereby, in *boikwoiks,* the love of meadows could take on onanistic connotation. Cf. in "Prince Llan," the passage in Latin, p. 232 of new edition. I take it that Gudruff is the call of an adolescent self. ("God-rub"?) Your attachment could go back thus. (But God damn the luck! I find that a typo has muddled things. *Debat* should be *dabat.*) All told: "The full recognition of his body's faculties was suddenly revealed to him; he loosened, he slipped softly to the earth, then gave himself to the temptation of his groins." That's what a "squandering of seeds" suggests to this dirty old man—and I thought of it ideally, in a pastoral setting that was to the Prince like a call. Perhaps the grander call was at the end of "My Dear Mrs. Wurtelbach," where it is ywrit: "David, my little man, sling your pebble at the universe." There are others.

As for that fart (or do I mean little shit?) who did the hatchet job in *Kenyon*: Your proposed answer would certainly not do, as you'll agree if and when you see the review. The issue really is quite simple: (a) The stinkerette did not review the book; (b) if he does want to hinge things around Dick Blackmur's twist, he (or she or it) should certainly have also considered my further remarks on the matter (LSA p. 492). But I tend to assume that editors get pretty much what they want in matters of this sort. And that's that. (Hence I guess you'd best leave it lay. But I am most grateful for your thought of answering what *I* certainly could not answer without demeaning myself, in even acknowledging the existence of such a low organism.)

Meanwhile, I move towards the New Isolationism (which would "normally" have begun the day after Labor Day, but happens to be delayed by the fact that some members of the clan are still around irregularly). My main problem is: How can I talk to myself with the privacy to which I am entitled, if the guy down the road is bugging the joint? Or could I jam his bugger? I await advices.

> And may youenz all rejoice,
> K.B.

Self-talk 10/1/69

Dear Bill,

Stanley Hyman asks about the elusive RESPONSES. He is apparently living under the fantastic delusion that it might be possible to wangle a copy from your Press. Ennihow, here's his address: Fairfax Motor Inn, 715 Delaware Avenue, Buffalo, New York 14209. He is teaching at Buffalo this year—and he plans to do a considerable stint on me next term.

Meanwhile, it's just possible that I may be getting out of my doldrums, at least somewhat. I shall probably stay here, at Self-talk, into December. And it 'gins look as though I may spend quite a fraction of the winter at Yaddo. (Otherwise, having definitely decided that I was in no mood to teach consecutively, and did not want to bach in the city, I had decided that I'd put books, MSS, and typewriter in the car, and drive glumly south alone.) The Yaddo prospects have cheered me up a lot, a whole lot, even to the extent of making me feel like getting back on the Motivorum job, and finishing it up this fall and wint.

Just now, my most immediate task is that of replacing the screens with storm-windows. "I put 'em up," the bard says, and then asks, "Who'll take 'em down?"

Though I vetoes consecutive teaching, I have been doing some kvickies, and have some further ones scheduled. (One of my deals, astoundingly enough, involves participation in another program anent, N.O. Brown. A nice guy who is kind to my stuff thinks that the BODY is wunnerful. And since he is an exceptionally bright man, I am tied in knotten. My two recent slogans, under pressure, are: "It's clock-work without a ratchet," and "Uncritical readers mistake its logical non-sequiturs for imagery." The second has to do with those who wd. have the book read as "poetry." I sez, sez I, "If that's what you want, compare and contrast it with the first Emerson essay entitled 'Nature.' ")

Well, we'll see. Just now recently, I have been punishing myself with Cleaver's *Soul on Ice* and Malcolm X's Autobiography. Such pounding, and so justified! The reading of such works at any time wd. give Whitey acute image-trouble. But blee me, frenn: The expeeerience is tougher than ever now.

It is quite possible that, by the combination of my age and Libbie's death, I have been beaten as never before. Not being sure yet, I am still spying on myself. Sometimes there is a sense in which I am as though glazed. But there are also the occasions that put on one or another of my old records, and they grind out much the same as before. And at times I fear the recurrence of an old malady, when I seemed to be split in two. But I dare hope that, at the very least, mine enemies will keep me in there swinging somehow. Surely I could not let them let me down.

And may though and thine rejoice,
K.B.

(next day: I neglected to mail it)

Andover
11/10/69

Dear Bill—

I see we got a small review, but a pleasant one, in the Sunday N.Y. Times. And I hope you try out the poem in the last (Nov. 8) New Republic.

May all be going well with thee and thine.

Avec Liebe,
K.B.

Lone Noisings 07821
11/22/69

Dear Bill,

All hail to the population explosion. I thought you were enough of a Boy Scout to be prepared. But if, as you say, it was a moon shot…

If you expect to find the ideal job at Ohio State, I take it that you plan to be a football coach. Otherwise…

I can only assume that the present editors of Kenyon got exactly what they wanted. The item reviewed my criticism by supposedly reviewing the stories; and it dodged the stories by supposedly reviewing my criticism. It is an irony that the "Anaesthetic Revelation" was published in that very gazette (featured even), and got an award of three hunnert bayries from a lil foundation then guided by Rosenberg. There was devotion to somebody in that review, possibly Wellek.

When driving West up there, don't miss a stay at Glacier National Park. Cf. my testimonials, in "Tossing on Floodtides of Sinkership." Damn it, when I wrote that, I didn't suspect how much sinkership the poor old bastard was in for. I always selfishly took it for granted that I'd clear out before Libbie.

Please don't insist that I be but FOR. Oft-times now, gloom-pervaded, I seem to feel that only the AGAINST is worth the … etc. As regards the Brooks piece: It was written in the first place because I was asked to participate in a panel on Formalist Criticism. I thought it gave me an excellent opportunity to define my position, and in ways that I thought of as suave and ironic. Perhaps you interpreted the signals differently. The McLuhan piece also was the latest, *Counter-Blast,* for ye olde New Republicke. … No, to my knowledge, nothing went wrong at Pittsburgh. Nor was there anything gleamingly right. I'd give myself a B-plus. Recently, at Temple U., there were ups and downs which you might find amusing. But it would take too godam much time to trace them all. Maybe we should correspond on tapes. I was at two branches of So. Illinois U. At the Edwardville spur, I gave a talk on the Twenties. "Thoughts on Literature, Living, and Livelihood in the Twenties," gravitating about my relations to The Dial. It was poorly attended, but well-received. At Carbondale, doubtless thanks to the fact that Hugh Duncan is there, and loudly proclaims my virtues, I went over swarmingly and swimmingly. Also, Stanley Hyman had been there a few days previously. The only other orating job I have this year is a day in Delaware, being asked questions at, for six hunnert bayries. I go to Yaddo on Jan. 8th, and linger until March 8th (except for a talk I give at a gathering of English teachers, in central Washington, Yakima, near end of Feb.). But I may happen to be in Rochester (unrelated to the Academic Circuit) sometime twixt Dec. 20 and Jan. 8. If it is so to be, I'll let you know.

Meanwhile, here's a Major Problem: I have had a byooteously tempting offer, for one course next year. But it's in St. Louis. And when I passed through there recently, the stench of the oil refineries hit me like a clubbing. I could probably put up with the *smell*, but could I stand the *idea?* At the mere thought, I feel my blood-pressure mounting. In any case, I plan to be gone fairly soon. And why should I put up with a spell of Acute Olfactory Excruciation, even for the glory of having, for once in my life, a one-year heavenly income? ... But hold! Since I wrote them words, a friend called, to assure me that the stench I exp*eee*rienced was not reglas. So I'll go to get my fortune told, early next week. (I've been getting some hospitality done at me, diagnosis-wise.) And if I'm allowed to live a bit longer, bejeez I'll take the job.

But the main thing is: Yes, I'd be most grateful for any suggestions you have regarding the contents of my Poetics enterprise, which I hope to finish up, while at Yaddo. I have some ideas, but I'd rather hear yours. And if you ever feel like telling just what worries your students about the LSA collection, pray spick.

Meanwhile, may all of you

Rejoice!

K.B.

LETTERS
FROM
1970 TO 1979

Yaddo
Saratoga springs, NY 12866
2/8/70

Dear B&B,

Of a sudden I hit an idea, or an idea hit me. I wrote to my friend, Malcolm Cowley, who is a trustee at Yaddo. I asked about chances of storing me here for the wint. Granville Hicks, who is the present acting director, was agreeable. And Mrs. Ames, who has since retired. So here I am—and given the opportunity to stay as late as the end of April, though I may return to And/or a short bit ere that.

I'm accoutred wonderful, enjoy the set-up and the company—indeed there's nothing at all wrong except my increasingly frequent attacks of Burke's Disease, which in its way is almost as bad as Rueckerts' Disease.

If you really wanted the Ohio State job, then you must have gone at things wrong. Here's a hunch I'd suggest: Maybe you're trying to be too bing-bing-bing. Maybe you're talking too much about what *you're* doing or planning to do. Don't forget, you can keep from being too much on the auction block if you keep asking everybody else what *he's* doing and how it's working out. And you're more likely to be loved if you're on the dull side. Also, be cautious with the alky (sez I, who so rarely am, alas!).

Yes, I'd be glad to see the hilarity of which you make mention of which.

Our articles have appeared in *Shenandoah*—but so far I have not been able to elicit a copy. (I reviewed another McLues book in the latest N.R.) Glad to hear that things progress well with the book. And best felicitations anent the coming further parenthood.

Me meanwhile, beneath all my daily and nightly rounds, I find that I am beginning to miss Libbie more and more. I often write diaristic lines to her, though most have to be discarded. Here is a couplet that might conceivably serve to wind up a Shakespearean sonnet: "Your death leaves such a tangled aftergrowth,/Dear Love, I fear I have outlived us both."

Rejoice,
K.B.

Yaddo, Saratoga Springs, NY 12866
March 16, 1970

Dear Bill,

Over the years, my total impression of you has become reduced to this: "About every six months he writes a clamorous letter suggesting that one is henceforth to be bombarded with letters at least five times a week—whereupon he lapses into another six months of total silence."

Here's hoping that your latest lapsarianism does not argue, or augur, any important disruptions. At least, write and assure me that all goes well (or at least as well as you will let things go).

I wonder if you saw the full-page advt. in the current issue of the New York Review of Books (including, thank God, no mention of M. Brown's stinko pamphlet). And I wonder if you have seen a copy of Arminius's digest, in the Twayne series.

Recently I did some verbalizing in Washington State. I flourished on hard work. Then o'errelaxed for two days in California, and came back one hell of a wreck on the rack.

Now I'm trying to finish a review of Denis's book on Swift (for the N.R.). Nthen I must send in a report for a meeting on N. O. Brown, the meeting not until April, but the report due before then.

Praise God, Granville Hicks (the present acting director at Yadder) extended my stay into April. Uddawise, I'd now be back at And/or, all loneliness and austerity such as me no relish. As it is, by the time I return (at or near the end of April), the seasonal inclemencies will have abated, and I'll be able to stand myself there.

The deal has been definitively settled for next year. Beginning in September, I'm to be the FANNIE HURST VISITING PROFESSOR until the following May, at Washington U. Then the next winter, if I'm still around, I think I'll trek south. (My seminar should not be over-exacting. It's on Burkology, a task for which your herculean labors in the Augean stables should be of great assistance.)

That start for a poem I mentioned turned out thus:

Postlude

When something goes, some other takes its place
Maybe a thistle where had been a rose.
Or where lace was, next time a churchman's missal.
Erase, efface (Life says) when something goes.

Her death leaves such a tangled aftergrowth,
by God, I fear I have outlived us both.

Malcolm C., who likes the poem, rightly objects that the third line (while good for purposes of internal rhymes) suggests more than I want to say. The missal, yes. But for the lace, cf. *Invitation à Cythère*, C.P. page 137.

Be gay,
K.B.

Yaddo 4/19/70

Dear Bill,

Here's hoping that all goes gloriously with Momma and the New Annex.

If you haven't yet mailed that item you mentioned, I'd suggest that you address it to Andover (whither I'm scheduled to return on the 25th).

The Brown seminar turned out to be a bit vehement at times. (Mea culpa, mea maxima culpa.) I have added some other angles (an account of which I hope to show you later). But basically my position remains as per my review of LB in the Nation.

Crescite et multiplicamini,

K.B.

1970

Three Poems of Abandonment
(to Libbie, who cleared out)

I - Genius Loci

Until you died, my Love,
somehow I had belief in fear of ghosts.
But now, in this lonely place
that is so full of you
whereby I am not in my essence over-lonesome,

what lovelier
than if your spirit,
the genius of this house,
did materialize right here before me?

Dear Love,
always I tried to earn you,
but now you are the absolutely given

while I each night
lie conscious

of my loss

II - Postlude

When something goes, some other takes its place.
Maybe a thistle where had been a rose;
or where lace was, next time a churchman's missal.
Erase, efface (Life says) when something goes.

Her death leaves such a tangled aftergrowth,
by God I fear I have outlived us both.

III - Part of a Letter

Your words to the both of us ...
For some time there has been of her
only so much as lives in the memory
or in the things that bespeak her. ...
I should have written months ago.

. . . the only solace:
she died just before her affliction
was to enter a phase much grimmer ...

in May ... the scent of lilac ...

I wrote several,
but I enclose the only two that came somewhat near to what
  I needed ...

the first when I lingered in our house alone
in late autumn ...
the second in a colony called "Shadow"

(the good rapport there, especially remarkable,
what with each an aching ego
to whom even great fame would be embitterment
through not being fame still greater ...
no pecking order
except for my ways of picking on myself)

The delightful conceit of that calendar you sent!
. . . from March 21 to March 20 ...
a perfect cycle!
As The Bard said:
      All seasons have their season
      only if
      each after its fashion ... only if
      all seasons lead towards spring ...

Agh! Spring!
to the gloom of personal loss
add the mean prospect
of man's compulsive, unstoppable Hypertechnologism
that gluttony
with its microgadgets and its macrogadgets ...

Your mention of her drawing (the handsome wierdy cat)
...
it reminds me of the times when we were greatly privileged
(now I know how greatly) ...

now much less efficient than I was ... often lack zeal ...
but keep batting away ... what else to do?
and at times the gratification of a sentence
that seems to turn out at least almost just right.

. . . spring once again ...
the cycle completed! ...
soon to be flowing
with the death-scent of lilac

Kenneth Burke

K.B.

[Note written on poems.]

Yaddo, 4/24/70

Dear B&B,
Leaving tomorrow for Andover.
Be gay,

K.B.

And/or 4/27/70

Dear B&B (Multiplicationists Extraordinary),
It just occurred to me:
I don't know how, or exactly when, Bill goes to Binghamton
(Harpur). But I'm almost certain that a bus from there to NYC passes

through Netcong. Hence, it would be a cinch for me to meet a pilgrim on a route of that sort.

I mention it, just in case. (Phone here is as was; namely: 201-347-3249.)

Damn it. Having indentured myself from mid-September to mid-May at Washington U. (*in St. Louis*), I am now being tempted to sign up for a seminar at Berkeley, sometime soon thereafter (though not at such a booful figger as with the Wash. U. job).

I don't know what to say. Apparently I'm gwanna die with my boots on. Wouldn't it be wonderful if, in a classroom, after just having said, "Pardon my French, but that filthy hatchet-man, Shitney Hook ..." and I passed out, while all present saw a dove fly out the window?

How long is it yet, before Bill holds forth at Harpur? There are some later items I'd like him to see, e'en though he might hate me for them (at least a little bit!).

Meanwhile, I have just seen a book, *Essays in Shakespearean Criticism*, edited by two Irvine gents, Calderwood and Toliver. I see that I got in with my essay (and comments) on *Coriolanus*. Published by Pr*nt*c*-H*ll.

They say we got 30 years to go yet. How sweet! When I am gone, mankind will still have a bit of future left, if the atomic war does not break out, and sheerly peace-time technology does all the damage.

Love, love, love - kill kill kill kill kill

Be gay!
K.B.

R.D. 2
Andover, NJ 07821
May Day 70

Dear Bill,

First, as to your inquiry: I have been to the University of Pittsburgh twice, once in Speech Dept., once in English. I think I got along better with the Speech Dept. But that's usually the case with me. Pittsburgh is in many ways an appealing city—very civic-minded and apologetic. And hospitable. And picturesque. I gave my *King Lear* bit (in the evening; I had peddled my verse in the afternoon). What happened was that some guy who was not connected with the school crashed the party and took over. So I did not get a chance to establish as much of a contact with faculty and studentry in general as I'd have preferred. But I don't see why you shouldn't like it there, except in the technical sense that everyplace is a vale of tears.

If you go to Santa Barbara, by all means get in touch with John Macksoud, and his wondrous-eyed wife, Jackie. They are an intense family unit (with one child whom they doubtless revolve about incessantly). John teaches in the Speech Dept. He has great energy, and a mighty, though friendly, ego. And he could probably give you a tip about a place. Home address: 450 Los Verdes Drive, Santa Barbara, Calif. 93105. The trouble with the place is that, even under "normal" conditions quite a lot of oil washed up on the beach. Living quarters are scarce. We stayed in a kind of Old Folks Home that would frown upon even a visit from the proliferous Rueckerts.

Another possibility (though it's a long shot): You might write Mrs. Mildred Ligda, Hermes Publications, Box 397, Los Altos, Calif. 94022, asking whether she might have accommodations on the hill. Joan Baez is living in one part of the place (or was). Mildred *might* be helpful. (Our relations are about 40 below zero—but she is unpredictable along those lines, and might be helpful.) Another possibility is John and Esther Sills, 20,000 Skyline Blvd., Woodside, California 94062. They are warm and gentle souls, sure to be on the good side of every movement, ecology-minded to the extent of raising their own goats. They make their living as potters. Woodside is in the Stanford area. Their place is on a steep slope, overlooking the Pacific. With Mildred Ligda they are on very bad terms.

Just got an inquiry from a gent in the Sociology Dept., U. of Manchester. Wants to reprint (in a Penguin paperback on sociology) 2,500 words of excerpts from the preface to GM. ... Got the item by Bill's student. But haven't yet had a chance to read it. Oof! what a super-tangle I'm in now. Plus a scare: Yestiddy, much Blut in the stool. Several times. Is it The End, or some diarrhoeic rage? Symptoms nearly but not quite vanished today, I dare think it was a temporary infection. ... Cancer of the gizzardry would be one way to escape the coming gloom of the lilacs. ... Incidentally, Reed Whittemore voted for the first two of the three poems. He was especially strong for the second, which I too think is the best. The third is a bit loose. But I may restore it if the poems are published in book form.

I have been sporadically unpacking. I enclose one of the articles which I wanted you to see. It gives some hint of how I would replace "ar-

chetype" and "prototype" with "entelechy" (and I think Brown's mytho-
mania gets things backwards, the perfect recipe for what *Marx* means by
"ideology"). The related piece (the basis of a talk I gave at Temple U. last
fall) cannot be sent, binnuz I lack a duplicate. But I'd like you to see it,
if poss., before your stint at Harpur. When exactly are your dates there?
And if I do manage to get a copy made in time for you to receive it, if
not at Rochester, then at Harpur, whom should I send it in care of? It's
called "The Doing and the Saying," and concerns what happens when a
practical act such as planting gets its "mythic *dédoublement*" in the realm
of ritual. It o'erlaps upon the concept of the "socio-anagogic" in RM,
and my speculations, with Fontenrose as point of departure, in LSA. (In
brief, it concerns ways whereby processes that "belong together" by the
tests of "piety," as twistedly discussed in P&C, can come to seem *causally*
related. And there enters mythic or ideological reversal, as the rite that
rounds out such a practical act as planting, comes to be interpreted as
causally necessary for the success of the practical act. In one sense, we are
all myth-men. But in another sense, there is the expert in mythopoeia.
And thus there is built up a special office, with corresponding claims to
authority and privilege. I say that this notion is analogous to Coleridge's
thesis that all men experience in terms of the "primary" imagination, but
only the special class of artistic genius experiences in terms of the "secondary" imagination. Drop me a card, with the necessary info—and if I
do get a chance to get the essay duplicated at a local Benedictine abbey,
I'll send it along. But I must admit, it's a quite mussy copy, at best.)

Meanwhile, here's hoping that all goes gloriously with youenz all.

Sincerely,

K.B.

Yasnaya Polyana

5/12/70

Dear Bill,

I'm sorry to hear of your troubles back home. Please tell Betty of my
sympathy.

You can complicate things a-plenty just by your lil self; but by God,
the Fates are certainly helping you out.

In the meantime, I have read your student's lively, amusing dialogue.
It was good clean intelligent fun—and please tell him I said so. But there
was one almost unforgivable mistake.

I refer to the places where I address Hook as "Sidney." If your student really understood my essence, he'd know that I could at best address the guy as "Hook." But I'd feel more like myself if I just introduced hit-and-run expressions such as "by hook or crook." And, around the house, he is fondly referred to as "Shitney." Otherwise, all is O.K.

Meanwhile, damn it all, this may be the last chance we'll have to see each other, until the infinite number of cycles repeat themselves, and everything, down to the tiniest detail, is once again as it was this time (and we somewhat understand each other because of the infinite times in which this special combination has prevailed). I feel thus about all the people I care about.

But in any case, if we're not to meet again, please at least do this:

If, when you're back on the job there, if some issue turns up that you think is worth discussing with me, please phone me COLLECT. (I'd prefer, of course, that you do so at the cheapest hours.) I forget whether I told you in an earlier letter, but I think there are places where you let them baystards push us around more than need be. However, the difficulty there may be more basic, since it involves in you a greater respect for Frye, Brown, and McLues than I can make sense of, though I'll pay them a lot of respect.

Here's the problem, as I see it (and you might bring it up to your class if you care to—and even tell 'em that I asked you to do so): Might you overrate Frye because he oversells The Department?

NO! You'd get so sidetracked, you'd not be able to say it like it is. I should keep outa this bizz.

Put down April 30 as The Day When I Had One Hell Of A Scare. Blut in the stool. I said, naturally, "This is the end." But no, indications are that the symptoms are a tribute to the murderous stuff you get from these bastard supermarkets. For, though I damn near pooped myself apart after eating some dubious-looking chopped meat, here I still am (thanks, I think, to the fact that I threw the rest out). I should add that *I* didn't buy the chopped meat. But it is a terror to see Blut in your stool, unless of course you're not, like me, beyond the age of menstruation.

Roll on, oh seas, roll on. Roll on, B&B, roll on. And contribute even as much as I did, to the criminality of over-population.

And if my letter seems unfeeling, please let me tell you why I am in mine anaesthetic stage. A student-type turned up yestiddy, to interview me. (In view of my notorious prowess as a rapist, she brought a girl-friend along to protect her.) I yiped for three hours—and bejeez, I slept all night sans pillulation. But when I did get up, I was beside myself. It was horrible—for now I had lost Libbie, the house, and myself. I usually talk to myself, but now I heard myself talking to myself (and there's one hell of a difference). I think I have figured it all out. And now, after about five hours of effort, I think I am at least on the slope of the sub-personality that I think of as really me. But I had to use some alky as a bridge towards the way back. To cut a lot of corners, I think the tangle turned up thus: My intervieweress was so clearly a student-type, I talked to her as with a student at Bennington, or someone else along the academic circuit. So the distinction btw. here and there got bridged. How then could I know my own house? And thus, how not have my identity (this identity) get muddled? It all has to do with such things as I discussed in Gramma as scene-agent and act-scene ratios. But in the meantime, I'm still fighting to recover. For this morning, after this incredibly long night-sleep sans dope, I awoke feeling much like a man who had forgot his own name. As a now-dead commedian used to put it, "Monkeys is the cwaziest pipple."

Please forgive me if I seem unfeeling. It's just that I'm plastered.

Sincerely,
K.B.

Slumpwump 07821
7/8/70

Dear Bill,

You ask where I'm at. I don't know, because I don't know what I'm after. How can I know the position, when I don't know the direction? I just wrote a guy towards whom I said it thus: "I think so constantly of corruption and pollution, if someone could persuade me that things are developing otherwise, I'd probably feel robbed." I also uttered: "I have become the very soul of inefficiency, bordering at times on total diffidence." I began that one by saying, "Since my wife's death."

In any case, since we last discussed such matters, I have received honorary degrees from Dartmouth and Fairfield U. (a Jesuit school), also an earlier one from Yaddo, on April Fools' Day. And the New School for Social Research up and gave me Two Grand, for being a distinguished rundown educator who was thought to need encouragement in his dotage. And at least I'm among the nominees for a National Book Medal, plus One Grand. (Don't bet on me.)

I salute your great heroism in joining the priesthood of Cybele. (Cf. Catullus's poem on the *Galli,* though I admit that I'm over-idealizing your sacrifice.) And I trust that you appreciate the privilege of being carefree.

The only way I can have Butchie as company on my drive to St. Louis is by leaving here sooner than I otherwise would. So I may be starting West just about the time you are starting East. I don't yet know where I'm to be domiciled. I'll let you know when I do. But if you do turn up at some odd moment, and arrangements have gone wrong, you might locate me by calling Howard Nemerov, whose address then will be: 6970 Cornell Ave.

Since both the cutter-bar and the lawnmower were out of order, things have been a wilderness here. But some of the rank growth has recently been hacked away—so the Domain of the Sleepless Ugly has been trimmed up somewhat, e'en though no kiss from a Princess came to dispel the curse here all about us. There was so much rain, the fields have a correspondingly rich stand of hay—and I think it's a shame I'm not that particular kind of ass.

Jeez, if only you and Stanley Aitch had blowhorned about what wonders you did at Harpur! But wow! what reserve and modesty! It causes me to tremble. "Oh, where was Moses when the lights went out? Down in the cellar eatin sauerkraut."

Meanwhile, best felicitations to theenthine.

Sincerely,
K.B.

8166 Whitburn Dr., Apt. 13
Clayton, Mo. 63105
11/7/70

Dear BillR,

Plastered, I wrote you a letter pronto—and it was stupid, so I haint sending it.

It's just as well you didn't turn up here. There were some picturesque disorders of travel and installment (though everything is quite pleasant at the school).

I don't know what to do. I like to teach. But I'm already beaten down by the sheer mechanics of living. Both academically and extra-academically, life becomes nothing but the filling-out of forms. And either answering or dodging inquiries. (Your Mr. Heath is all set to put the Heath on me. The computers are teaching all up-and-coming scholars how to make interviewees do their work for them. Recently I have done some rebelling, but it's suicidal.)

Doubtless it's only force of habit that makes me want to live at all. Many people are friendly, and I have my ever-zingoing family—but I miss Libbie more and more rather than less.

Simultaneously, I am lonesome and lone-seeking. Me and Garbo.

Wow! You're lucky that Betty's symptoms at Zion were but a passing phase. I wonder where you stayed there. And did you (if I may quote The Bard, p. 286) all night hear "the deep convulsive intake of the desert/through the gulches"?

Gass is not here now, but is expected back next term. And I expect that we'll get along quite well—for why not? Which reminds me: I finished my "Brown Study," to what I added a "Postscript" and a "Post Mortem"—and then a "Da Capo" (in keeping with modern teachings that trash should be recycled).

I forget whether I showed you a rough draft of my bizz on "Doing and Saying," an item I talked at Temple U. about a year ago. I greatly revised it (not for sense, but for sentences), and gave it a box-office subtitle ("Thoughts on Myth, Cult, and Archetypes")—and it's to be published in *Salmagundi,* now subsidized by Skidmore, near where I was last wint. … And if all goes as Andrew Lytle tentatively planned, the winter issue of *Sewanee* will have my Helhaven satire, an article (doubtless shitty) by Wellek on my criticism, and an article (doubtless an ingenious what-is-it on what-am-I) by Howard Nemerov. Next week I fare forth for four days to Chicago, where I hope (in friendly company) to consolidate my logological critique of the mythologers by demonstrating the need to interpret "archetypes" in terms of "entelechies."

I'm scheduled to be here until sometime in May. I have been asked to do a term at Berkeley, but have been loath to sign up definitively. You speak of moving on. It's a language I speak, however differently we may understand it.

May youenz all rejerce,
K.B.

Department of English
Washington University
St. Louis, Missouri
12/8/70

Dear Bill,

It just occurred to me: In case you happen to be around Nov Yorick during the holidays, do try to get in touch. Try phoning Eleanor Burke or France Burke in Manhattan (Horatio St., or Avenue B respectively), or Michael Burke or Elspeth Hart in Brooklyn (Middagh and Hicks, resp.). I thought the MLA racket might be in NYC, and you might be attending.

Recently, in my seminar, I went over my section on "The Dialectic of Constitutions." I was astonied to note how thoroughly it gets neglected in the reviews you assembled, except for one paragraph in Fergusson.

I wonder if you feel that Kaplan's statement of my case fits with what I say in paragraphs 3 and 4 for GM, p. xvi, as continued in top paragraph of xvii. As I see it, by omitting references to my discussion of "Constitution-Behind-the-Constitution" and kindred observations (for instance, regarding the way in which the U.S. Constitution eliminated the authority involved in its founding, hence led to quite different notions of the enemy), Kaplan could continue, throughout his article, doing what he did when *giving in his own words* what I said I had done, as vs. *explicitly quoting my distinctions between "strictly speaking" and "speaking broadly."* You praise Kaplan for the tone of his review - OK. But surely Rule 1 in discussions of this sort is to quote the author in his own words. Had Kaplan explicitly quoted my sentence about "strictly speaking," it would have been obviously indecent of him to omit my next reference to "speaking broadly." But by omitting this statement of myown, *along with total silence* about my discussion of Constitutional Casuistry, he earned your respect while refuting a book of his own making. I don't say that he misrepresented the situation intentionally. I simply say that he misrepresented the situation - and gets patted on the back for doing so. And he completely failed to realize that my thesis about the "scene-act-ratio" is the basis of my claim that our concepts of ultimate motivation are grounded philosophically rather than scientifically. For the theory of the scene-act-ratio (i.e., the act is to be interpreted *in terms of* its scene) *must* be philosophic rather than scientific in the modern sense of the term scientific - since there can be no specialized "science of 'circumferences.' " The specializing in generality is philosophic (or, as regards Dramatistic comedy, "logological," a term that I wasn't using then, but that Kaplan himself is groping for when, on your page 171, he refers to transformations that "are not strictly logical, but socio- and psycho-logical").

As regards Kaplan's statement, "And Burke's insistence that the book itself 'is wholly scientistic in its aim' is hardly credible when he indulges in journalistic attacks on animal experimentation as 'sadistic' and serving no useful purpose," I wish you had asked him to specify the text. Here's the sort of thing I have in mind:

As regards all the scientists who are engaged in the production of so many hellish means of torture, maybe it's actually true that not a single one of them is a sadist. Maybe they're all just technicians, and simply lack imagination. Maybe all the Nazi scientists who tortured not just animals but Jews for contributions to knowledge, maybe they weren't sadists, but just obediently going about their dirty business. But even so, I have in mind a notion of this sort: I remember when a friend of mine, a sweet fellow, saw possibilities of getting some money for educational experiments on animals. He was all steamed up - and began thinking of how one might, for instance, work out still more experiments to show how an animal can be driven crazy. I said I though that animal experiments had already proved this point. So why not leave it at that? Must we repeat these experiments, for every class? And I knew another sweet guy, as gentle as they make 'em. He had figured out a lot of new tortures for animals - and he had the data, and it was quite convincing. There's no doubt about it; when you scientifically torture animals, you'll be able to prove scientifically that the poor devils gets quite stirred up. I asked the guy, "Did you ever think of trying to find out what happens to animals if you are nice to them?" Wow! I saw the gleam in his eye. Two years later, in a magazine section, I read a story about that guy. His whole house was full of animals who were getting along hunky-dory with one another. Then I understood the gleam in his eye. He had had a vision of another grant - and it materialized.

Maybe it isn't sadism. Maybe it is but lack of imagination. Maybe that's why it's acceptable for us to obliterate villages from a distance, but horrible if someone does the same thing close up. And of one thing at least I feel sure: I feel sure that the people who give such orders in the first place have "transcended" the realistic truth of what they are after, and how. My hunch is that if our leaders had either scientifically or imaginatively known what our Vietnam deal would lead to, I doubt whether a single one of them would have ordered our invasion, so many thousand miles from home. ("He got entangled in a situation/ that would defy the best of us/ through having access to misinformation/ that was denied the rest of us.")

Agh! Gawd! Of a sud. I 'gan trying to memmer what you had said anent Constitutions. I dug up the Sacred Text - and the indexer gives me not a hint. Plizz! Plizz!

Ennihow, you did a (an) herculean job. Recently, by the way, it was an exceptional pleasure to meet Leland Griffin. He is as decent and kindly as they make 'em. And I'll tell you more anon.

Meanwhile, may thou and thine,

Rejerce,

K.B.

I leave for NYC on the 16th.

8166 Whitburn Dr., Apt. 13

Clayton, Mo. 63105

2/17/71

Dear BillR,

Thanks for the offer to be mine own necrologer. I happened to be writing Happy—so I asked her if she had handy something that I did for her once. It might serve you as a point of departure, at least. (Also, though I've never been able to find who did it, I thought that the definition of Dramatism in the recent disgraceful Websters was pretty good. And I think that the opening sentences of the article on "Dramatism" in the *International Encyclopedia of the Social Sciences* is fairly to the point.)

I have met Gass, but haven't yet really had a chance to do more than say hello. Apparently his new book of criticism is going to take on. And whereas the philosophy department was in a bad way here, his course came through with a bang, chalking up an enrollment of 240 students.

And I salute your ecological poem.

As for me, meself, and I—we are all quite moody and where-is-it.

Sure, you should arrange for a visit to And/or this summer. I expect to be there. I have sworn to do no more course-work in teaching, though I'll go on welcoming quickies. Since the Cowleys are freezing in Minnesota, for the present at least I have them sold on the idea of our going south next wint.

I had a big scare. Possibility of cancer in a big way. Things now look otherwise. But I haven't yet got my diploma definitively. I had some spectroscopic cauterization done—and am to get a final inspection a week from now. Was in the hospital for some time, though sans pain. On the whole, the interlude was quite restful, and even enlightening.

I enclose an item for your edification, if any. Meanwhile, all best to theenthine.

Sincerely,
K.B.

The Gass-line you quote reminds me of a relevant story that you might find amusing. A guy had gone to a dance, he was a bit fuzzy with alcohol, and he 'gan finding himself caught short. Someone gave him instructions as to where he might find the men's room, but he got muddled. And he was more and more in trouble; for he had to poop in a most urgent way. Then he ran across a door that led to an upstairs—and that in turn led to a big empty place. He knew this wasn't it. But it was quite deserted. So he was safe enough, and there was a place that seemed feasible. He took down his pants and did the job there. He had some trouble finding his way back, so it took a while. And to his astonishment, when he did get back to the dance-hall, the place was damn near deserted. But he saw one member of the orchestra, who seemed to be putting away his drums. So he went over and said, "Say, what happened to everybody?" And the guy answered, "Just where were you when that shit hit the electric fan?"

Longlivelongevity,
K.B.

8166 Whitburn Dr., Apt. 13
Clayton, Mo. 63105
March 4, 1971

Dear Bill,

Hold the presses. Does the stuffo on the other side give you any notions to work in, or work from? (Notice, by the way, the vexingly strategic error. I have decided I must give up using the words "now" and "causal," for "now" is always susceptible to turning up as "not," and "causal" is ever lurking for an opportunity to sneak by as "casual.")

Just a few days ago, by the way, I felt as though the NYT obit had been ordered just in time. I felt so down-and-out, I thought my heart would stop. (At my age, a mood of thick gloom can be fatal.)

I quote a quatrain that may not be the best of poetry, but is diaristically as accurate as one could ask for:

3/3/71

How could those times be now so wholly gone,
blackened into oblivion?
Now all is emptiness and fear—
Christ Jesus, get me out of here.

It had been led into thus (by adapting ironically Henley's Great Sales Talk title):

Invictus

If things are bad, and I can't make them better,
then all the more I'll be mine own begetter:
Adversity will be my universe,
making me free to act to make things worse.

But now all has cleared up; and I'm feeling so good I don't even give a godam if tonight's public performance is a flop. (Howe'er, I'm working like a fiend all day, to make it, if poss. be wholly otherwise.)

Meanwhile, a new symptom, damn it. It begins to "transpire" that Nembies are developing side-effects, most notably a lot of flickering around the immediate object of my vision.

Rejerce,
K.B.

07821
7/19/71

Dear Bill,

Smatterafact, the later in the season you came, the better. I expect to linger here until circa the end of November, then migrate to Floridoah, there to linger until April. But at this time of year there are usually members of the clan hereabouts. It's with the oncoming of autumnality that my selfness grows more severe (though I must admit that I'm pretty sick of it all the time).

Despite the annoyances, it must be wonderf to be building. I'm thinking in the other direction (planting pine trees in the fields behind the house, since I get tired of laying low the grassnweeds). Gradually things keep disappearing or getting misplaced or worn out—and to those degrees I infold further. I have started saying a glum good-bye.

If you haven't yet read Wellek, please delay further, until you have my artikkel in answerve. After raging around the house, I wrote a Buddhistically non-peevish piece. Fulminations are for first drafts. My theory of the last draft is that one should use an opponent as a way of getting something said. But Wellek has an exasperating trick of mussing up just enough almost everything he reports. And to answer him point by point would require answering each of his paragraphs with a page. I think I solved the problem. But let's wait and see.

Having sworn that next year I will creatively rot, I have turned down Seven (7) offers to teach part or all of 71-72 (incl. one in Berlin, the one I most felt like yielding to. (I think I'd like to do no more regla teaching, though I still love semi-Revivalist quickies, when I hold forth for a day or two. So I'll probably take on some of those, if opportunity offers.)

Yes, I was in the hospitality, and under a really gruesome threat. They were going to do so many tricks with my guts, I'd have gone down in history. But I decided: No; if I have to go through all that, and end up shittn in my hand out of my side, I'd rather clean up my accounts and bump myself off. Well, in that case, they settled for a quite minor operation—and I am out of that threat entirely, free now to suffer and die in some wholly different way. But though saved from that threat, I must admit that, at least, I still like the idea of an item to be called "Notes for a Poem on Suicide."

I don't know what "high honor" I was in danger of. I did get a grant of Five Grand, and my job at Washington U. was for thirty grand, except that my Uncle Samuel has been eating into it like crazy, to the greater glory of the Pentagon. My next job is to clean up two talks I gave at Clark U. for fifteen hunnert bayries plus expenses—and it's in a good series. My problem is that I want to do something in the medium of The Other Side; but since there haint no Other Side but Oblivion, I would write of what is doubly ineffable. So, a lot of the time, I just putter, and write letters to guys like Rueckert, who don't know from a hole in the ground.

And that's how it all sets up, towards a Next Phase. Meanwhile, may thounthine

Rejerce,

K.B.

07821

10/4/71

Dear Bill,

Just before entering the salt mines for the day, I chawnst upon thine of 9/19, nearly lost among the various piles that tend to accumulate about me.

As for my item anent Welk's Pestulations: The sichaysh is that Lytle dint want to publish it. But I had shown a copy to Allen Tate, who liked it, and suggested that I try Radcliffe Squires, author of a book on Tate and freshly editor of Michigan Quarterly Review. Squires promptly took same, but suggested some minor changes, to fit it better for its new habitat. And (such is the curse on my House) in making these minor editorial changes I just accidentally made the article twice as long. So I may have undone myself. (I just sent it off recently, and haven't yet had time to learn what next.)

Job for this week: to fickness up, for a Henry Sams Festschrift, my Eye-Crossing poem (to fit the pattern, it needs some prose comments).

I have definitively arranged for four months in Floridoah this wint: Stanford Resort, 1765 Gulf Blvd., Englewood, Florida 3353. Godwillens and Deo volente, I'll be there about the fid of November. Several bids for barn-storming have turned up, but I'm trying to get them shifted to dates in 1972. Otherwise, too much of the take would be sacrificed to the Methodical Madness of the Pentagon. I expect to be in Flrd for four months; the Cowleys have arranged to be neighbors for the last three. All is well, except that I don't like the idea of driving south alone, and have no intention of picking anybody up along the way. A chap who heard of my impending trek suggested that I give an oration while passing through Virginia. That would pleasantly ease the dreariness of the drive, and more than pay for it; but I'm suggesting that that, too, be shifted to spring, even though there's some likelihood that the trip back would not be so austerely solo. If I delayed going south, Butchie could probably drive down with me. But his dates were still too uncertain, binnuz he didn't know what last-minute obligations might turn up as regards his teaching schedule. That was a hard decision to make, for though I loathe driving, I greatly enjoy driving with him. But duty calls. Meanwhile, this bit of demagoguery is my latest poesy-wise:

Thoughts on Latter-Day Attica

Our nation suffers martyrdom
from having torn apart Vietnam
where every time we dropped a bomb
it now explodes again back home.

And so, to that disquiet
add history's further jolt
that turns each prison riot
into a slave revolt.

Love to theenthine,
K.B.

07821 11/23/71

Dear Bill,

Getting ready to clear out. (I mistakenly referred to my arrival in Englewood about Nov. 5. I shd. be Dec. 5.)

The Anti-Welk is in galleys. Due for publication this wint. I'll send you a copy of the (considerably lengthened and improved) final version when I get reprints.

First below-freezing weather has hit here. I hope to Gawd I can get out before I have trouble with the pipes.

Probably a granddaughter and her boyfriend will be driving down with me. I'd loathe the long drive alone.

I surrounded the "Eye-Crossing" with a batch of prose comments. Mine enemy can thereby object on the grounds either that the comments were necessary or were not necessary. (They were adventitiously necessary in the sense that some such addition was needed, to fit the conditions of the Festschrift—in honor of Henry Sams.)

I am now in the midst of decisions-decisions-decisions-decisions (in re what to take on the trip).

Here's my latest sunshine thought:

> What in God's name can I do with me
> to whom Death means Eternity
> and everything seems so awry
> I do and do not want to die ...

May thounthine
Rejerce,
K.B.

c/o Stanford Resort
1765 Gulf Blvd.
Englewood, Florida 33533
January 5, 1972

Dear Bill,

Delighted to hear from you, and to see the testimony of your joint productivity. After several months of gloomy weather (which I reflected with almost total fidelity), I arrived here on Dec. 5, and have lived under the sign of the naked sun, almost every day since. As a matter of fact, I actually began wishing for some bad days, the better to help me clear up some Unfinished Bizz. But no, the days have remained inexorably halcyon—and except for a very few I have wound up each afternoon with a four-mile walk on the beach, then I gravely sat on the beach and helped the sun go down. My magic has worked extremely well—and though I didn't check every day, on all the ones I did check it went down exactly on time. Mostly I used vodka martinis, plus a bit of note-taking.

Over the Christmas holidays, first Butchie, then Dutchie and Happy came down, to get me out of solitary. And tomorrow the Cowleys are due, to stay until the beginning of April. (I'll probably linger here for about a week thereafter, then wend north, visiting friends in South Carolina, and verbalizing at the U. of Va. (Near the end of this month, I fly to the U. of Texas for two days.)

I am plagued by inefficiency, though not all of it is my fault. A great deal of it is due to my loss of Libbie. And the insomnia continues to be damned wasteful. Still, I am getting things done. And though I am by no means what could be called joyous, I seem out from in under the gloom that I feared might be a major aspect of this next Phase.

Just now, only thus belatedly, I am trying to finish the revision of my Clark U. talks. Then I must swing into preparations for my talk in Texass. (In a Supplement to The Saturday Review, Isaiah Berlin had a long article the first part of which surveyed theories on Machiavelli. 'Twas made to order for me, since my chapter in RM swings in from an angle that he doubtless knew nought of—so I'm using that as my point of departure for the Texas project. Also, Silvers has agreed to let me have seven hunnert words, which I'll also use for my lecture.)

The possibility of a fifth knighthood especially entices me binnuz I'd being seeing youenz. Also, I'd greatly like to see Watson, who is crippled with some kind of hip trouble. (I myself have a vexingly lame right arm which may be bursitis or may be the ultimate pay-off for my broken neck, a possibility that was held out to me some decades back. At times it becomes so bad that, if my left were equally in trouble, I'd have a very tough time even getting out of bed. It usually doesn't bother me much when I'm up and about. But at night, no matter how I lie, it becomes damned painful.)

If I can find a xeroxing joint down here, I have a few items I'd like to send you. But I don't know of the historiographic developments you mention, though I believe that, if there is such a logological monster as a "scene-act ratio," its historiographic implications (incl. problems of the scene-behind-the-scene) are considerable. In my first Clark U. talk, I have a section pleading anew for my pages (in GM) on "The Dialectic of Constitutions." By the way, I believe I sent you (dint I?) a xeroxed copy of the artikkel, "Doing and Saying," that was published last wint in Salmagundi.

Yes, I must read the Merwin volume. But the "terrors and voids of our time" are at least not nearly so bad as they would be if we didn't have The Documents. Let's each try writing a poem to The Documents. I guess that's what Cicero meant by the consolatio philosophiae. "*Si hortum in bibliotheca habes, nihil deerit* ... said that great platitudinarian, Cicero, that unfortunate, knowing the laws of good fortune. But you will pardon the author, dear reader, if at this point he interrupts himself. For your author is dying. I, Morducaya Ivn ..." etc. But I may have mistranslated. He may have been using "garden" figuratively. But no, I see I took care of that.

But 'tis the next morn—and time is up. I must back to the salt mines.

Love to all, from rundown Uncle Kenneth.

Holla!

K.B.

c/o Stanford Resort
1765 Gulf Blvd.
Englewood, Florida 33533
March 15, 1972

Dear Bill,

Many thanks for thine of recent date inst. I answer seriatim:

I'm most grateful for your divulging about Texass. I *knew* there had been a surprisingly large audience, and I *thought* that the show had gone off well. But binnuz there's no fool like an old fool, I didn't dare to assure myself until I heard ab extra. Thanks for reinforcement (if I may use a bit of Behaviorist cant).

Whate'er they decide to do or not to do about my doctoring, this ole rundown dropout is scheduled to be, for the fifth time, honorifically demuttized (at Northwestern, June 17th).

Your CLIO project sounds interesting. But it seems to me that your colleague, Hayden White, should start it (by stating a general position, hence related doubts and questions). If he wanted another turn later, after I had uttered, that would be oke with me. But I don't feel that I should begin.

That Saratoga deal sounds full of possibilities.

As regards GM, when on "act," be sure to stress the *Attitude* angle, as per the section on " 'Incipient' and 'Delayed' Action."

Incidentally, though I know you think I shouldn't answer diseases like McLuhan and Wellek, my theory is that I should use any angle as a way of rounding out the statement of my position. I am now in a position to do that, and I don't at all consider it a "waste of time." More on this point later, when I have time to tell you what I want to publish next. Among other things, I have taken quite a batch of notes for a Dramatistic analysis of Skinner's Behaviorism. "Cycle of Terms Implicit in the Idea of 'Control.' " That's being "impervious," eh?

It has been a good winter, but inefficiency gains on me—and the battles with insomnia are aggravated by mounting troubles with a neck-shoulder-arm nexus.

After returning North, I'm to be at Penn State for a week. Also, the Wenner-Gren Foundation is financing some sort of a dinner for me in Philadelphia, in some way connected with Dell Hymes and some of his anthropology colleagues. (He has an Urban Ethnography set-up.)

I'm sorry to hear that Betty was ailing. All told, the season hereabouts has been quite salubrious (except, of course, as regards that morbus insanabilis, senectitude).

My plans are to leave here on the morning of April 5th. I publicly verbalize at Charlottesville on April 12th (a piece I am now writing, not sans considerable vexation).

May youenz all rejerce,

K.B.

R. D. 2

Andover, NJ 07821

4/29/72

Dear Bill,

As you doubtless know, you schemer, you low organism, I shall have a chance to see youenz and my ole frenn JSW—binnuz my muttitude is to be honorarily bedoctored by the U. of R., come June.

I'm back here, with lotsa things to say. But why say them now, when we might later have plenty of time?

And your Firm is setting me up for the night—so there's no problem along them lines.

But there's a Wenner-Gren job being set up whereby people come to feed their valuable faces in my honor, with the outfit (as I get the deal) paying their way. So I'm putting your name on the list, though I don't know how the whole things gets set up, or whether you could occur in Philadelphia at the time (May 19). Ennihow, it won't hurt to try.

I must trek to Penn State across Route 80, on May 7, there to get pushed around for a week, at not too grand a figure. And all kinds of other things threaten to befall me. But of all that, more anon.

Meanwhile, haint it nice that I'll be seeing youenz soon?

Holla!

K.B.

> R. D. 2
> Andover, NJ 07821
> May 25, 1972

Dear Bill,

This is the anniversary of the day when Libbie abandoned me (5/25/ 69)—and I miss her more every day I last. (Lilac-time.)

Thanks for thine of the 23rd. Sorry to hear that you're fighting the blood-pressure vexation. For long I have boasted of how I fought it and won. But now, God damn the luck, mine has taken a big jump. I blame, most of all, the punishment of driving all the way back solo, while under pressure to finish some preparations for lectures. And it begins to look as though things won't quiet down nearly as soon as I had hoped. Sorry that you couldn't come to feed your face in my honor, at the Wenner-Gren deal last week. But you missed no great words of wisdom.

I am glad to learn that you are to oversee my processing. "Twill be my fifth such knighthood—and there's to be a sixth at Northwestern, come the seventeenth. But this is the first one at which I e'er had to dig up an utterance. I have first-drafted something. Too bad I can't think up an item really hot, like "being at the crossroads." The nature of the *problem*, at least, is clear and simple; namely: How be an honest man without saying and resaying, for five minutes, that everything is going down the drain? Believing in the propriety of occasions, I think that we should end on ASSERTION—so I have a first draft that builds up to my most triumphant pronouncement, the lines entitled "Stout Affirmation." At least, that's how things tentatively look at present.

My plane is due to arrive by American, flight 439, leaving from Laguardia, and arriving 3:47 P.M. on June 3. I have an invitation to an informal supper at home of the President (exact time not mentioned). And I'm invited to stay at the Chancellor's House ("over night June 3rd-4th"). I shall accept the invitation for Sat. night. But I think that I should wend back hither towards late afternoon or thereabouts, on Sunday. We can figger out things when I get there. (I think I'll write Watson, suggesting a visit on Sat. aft. So keep that in mind, in case you'd like to go along.)

I'm sorry the Dr. naysaid about a knighthood for him—but it's wholly like him. And I'd have found it hilariously amusing to have Skinner for my pal.

Yes, Wesleyan proposed a deal (six weeks in Nov.-Dec.)—and I yeasaid, though with doubts. After I've said something for as much as ten minutes, I have a burning desire to shout, "It's a godam lie." It's a tough life being 75—and thank God one has to go through it only once. But no; if one lasts out the year, one will have gone through it thousands of times.

I wish you had let me know about the student, in advance. I'd have been on the look-out for her (though I always have one heck of a time with names). The occasion assigned to the graduate students, incidentally, was on the flop side. Only three turned up. And I was spoiled because I had had an especially good session the night before (with stages beginning, cum dwinks, at 5:15, and lasting until 10:30. If one of the girls that did show up was your Liza, it remains a scientific fact that neither of them was happy, and they cleared out quick, by what I interpreted as a prearranged signal. All told, I was involved in nine shows, which had their ups-and-downs. The toughest one (or what I expected would be the toughest) had to do with Joe Grucci's two classes (*sixty* kids all *writing* verse!). He had combined the classes—and not until some cocktails just before supper that I think of A Way. There had been a bit of revoluting on campus that day. So I said: "Suppose I read you some of the poems I wrote during the Thirties. And you take off from there. Let's not discuss whether the poems are "good" or "bad." Rather, let's discuss how things now similarly current should be dealt with: what should be added, what left out, what style would seem a better fit for now, etc?" And begad, they were in it, in no time.

More anon. Hope to be seeing you soon.

Holla!
K.B.

Tanglefoot
6/10/72

Dear Bill,

"Twas good to see youenz. And I hope that our mussy scheduling at the end dint do any great damage to Public Relations.

"Twas good to see the family all so joyous.

Wouldst kindly tell your friend, Jarold Ramsey, that I was delighted to get his artikkel, and shall answer him later, when my turmoil subsides. (Jeez, just when I'm still winding down, the Wesleyan outfit is after me to start winding up again already. I'm already being pressed to make decision that I hoped I could delay until at least September.)

Do you remember the name of the gent who did my salestalk? I fear that, in the general hubbub, I forgot to thank him (though I do recall waving an acknowledgement to him just as he finished.)

I leave for Evanston on the sixteenth, returning the next day (unless we're lucky enough to get a roundabout trip to Cuba or Algeria).

I patched up my "Ms. Universe" bleat a bit. But I guess I must accept it (though not without embitterment) that the Women's Lib. movement frowns on such clowning. In any case, I can at least enclose a copy of the Revised Version. Maybe it would get by if I changed, "by heck, a bitch is wonderful" to "By heck, a she is wonderful"? Or is my effort beyond saving? At least, God damn the luck, it keeps moving, ticks things off step by step.

Flourish, all,
K.B.

[Poem attached to letter.]

Ms Universe

After God did His Creating
and decided He had done a good job,

One Vast Womb
perpetually bearing its own development,

"By God," He said,
"I have created Woman."

Whereat anyone
with the slightest sense of dialectic

could realize the problem
He had set for Himself.

"How make it possible," He asked,
"for this contrivance

to realize
how good it is?"

Whereat again anyone
with the slightest sense of dialectic

would realize why He solved
this secondary problem

by creating Man
in His image.

For thus was Man set up to say,
"By heck, a bitch is wonderful."

But Man got so damned full of himself
he made up myths backwards whereby

the Principle of Womanhood
was said to get born of Manhood.

Thus as one thing led to another
it all added up to this:

All is but Woman
and deviations from Woman
and deviations from
those deviations

                  K.B.

                          Nixon Nook 07821
                                9/12/72

Dear Bill,
    How goes it with self and family?

I'm about 3/5th out of one hell of a log jam. Have been writing a talk for a Communications conference at Barcelona, Oct. 3-6. In case you're passing that way, I'm to be domiciled at Hotel Bonanova Park, Capitán Arenas, 51, Barcelona.

I guess I should at least warm up on my French, but lack the time. Always in the way.

Family has cleared out, except for week-ends.

I attach a scientific sample of my attitudinosity.

I have grown some facial spinach. Shall send you a copy, if I can ever get the photos developed.

I forget whether I told you: I'm to be at Wesleyan for six weeks, beginning at end of Oct. A seminar that meets once a week. At least, since several people (with me among them) are to deal with the same subject, Mimesis, I have a grand title for my offering: "Mimesis, Imitation, Symbolic Action." Public talk will be: "Imitation and Stylization." Except for an occasional sally, I think of spending Jan.-Feb.-March in a college town (possibly Princeton), not trying to make a cent, but just indulging a long-delayed (for half a century) desire to roam around the stacks, reading whatever I feel like reading.

All out of Nembies, and my transistor radio isn't working. So I guess I'm in for a sustained sick-of-oneself night, in a big way.

May youenz all be joyous.

K.B.

[Poem attached]

Sick Mind in Slightly Less Sick Body

Of all the things I am undone among,
come, sing a song of loss-loss, come you all.

Hating my years, yet I would not be young,
what with my lonely, ineffectual wrath

adding to hate of my age my thoughts on death,
—then, even while I think of falling, fall.

Triumph: me there, pitched headlong on the ground,
once more at least these brittle bones proved sound.
K.B.

Nixon Nook
10/12/72

Dear Bill,

'Twas good to hear from thee in any case, and all the more, thanks
to the enclosure. The guy's on the track of something. And what with
guys like youenz to guide, I think much can be done by building from
my verse and fiction as central. As I prombly said somewhere (at least in
correspondence) I consider TBL the ritualized expression of what I develop analytically in my criticism. Having by proxy gone crazy (piously
bringing gifts to the altar of Insanity), I realize more and more clearly
how my life has been but a symbolism. And I study other texts as dreams
of which I am a fragment.

As I see it the major design that the guy missed in the novel is the
symbolism of *division*. It's everywhere. For instance, Neal (kneel?) bel-
lyaching to Florence in a pay phone, and smiling so that the guy outside
(who is waiting to call next) won't get the point. I'm not sure that it's
humanly possible to dissociate thus. But *symbolically* it's just right. Twice
I have given a talk, built around that theme (beginning with details of
my childhood)—and it worked out well.

But the guy did admirably by the circle theme. And I'll write him
saying thanks enthusiastically. Yet I think that an ultimate dialectic here
would work the two circles (the benign and the vicious) in with the
theme of the *divisive*.

And now, where in Hell's name did your letter go, which disappeared
in the middle of things? I live in a constant round of such vexations. Ennihow, at least I have your address from the envelope. I expect to leave
for Wesleyan near end of Oct. And wd. rejoice if somethinx could be
worked out, for my verbalizing in your area (perhaps after the first of
the year?) Also, tentative inquiry from Storrs has turned up. Also, I'm
thinking of writing Parsons, about the possibility of my doing my Skin-
ner-skinning at Havvud. Regrettably, I'm being asked to give my public
lecture at Wesleyan soon after I arrive. I'd have preferred to linger longer
on that one, particularly since I have to do a talk soon thereafter, in commemoration of Bill Wms. (at Fairleigh Dickinson).

I wish I had time to tell you about the doings in Barcelona. I gave a talk that wound up in admonitions against the evils of "Technologism"—and it turns out that I was talking in a school of *industrial engineers!* But the earphones and the translations were so bad, I doubt whether anybody but the few who understood Amurrican had the slightest idea what I was talking about. My talk came second. But by the end of the series, the attendance had fallen off so drastically, there was literally no one present but the speaker. But we were handsomely housed, and ended on a grand banquet (a different wine with each course).

Love to all, and may your new enterprise fill you with enterprise.

Sincerely,
K.B.

I discover I couldn't find your letter because I was writing this on the back of it.

The Center for the Humanities
Wesleyan University
Middletown, Connecticut 06457
Nov. 25, 1972

Dear Bill,

Heldamnaysh, I feel rotten about so mussing your plans. But I am in a tangle beyond belief. The tangle of uncertainties, inquiries, and Unfinished Bizz now besetting me makes it almost impossible to concentrate on anything. I am like a country dog suddenly loose in the traffic on a roaringly busy city street.

In addition to everything else, I assigned Auerbach's *Mimesis* for the class text. And the way Imitation does and does not coincide with Symbolic Action got me into some expository muddles that I should have foreseen, but didn't. Finally, when I wept to the Herr Direktor, he freely agreed that I should let things loose on the Symbolic Action side of the seesaw, thereby relieving me of my valiant efforts to maintain the role of candlestick. So, for the rest of the term, it won't be a seesaw. I'll be on the ground again.

Meanwhile, ambiguities of travel (when and where I am to set up my basic headquarters for Jan-Feb-March, incl. some intermediate time around Christmas) have filled my cup of Disorder until it runneth over. (Not only your proposal, but several other offers are varying sorts and duration, have had to go unanswered. If only I could wake up and find out that it is merely an exceptionally troubled nightmare! Or, better yet, I guess it would be best that I simply go to sleep and ne'er wake up.)

Maybe, in any case, we shd. shift from Jan to Feb—for by then I think my special burden of entanglements would have abated. Also, by then I'd know (as I don't now know in the slightest) how I'd travel from where. Sometimes I have dreams of being totally lost. That's the muddle I'm in.

Also, incidentally, I have an inquiry signed "Betty" (sans address but with a Saratoga Springs postmark). About a possible trip to Sanibel, for recuperation after "some repairs and removals." Is that thy Betty? And I hope the operation is not serious. Sanibel wd. be good, but expensive. And yes, I guess the best way to get there would be from Fort Myers. There might be a better chance of getting a place right by the beach at Englewood. 'Twould be less swank, and less expensive. It can be reached by Limousine from Tampa—and there are some planes to the airport at Sarasota. Bonita Springs is also a good possibility (Libbie and I lingered there for a while).

Gawd! what a jangle my own affairs (sheerly business) are in. There are just too godam many things to fill out. And the situation is going to get worse, every time another computer is born. They have added the final perfection to the job of keeping our machines busy.

Avec Liebe to all,
K.B.

Among my wrack of duties, please include an exceptionally pleasant one, namely: to acknowledge a charming letter from Wayne Booth, who had 55 graduate students read C-S and LSA ("most of each"). "I want you to understand that there are just the two of you that the students spend much time on, you and RSC. Him first, to keep them honest, then you to prick them into full life again." "We have Very High Level Discussions about you." The letter also included notes on a dream he had written down in 1951 (as per the stuff in my "*Somnia ad Urinandum*"). In writing him I shall offer my tentative explanation as to why, though the dream itself so "authoritatively" established the fact that he was *not* dreaming but was awake and taking care of himself properly, it did not eventuate in actual bed-wetting.

K.B.

Residence phone number, if you want to cuss me out: 203-347-3211. I live alone, and am usually here every morning.

> 204 Graduate College
> Princeton University
> Princeton, NJ 08540
> January 9, 1973

Dear Bill,

Helndamnaysh. First, I was the Man Without a Forwarding Address. Now, I have been here for several days, all set to be forwarded at—and nary a peep outa anyone.

As I recall, you contracted to send me some data anent trains and I was to let you know accordingly. If that haint on the way, plizz make haste.

There is a phone outside my door in the hall, but I'm not likely to be near it, as I'm mainly working at the library. So if there's anything to be settled by phone, I had better phone you. In which case, plizz say when.

But I did, before moving on, get Betty's seasonal remembrance, plus welcome visual data anent the clan. I hope that her time of recovery on Sanibel is pleasant, though I doubt whether the place is as much on the plus-side as it was before the current causeway replaced access by boat.

Meanwhile, tough luck: Though I'm not exactly sure of the dates, it looks as though Isaiah Berlin will be verbalizing in the Gauss Seminars just about the time I'm faring forth to Make History in Saratoga Spr. Ennihow, binnuz he is to give a talk on Vico, I spent the day doing my homework on same. Should I tell him of the doity trick they done on me, when publishing my letter anent his supplement on Machiavelli (in the NY Rev. of Bks)? "Sir Isaiah" being a bit hard for me to manage, I referred to him as "Dr. Berlin." My letter was published without my seeing galleys. Some poop (doubtless of Phartisan allegiance), changed my four "Dr's" to "Mr's," where upon Sir Isaiah could delicately answer me by first addressing me twice as "Professor," and then demoting me to "Mr." In all likelihood, the best thing to do in such a sichaysh is simply to write it off, ptikly since his letter was otherwise quite gracious. (I speak as a six-times bedoctored drop-out, who is ashamed even to mention such things, yet can do so at cocktail hour now being enacted in my severe bachelor quarters here alone.)

I believe you were also to tell me what I should be setting up, as some kind of WRITTEN STATEMENT. Would I be needing some of my stuffo, for that purpose? Or are the necessary documents available thereabouts? (I ask in my capacity as one who is sick and tired of tearing his guts out* by lugging his books around.)

Holla!
K.B.

*and gettn pinsnneedles around his heart

204 Graduate College
Princeton, NJ 08540
Feb. 2, 1973

Dear Bill,

Here 'tis, bejeez.

If youenz guys think it's a bit too much on the breezy side, I'll consent to have it debreezed, if youenz guys do the debreezing.

If, on t'other hand, you want to pitch in by making it solider, I'll be as grateful that way, too. Indeed, e'en more so. For who other than you would be better able to judge what I thought I said and didn't?

I can imagine, for instance, your up and saying and perhaps adding at the end: "To my mind, Burke didn't do well by, etc." And you'd say how Burke might better do well.

Please thank the Herr Direktor for his letting me in. And I do pathetically hope that he and Phyllis and the camera crew can figure out acceptable ways of salvaging at least one program out of my two. (Perhaps the most brutal expeeerience of my life was when I perforce walked out on the rerun of my performance, which I wanted to study for both morbid and professional reasons. But no one else loved me. I was all alone.)

And tell Pat that, any time she wants me to, I'll brush her lovely hair for nothing. (Don't you dare!)

Meanwhile, all sorts of new offers have burst upon me, NE, SW, and NW. And further good news arrives from France. But heck: How can I write a satire, if I am eroded with gratefulness?

"Twas a delight being with you, me frenn, and seeing the fambly ("Country Full of Swedes," says I, if you remember when Caldwell was a good writer).

Universal love, (even for
Nixon?!)
K.B.

204 Graduate College
Princeton, NJ 08540
2/3/73

Dear Bill,

After hurrying to send you back the Burpian Modulation, I later realized that I had not been accurate enough.

I mean: I dint at all convey my joy at our times there togidda. And note: I took out that tiny toydlet I let slip in. For though it meant nothing at all to me, it could look more looming, to others, from a distance.

Meanwhile, I have bethunk me of a great idea. If and when the whole exhibit gets set up, why don't you suggest that, any place where they might use it in the State, you could fare forth thither and offer to pitch in by adding what proved to be still needed?

What I mean is:

(1)the whole project is still in process of formation.
(2) Why not suggest a further twist of that sort?
(3) A further step of that sort would be a clincher.
(4) Other shows could be similarly treated.
(5) Or am I a Visionary?

I returned, to find others knocking at my door, from as far as the whole Continent apart.

Jeez, I glimpse the possibilities of a whole new Enterprise. Imagine that, where I'm asked to go and speak in some other State, it were possible to rent the exhibit, put on the show, and take over poisonally from there. Even *during* the show, I could heckle myself a bit. Here's a whole new medium, arising out of such material.

The Herr Direktor might work up something of that sort with his whole stable. (I speak as one who was just a Saratoga Springs, with its nostalgic memories of a great horse-racing past.)

I now fare forth to have dinner with the Fergusson clan. Last eve I had a grand time feeding some of the local studentry, and in general upholding the need for the momentous step from *mythos* to *logos* (hence, from archetype to entelechy).

I have indentured myself for a ten-day deal in early May. But thereafter, I hope to be doing nothing but creatively rotting. So, if youenz all want to invade, making it a "Country Full of Swedes," think on't.

Meanwhile, thanks for fine times thereabouts.

Holla!

K.B.

204 Graduate College
Princeton, NJ 08540
Feb. 17, 1973

Burpius Billioso Sal.

It's good to hear that Betty is recovering so felicitously. That was a good break for her, out of a bad break. May all go as per like that.

As for me, I've been suffering from an acute, an extremely acute, attack of car-trouble. Already the hospital bills are nearly up to $80.00, and there's more in store, more in store. Added to everything else, I left the parking lights on, just when the weather dropped to sub-zero. And when I tried to start the motor, it didn't even have power enough to moan.

Your pernts about my modulation are quite correct (though I speak only in the light of your letter, not yet having received any comments in detail).

Herewith a tentative draft of my trumpeteering in thy behalf with ACLS. Please inspect same, and return to me with your suggestions. Or, if you don't think I did at all well enough, write me a song for me to sign. (I wrote as I did with the idea that Burkhardt would see it; I knew him at Bennington; and he was a close pal of Stanley's.)

. . .

Time out while you read my blurb, and write out your comments. (From now on, you see, I'm to be a confirmed modulater.)

. . .

Now that you have completed your reading and comments, and have rushed out to mail me your answer, let's further discuss my piece.

I'll have to delay the revising for a bit, since I'm in the thick of the L.A. bizz (anent satire). And jeezoos-keereighst, thick it is (binnuz I'm jes lettn it roam whither it listeth, and I'll cut it down after the steam has all blowed off).

Add anything you want, plus your name. I say "plus your name," not because I would disclaim your additions, but because you should get credit for them. Meanwhile I note that, despite my abject pleas, the addition I wanted quoted from PLF didn't get added. (Cf. btm. p. 34, when the whole thing is returned to you.) Above all, I was aware that I was back-sliding, as regards assignments to the studentry - but time was pressing, and I wanted to get the general outline slapped out. I very decidedly want to make emendations. (Incidentally, I'm signed up for Stony Brook, ten days, in May - and praise God, at a better figure than you poops pay, though tell it to no one, if you love me. There was tentative talk of my addressing some local high school seniors in English. And I believe I might well try out the first few pages of the mdl on 'em, perhaps even unto asking that they write the two letters and let me see the results, before I get there.)

Oof! what a jam I'm in!

Rejerce,
K.B.

204 Graduate College
Princeton, NJ 08540
Feb. 24, 1973

Dear Bill,

Godam the lousy luck. Your letter anent my bleet in your behalf is dated Feb. 20. I note that the deadline for applications of that sort is the fifteenth. Itshay.

Anyhow, I sent it, somewhat revised. (I took out references to Stanley Hyman and to my "reputation-if-any." I decided that the tone of the second was not proper for that august body.)

I am so godam scatter-brained about the pragmatics of things. Had you called the deadline to my attention, I'd have sent off a statement without waiting for your comments-if-any.

Have been having a history-making correspondence with Pat, binnuz the Personel Office wanted me to sign a "technicality" avowing that I had been up there for 20 days, the which me no wanna do. I assured her, it's not that I'm an honest man, but "I'm wary, which almost rhymes with Pat McGarry." E'en though I'm getting to be a bit hard o' hearing, I can hear mine enemies saying, "Get the bastard on a 'technicality.' He perjured himself before the Great State of Nuevo Yorick." (or, in the cause of greater resonance, "in a statement before the Great State") Meanwhile, I have used the opportunity to pour forth timid hints of my great love. And when I wrote something along the lines of "Does he look suspicious/ or docs he just think he looks suspicious/ or does he really look suspicious/ because he thinks he looks suspicious?" Pat wrote, sweetly assuring me that I don't look suspicious. Pat's a dawlink. I must remember her in my will. What should I leave her? Then I'll hurry up and die, of a broken heart.

Meanwhile, here's hoping that all the news is goodnews about Betty. Your previous report indicated that she was getting along wonderf. And doubtless every day thereafter things grow easier, so all should by now be poifick.

As for your letter-project, I can probably think up somethinks, possibly satirical (binnuz I'm now in that vein, but beneath my grease-painted smile my phizz is drooping). Meanwhile, I have added some lines to my Invoking of Peitho, so I'll quote the whole:

> Suave Power of Persuasion,
> help me to persuade you
> to help me be
> persuasive.

> May I be as profound as a bass drum,
> without the emptiness

> and as clever as Oscar Wilde
> before he went to jail.
>> Holla!
>> K.B.

204 Graduate College
Princeton, NJ 08540
3/6/73

Dear Bill,

Helndamnaysh. I'm so uneasy about the godam job I'm set up for, in LA come Thursday, the best protection I can think of is to lay the woiks all aside and write letters.

So, this is to join the welcoming Committee for Betty's return. Here's hoping that all goes joyous.

Meanwhile, I'm after wondering what the hell you think of this godam thing (though, if you're agin it, you caint tell me in time to save me).

The pernt is: It doesn't exactly ask to stand alone. It is meant to serve as a somewhat rowdy summing-up of my artikkel. Hence I'm not sure that my statement on p. 26 will wholly set things up for you, if you haven't suffered what has gone before. Also, I want somehow to work in the lines:

Levitation, ah Levitation,
O dithyrambic moment
than which how much the more can there be like!
All hail to Levitation.

I happen to have a particular fondness for nonsense as per line 3, but some people don't. (Incidentally, the only porno in my 32 pages is in my lines from Whitman, on p. 30.) As the piece itself makes quite clear, the Apocalyptic angle makes things so that we have The Chosen and the Damned, which is my contribution to a satire on Pollution (with the Lunar Paradisiacs clearing out, and leaving pollution for the poor baystards who can't get saved, and are left gasping here below). I end up with two characters: The Master is the Personalist Supreme, the Whitmanite who sees beyond Whitman; and the Vice-Personalist is the coarse administrative type, whereas The Master is pure Visionary.

I have a tangled theory as to why such tangles are needed—but God only knows ...

Holla!
K.B.

[Postcard]

Princeton
3/21/73

Dear Billiards,

How go things (a) family-wise; (b) with modulations?

And please remember that anything likely to reach me later than March 29 should better be sent to And/or.

Have been having some fantastic eye-ailment, which I am treating by not taking the stuff the doctor prescribes. I have decided that it's psychogenic, due to a tangle in my work (in particular a review I'm involved with).

Avec Universal Liebe,
K.B.

Olde Stande 4/4/73

Dear Pool,

Jeez, the fambly seems to have been behind the eight ball. Here's hoping that, by now, they're all racking up a splendid score.

As for my Flowerishes, unquestionably the profoundest one I ever arose to, or delved down into is: "Why does a chicken cross the road to get on the other side?" But doubtless that's too tough.

But I am sorry to hear that The Establishment won't let us make my Offering better. Why don't they want us to make it as good as we can? I saw places where we could make it better. And I hoped that we would.

As for mine eyes: They are completely better, because I didn't take the crap prescribed. When I realized that I was being put through a ritual, forthwith the pain was gone like magic. Betty had to find out that sorta thing the hard way. But it was astounding how intense and real the pain was, before I, of a sudden, understood its sheerly psychogenic basis.

And I'm sure that poor Pat's ailment is psychogenic. It's even possible that I scared her into an ailment when I refused to perjure myself in keeping with her friendly modes of accountancy. She may have suddenly been startled, on realizing that a whole batch of such "technicalities" (her word) had crept up on her. Don't say this to anybody, but snoop around and see if it's at all likely. For I'd certainly be scared if I were she and had gone along with several of such "technicalities." For although there was no underlying crookedness at all, The Enemy could make it look bad. The Personnel Office is still trying to work out a fiction. And it's not inconceivable that, as things are now set up, they could do me out of $500, if they wanted to. For the situation at the moment is such that I couldn't insist upon my full amt. as per our contract without embarrassing you—and that, of course, I'd not do. My dealings with the State University are not confined to the Saratoga Spr. division. So, unless the ESC is not on a par with its sister-outfits, the laws of bookkeeping I'm invited to believe in jes haint so.

As for the kivver, I thought of a double-deal. One wd. be somethinks as per what you say (Betty's snapshot of me manic). T'other would be of me hiding my face, when the Herr Direktor asked about my academic record. But that's a mere conceit, albeit not conceited.

My sally into L.A. worked out perty good. Even a big accident was sent by God to be on my side. For the mike started shrieking back at me (I say "shrieking" literally). Whereupon I had the godam think shut off. And I bellowed forth to the five hunnert assembled, in intercourse sans cundrum. In keeping with the principle of "congregation by segregation," I shamelessly got them to join with me against the mechanism, as I left the lectern and went to the middle of the stage and held forth, while glancing back with detestation at the unruly apparatus. It all worked so well, some e'en thought it had been planned. I'll send you a copy of the item in toto. (Incidentally, on being asked to suggest a reader for a MS, I said Rckrt. My suggest no hit?)

Meanwhile, wd. say: Dear Rueckert Fambly, cut it out; get better. And as regards a possible *Book of Fragments*, I'd say decidedididly YES. And I mean it. Even when you already have a sustained artikkel, break it into bits. It's a good step along the way although (as per TBL) one might eventually batter one's bits into a kind of continuity.

Onwards, outwards, up!

K.B.

And/or, NJ 07821

4/16/73

Dear Bill,

Last night, at the fatal stroke of twelve, there began on Channel 9 a performance of Ingmar Bergman's *The Seventh Seal.* Though I hadn't slept since four o'clock that morning, in the light of my recent letter I decided to hang on. I'd tentatively line things up this way:

(1) The whole thing was so saturated with disaster-laden attitudes, within five minutes the audience is wholly prepared either to turn the thing off or to expect some kind of disaster-in-general.

(2) The fate of the incidental background characters simply dropped out of consideration. Insofar as you might ask about them, they were so thoughtless, ununderstanding, and uncharitable, if they did get a beating eventually, they had the lesson coming to them.

(3) The special case of the crucified girl was particularly effective, owing to the analogy with Christ's passion despite the quite different rationale for the *sacrifice* (which was decidedly on the *kill* side, in keeping with the general satanistic, sadistic, masochistic aspects of the film's overall attitudinizing). Thus, for all the difference in rationale, her "Christ-like" role made her victimization acceptable. She was a darling victim, thus to be typed with Desdemona despite the many ways in which she is nothing of the sort.

(4) The three characters who were *specifically* saved (in contrast with the general background figures who were simply ignored) deserved being chosen for salvation if only because there was no attitudinal reason for giving them up. An interesting twist here is that this couple, with the child they are so proud of, quite "transcends" the bourgeois-Bohemian conflict in Thomas Mann's "Tonio Kröger." Their artistic way of life is one with their idealized petty-bourgeois relationships. I think it is "formally correct" that they should be spared the general disaster. (On the side, I wonder how the plot may have tied in with purely personal situations, since something of that sort seems indicated as regards the saving of this actors' guild family. But such speculations are, of course, irrelevant to the work "in itself.")

Meanwhile, speaking of sacrifice, I'm putting this letter in the box along with my income-tax statement and cheques.

Ouch!

K.B.

Back at The Old Stand, Last Stand? 07821
5/21/73

Dear Bill,

Sorry to hear that things ended up for you financially not so well. At least, 'twould seem that you fared better than The Undersigned, who has no yet recd. one penny of his One Grand. Should I write the Better Business Bureau? Or the Small Claims Court? Or who the hell? And what finally happened to Pat? Did she recover?

My doings at Stony Brook and Hartford turned out well. But I use myself up on those deals, and when I get back here all I wanna do is fall apart for a few days. But Bob Zachary, my editor frenn, turned up. So I had to whip up the old nag, and that was not so good. I'm afraid he left a bit disgrunt. For I was decidedly on the down-turning side. (Include here a momentous triviality. Having cooked him some good meals, I told him I had no eggs for his last breakfast. After he left, I realized that he had in all likelihood seen the five eggs I had lined up in the refrij. The story about Those Five Eggs is that they were not good for eating by their little selves. I had bought some at a store that had a slow turnover—and after eating a couple some days ago, I had ruled against them except for use in somethinks like a meat-loaf. But I never thought of explaining all this. There was also the fact that, coming from the West Coast, he brought with him a different time-consciousness—and since he goes to bed late anyhow, I simply had to leave him with himself. When I was at L.A. on the Academic Circuit a couple of months ago, he'd leave at three o'clock A.M.—and although that was 6 A.M. by my schedule, I could take it; for I knew that I could fall apart when I got back here. But this time, when I got back here and all ready to fall apart, lo! his wife phones, to tell me he is on a plane, coming hither. So, all told, the auspices were not of the best.)

So I desist. This is intended but to meet your outcry with my outcry. Today I did none of the big-doings I had planned for today. As for tomorrow, I know not. No further business on the Academic Circuit looms until late June. And I'm pathetically hoping that Butchie will be turning up soon, from Canada, though the thought of my pleasure in seeing him is already poisoned by the thought of my gloom when he departs.

Meanwhile, there's a sore spot in my throat, just about where my mother's cancer started. It's a swelling, and it has been there for some time. I wonder, oh, I wonder …

May thou and all thine rejerce,

K.B.

Gatesville 07821
6/11/73

Dear Billyrus,

Forgive me for feeling in a sportive mood this eve. Most of it's doubtless due to the spirits one can buy in a bottle—yet not wholly so. For I do think I'm still in there punching.

In any case, though I did not yet dare hear the records you sent me, I did receive my One Grand.

But I wisht you had told me how poor Pat fared. And if she is in a bad way, I'd like to know how I might write her, with some of my fun-loving grandfatherly verbalizings. She'd love an old man's love.

Having set myself three jobs this summerandfall, I have just about finished the first (and least troublesome). In some kind of subtle way, I think that this outfit is Under New Management. For these whole three jobs (finishing up three books) seem to me like washing dishes (and if you have any imagination at all, you'll know what a sense of accomplishment goes with washing dishes—unless, of course, you put them into one of those shitty machines with no sense of anything).

In any case, I do hope that the sichaysh is not too inexorably HBP. You have piled up a quite wondrous Country Full of Swedes—and that's a great joy except when it aint.

All I esk is: Never write me, saying that you are going to write me a letter. Don't write me until you can send me the letter that you were going to write me.

I thought of you ptikly this eve because I was writing to Another One in Rochester. At my age, everything is somehow in some particular associational bin with somethinks else. And that's that, in this case.

Meanwhile, my affectionate greetings, to thee, and Momma, and the Country Full of Swedes.

Holla!

Incidentally, at a show in NYC recently, I sat next to the third Mrs. Erskine Caldwell. Everything went wonderf, except that I hadn't read one word of the guy except for the early things I had been quite friendly about.

K.B.

R.D. 2, Andover, NJ 07821
6/18/73

Dear Billoxi,

After much heatitude, we now have considerable coldicity. Or should I say: We now have considerable colditude after much heaticity? So I put on sox—and maybe that is what was wrong with me. For I had decided that whereas thoughts of things like John Wayne made me feel nauseated, things had got turned around whereby a feeling of nausea makes me think of things like John Wayne. And now, with sox on, I don't feel nauseated at all, even though this morning I read a nauseous item on John Wayne. I am The Man Who Invented the Migratory Symptom. And being such, I no longer have the ominous swelling in my throat. But en revanche, I have had a ferociously painful left arm, along with a kind of eruption which two local amateurs independently diagnosed as shingles, a not unlikely condition, inasmuch as I encountered some vexations after a period of sheerly physical strain. I did not consult a doctor because of my devout conviction that it is a doctor's business to sell a patient as many ailments as possible—so I incline to delay until I see whether something gets worse and worse. Though my arm is still damned unhappy, the localized swelling did not get worse and worse; nor did what looked like a kind of pus ever break forth. And today my arm is less painful than yesterday because, I think, I got into a kill-or-cure mood, and worked the devil out of it by clipping a hedge. So today it just hurts in a normal way, as though I were a southpaw and had pitched a ten-inning game yesterday.

As I believe I told you, the Great Empire State paid me my One Grand, though it still owes me One Grand and a Half for ten days I did at Stony Brook. And don't tell on me: but every night when, on saying my prayers, I come to the place where I ask God to take care of all the nice people I met at Empire State College, I put in a fervent aside: "And I thank God that I'm not Pat McGarry, and so I don't have all that boofulness to take care of."

I am scheduled, about the time you receive this, to be verbalizing at the U. of Kansas (Lawrence). They have worked up a two-day schedule that would surely slay me if I were but a week or two older. Seven hunnert and fiddy plus expenses. The one thing that will sustain me, if I am sustained, is the assurance "that most of the group will be familiar with P&C, ATH, PLF, GM, RM, and LSA." I'll probably stress satire.

Recently I summoned the guts to hear the tapes you sent me. I preferred the first to the second. Many places made me wince. (In particular, I got quite sick of my nervous titter, though that may not show up quite so badly when diluted with visual distractions.) I thought that you came to my rescue quite handsomely. But there are several places where I just plain muffed.

My papers may be appraised soon. And I may take on a three-month deal this wint, as Logologer in Residence. Though I am working, the Making of History is delayed by both my Gathering Gloom and my weakness for following the Watergate sessions on TV.

Meanwhile, my fondest avuncular greetings to the assembled multitude. May you all flowerish.

K.B.

Sounds at Dawn

It's not that birds so faintly sing,
but that mine ears so loudly ring.

Gatesville Still 07821 8/1/73

Dear Billify,

Indirectly, your letter brought me bad news. More books missing. (Recently I discovered that, although I had copies of just about all Richards' books, they are all gone but one I happened to have among some papers in a locked room.) Now a Faulkner lacuna (the Brooks book).

So I'll settle for doing simply what I'd do with "Mannigoe," simply as a word about which I knew nothing but the fact that it was the name of an imaginary character in some book or other. "Man," yes. But also "Man-go," possibly in the sense of ceasing to be man or in the sense of going (becoming) man, or both. I'd also try possibilities of "ego" in "igo." And could I find an "r" for "neg ( ) o"?

Working more circumstantially, I'd want a good index of "black," plus possible secondary meanings of whore and dope addict. (Might dope, for instance, be a surrogate for alky, a question answerable inductively by comparing the two clusters. Any lines whereby infanticide is roundabout for onanism? Might an "androgynous" black woman's "past" involve imagery that made "her" a surrogate for a white alcoholic author's problematical adolescence? What terms surround "nun" in the book? Obviously, ditto, "temple," either cap. or l.c.)

In sum, how would you set up a cycle of terms? But it's a lotta work ...

Meanwhile, wd. say: I have taken on a job at the U. of Pittsburgh from Jan 6 to Apr 22. Probably I shouldn't have, but I liked the idea of a return to the old homestead for a while, and I didn't know what to do with myself otherwise. After taking the job, I received a tentative inquiry from Princeton. I have bought a new car (doubtless my last), for three grand. Now I have to worry about dents, but my Chevelle 64 was becoming more expensive than a stable of horses. (Also, it was well dented.) I sent some answers to Professor Joji Mori, who has done a Japanese translation of items from PLF and LSA. I did a mussy kind of topical Index for the new U. of Cal. edition of PLF. (I shall, of course, also retain the former Index.) I hope that, after one day of odds and ends, I'll get to work on the definitive editing of the Devices which I wrote btw. ATH and GM. I expect to stay here as long in the autumn as I can stand myself. I have been asked to join several boards and write several articles. I have dodged the boards, and am weaseling about the articles. Sometimes I feel pretty good, sometimes I wish for the assertiveness to up and clear out. I have wasted too much time on the Watergate hearings, and I hope they'll soon end, so that I can resume the making of history with less of a subdivided mind. In any case, my three major ailments (doubtless synergistic) are: subdivided mind, loneliness, insomnia.

May you all rejerce.

Sincerely,
K.B.

Nixon Nook 07821
XI/25/73

Dear Biller-killer-diller,

How goes it with all youenz? How far did you get with your Falcon-er? Where are you, btw. Perfect Calm and Run-Ragged?

If all goes as planned, I leave here, around the first of the year, for 3 1/2 months at the U. of Pitt. My major worry is: Can I get the gas? For I must take quite a bit of my brain with me, and most of it is in my books and papers. Indications are that I must come prepared to be in multiple jeopardy (and of the most unnerving sort; namely: not from enemies but from those who look forward amicably). I have but two states of mind: Either I can't take notes on anything without wanting to work on seventeen articles at once, or I lie in bed wondering how I'll ever come up with one sentence more to say.

My lonesomeness becomes severe now and then. Yet I must admit to myself: I've become a professional Loner at least to the extent that I couldn't imagine shacking up with any living thing, be it male, female, or any variety of same. But a wholly professional Loner would never become lonesome.

At times, feeling sorry for myself, I suddenly realize that I had only one really dirty deal in my life: when Libbie cleared out first. Even without thinking of the matter, I had taken it for granted that I'd be out before her. (If I were superstitious I'd make much of the fact that, just as I was writing those words, there was a thumping in the house, on this dark day—and after examining every room, I can't account for them.)

As for current ups and downs: The U. of Cal. Press is having a so-called "Earthquake Sale" in which copies of my novel and poems are available for $1.00 per volume. Dante tells how, on the Mount of Perga-tory the whole place shook every time a purgand went up; here with the shake the purgand goes down. The sale goes on until the end of Janu-ary—and I know a bargain when I see one. So, since I have a public talk that comes to a focus in TBL (and I tried it twice, both times to good effect), I think I'll line up something as soon as I get to Pittsburgh and see just what the whole situation is. I think I can have some fun with that development. On t'other side: Henry Sams sent me xeroxed proofs of a quiye scrupulous article on *Rhet. of Relij,* by a Georgetown Jesuit (it's to be published in the forthcoming issue of *General Linguistics*). Wayne Booth phoned me to the effect that he is giving a lecture on me at Princeton. Also, he and some of his pals are getting out a new gazette, to be issued by the U. of Chicago Press. And he wants to include, in the first issue, his stuffo on me, along with my comments. He is quite on my side—and so, although I take it for granted that he'll have his wholesome Howevers, I expect to class our interchange among the Civilized Amenities (in brief, whatever the antonym is to the ways of Shitney Hook). I forget whether I told you about the monograph which a French specialist in political theory, Charles Roig, wrote on my Dramatism line (and, to my great delight, he did wonders with the section on "The Dialectic of Constitutions" which often didn't even so much as get mentioned by domestic thinkeroos). Recently the University of Geneva sent me the copy of a new book by him. And jeez, I do think you should ask your local Librarian to stock one. It bibliographically sings thus:

> Analyse de Système et Connaissance Sociale,
> L'analyse de système comme discours:
> langages, postulats, concepts,
> Charles Roig, professeur
> Département de Science Politique
> Faculté des Sciences économiques et sociales
> Université de Genève

I'm in. But of course I have to move over and make room for a lot of others. There is no price; but it shouldn't be much, since the text is only 126 pp. (I got 141 pp.)—and it's what they call *polycopié*, and we at the Stanford Center called multilithed typescript. I'm writing to Pittsburgh, asking that they get a copy for me to put on Reserve in connection with my doings. I promise you would be interested in it, though it's more socio-political in its slant than fits your focus. Eskem.

Meanwhile, since there's some space left, and I'm parsimonious, let me as filler slavishly type out a sadly funny poem—and if I sent it to you already, forgive me since I hope that it will eventually go through many more editions:

> But for these lucky accidents

> Were I not tall and suave and handsome

were I not famed for my glamorous Byronic love-affairs
had not each of my books sold riotously
had not my fists made strong men cringe

did not my several conversions
enlist further hordes of followers
and did not everything I turned to
make me big money

despite my almost glorious
good health of both body and mind,
how in God's name
could I through all these years

have held up
and held out
and held on?

Avec Universal Liebe from ole Boy-Scout Ignatz de Burp,
　　　　　　　　　　　　　　K.B.

　　　　　　　　　　　　　　　　Department of English
　　　　　　　　　　　　　　　　University of Pittsburgh
　　　　　　　　　　　　　　　　　　March 4, 1974

Dear Billious,

　　Yes, bejeez, 'twas good to hear from same. And I have put in a plug
for thee, though at the moment thy association with me couldn't help
out overwhelmingly even with me, who am a bit on the fed-up side,
binnuz everywhere I turn I am perforce burkologizing to more than my
heart's content. And how do uddawise? (What with having property to
protect.)

　　Tillich was a crook. Niebuhr ditto, but less so. If it weren't against
The Law, I'd say that Buber is a crook. All I claim is, along those lines, I
may be right, I may be wrong, but at least no bullshido.

　　You go buy a book. After much inquiry you find that it can be ordered for you if you pay half down. O.K. You give your name. Of a
sud. somethinks has happened. In effect it says, "So that's him!" So you
live on that level? No, you slink away. All you ask for is enough of that

whereby, when you're away from home, they'll leave your house intact. They will say in effect, "The poor old slob put our town in *Who's Who*. So let's him hang on. He hasn't offended anybody hereabout." From then on, all you ask for is that we all fight by the Marquis of Queensbury rules for ideal seminars. And I'm after tellingyuh, me lad, there's one of the last few civilized procedures still left. (But I doan need to tell you.)

Yes, Marsha Landy did run across me and invite me. I recognized her, sans relation to her name. I went to the party, taking a bottle, and had a good time. I left as an old man on the drunken side—and she was so pityingly sweet, she kissed me goodnight. I think she was saying in effect, "You were peddling your wares quite assertively, as you should. But 'neath it all you are an old man near death. By my kissing you on the way out you are proclaimed to be not a dirty old man but a sweet old man who needs just such kinds of graciousness as I, in my role as hostess, enact towards you." Or I could be insulted, if I so decided, or got decided for me. But of course I warnt.

I forgive you for not knowing what it means to be 76 years old, since even I am only finding out as I go along. And, still within this year of mine, tomorrow suddenly everything may be different.

Yes, I did say "By all means, Rueckert," but later on. For the time bean they have enough of me. No malice. Everything is on the friendship side—for here I am, back in my home town, and genuinely translated, except for even worse tricks of pollution when I survived tuberculosis (via the Christian Science Church on nearby Clyde Street) many years ago, without the medical procedures that killed my cousin of the same age, for I was spared the mistakes to which his then mistaken medicology subjected him.

[other side of above letter …]

III/18/74

Dear Billions and Billions and Billions,

Jeez, where are I? Of course I have plugged for you. And I'll try further. But the skientifick fack is that Burke is on the edge of what-is-it.

He has even got to the point where he has to do tricks. Whatever, you need not worry. Yet there he is, sick of his Selph, and all the time a-sayin. Give him one more chawnst, kid.

When you get to my ages, how you do scheme! Only yestiddy, right in the middle of what to say come late April, me elsewhere afore leaving here, I realized that I already had most of it set up. There must be Somebody Up There taking care of me—or I'm having luck, even at my sainted years.

Haint I worth anything to the likes of you? Certainly not here and now (or hic et nunc to you, or the likes of you) where I hold forth so often, I 'gin get sick of same. for the likes of us. And now I'm going to bed, at me—my Gawd, how did I spend the whole night through, it's seven of the morn. God jesus no, say not.

...

Now, twelve of the morn. The above gives the impression of being on the alcohol side. And well it should. Nor am I quite sure just what I always meant. And well I shouldn't. The IMPORTANCE is that, when knocking off Nembies, I natheless SLEPP. Today I'm playing hookie.

What I was trying to say, up there above, is that I worked like heck to prepare for a seminar yestiddy—and in the very midst of the deliverance, lo! I of a sud. realized that I had set up the first rough draft of a talk I'm shedyuled to give at Purdue, come late April. It builds around three texts, in the order of their appearance; namely: P&C, Richards' Philosophy of Rhetoric, and Turbayne's Myth of Metaphor. And its sumjick is: "Rhetoric, Poetics, and Philosophy." And I'm after telling you, youngster, the ole baystard has got it said, and it will knock out their eye if they got a knockoutable eye.

A few days ago I was up at Ann Arbor, knocking out their eye with another Grand Definitivo (at my age, all one does is Definitivos). The only trouble was that they gave me a lectern with but a pitiably tiny light—hence I perforce spent my time squinting at my MS rather than saying it all right out there to the assistance. And under those conditions it's hard to knock out an eye, though all went well uddawise, incl. a good pre-prandial pyawty and a superb prandializing. And if you jes hold your horses, wait till you see The Document, and how it all turned out.

I dare feel that I'll be out of here before I organize the opposition. In the meantime, I have some loyalists that will not piss on my grave, an dat's a datta.

Avec Universal Liebe to
theenthine,
K.B.

College Garden Apartments
8531 Walnut Street
Pittsburgh, Pa 15232
IV/4/74

Dear Billions,

Know that I did speak in thy behalf. But I have fussed about here
so ubiquitously (and am still not quite through same), just at present
they'd seek replacements from anywhere in the world but the likes of
us. However, on departming I'll again put in a plug for you. If you have
any specific suggestions in mind, spick. If not a job, for instance, then
something on Falconer?

My talk, "Satire, and Plans for Writing One," I finally rerevisionis-
tically definitivized—and I think it's perty good now. At least, it went
quite well at Ann Arbor (I had puttered around with it also in my seminar)—and it's to appear in the autumnality issue of Michigan Quarterly
Review, Radcliffe Squires being glowingly in its favor. My problem is: I
gave them such an illegible copy, I dint have the nerve to ask for more
than the amt. I got for my public vocalizing. But maybe if I weep elo-
quently enough I can at least get some offprints sans the horrendous
charge I paid for copies of my Welk Confrontation. Here's hoping.

Sorrows may beset me ambiguously at the U. of Cal. Press. Some
kind of inter-departmental agitation seems to be being-itself there; and I
'gin fear that I may have got hurt as an innocent bystander. (In matters
of this sort, I still can't distinguish, on my part, btw. experienced shrewdness and paranoia.)

One caint jes go about one's bizz, *more dramatistica.* Everywhere one
turns or doesn't turn, there are NEGOTIATIONS—and I'm not good
at same. My best hope is to be so pitiably incompetent that the other
side tries to help me out. Unlike poor devils who get in the clutches of
loan sharks, I have dealings with people who still have souls. So, beyond
a certain point, they quit trying to push me under and try to help me up.
But I'm improvising. Things are working out well enough.

But here's some inside info for you: If you happen to be near Central
Warshington State Collitch about May 8, ask around and locate a de-
finitive Dramatistic vocalizing to be entitled "Against Behaviorism." De
Burp plans then to get shut of the Skinner notes that have cluttered him

up consid. We gotta move on. ... And that's that. (If you happen to have with you the Country Full of Swedes, bring them along.)

Surely I told you about Florence who, at highschool, ran my calflove grades in our geometry class down from the nineties to the sixties. Two of my darling daughters came to visit me recently—and we all went to see Florence. She has held up so booful that, if I were still were susceptible to calflove (ah, loveliness!) I'd be mooning all over again. I left her a book of my poems. But I didn't dare mention the novel, in which the author had taken such obscene liberties with the dear name. Though girls are quite rough one another, my darling daughters commented on how La Flower had *improved* since her picture in the Peabody Graduation book that we all looked back through. And the truly remarkable thing is that I remembered her as she is now—and had I been shown that passport photos (or some such) of her as then, I'd not have recognized it as hers.

Turned on news. Pictures of the destruction done by the twisters. I started to cry. Then I cried twice as hard when I realized that, vicious as that "act of God" was, it was but a tiny fragment of what our military policies visited upon Vietnam. Please help me let it get said.

At thus stafe I realize that I sgould not have

(returning later, I realize that the medicaysh seems to have caught up with me)

May God have mercy on us all,

K.B.

Ignatz de Burp

Pittsburgh
April 22, 1974

Dear Billions,

Pretty much what you were saying straight about Walt, I have been giving a satiric twist. It's scheduled to appear (as wind-up for a talk I yiped at Ann Arbor some weeks ago). I tied my notion in with the idea of a "Master" who had been a disciple of Walt's, then began to lose his mind when he realized that the Whitmanite Song of Occupations, etc. had come to a grim "fulfillment" in the fact that all the promises led to pollution. He nearly had a breakdown—but it became a breakthrough when, with the philosophy of Helhaven, or my "Modernist Sermon," or of Revelations, he realized that Pollution can be *affirmed,* once you look upon it as the Vision of a Division whereby there are the Elite and the Damned. Speed up the pollution of the Earth, in order thereby to intensify a desire to transcend this world by building the Culture Bubble on the Moon.

I include the two "poems," though they depend largely for their effect upon their place in the article. By shamelessly mixing in some bits of Walt, I enabled it to noise well.

Meanwhile, I'm in one hell of a spot. I'd like to stop now and rot. But I had to smack out a talk for Purdue this Wednesday. And then almost as soon as I get back to And/or I must flit to Central Washington State College, to give a piece that still needs considerable work (for which where find the time?).

Sorry to hear of your ailments. What the heck must you be doing wrong, to be so beplagues? Might something that you're taking for something be having side-effects?

I doan no whether to congratulate you or lament that the book is sold out. It might be worth while trying Bob Zachary, though perhaps not at the moment, for things seem in a muddle there just now.

Let me know of your careerist concerns. And henceforth in NJ again. Since I got paid well here, I'm luxuriously asking Michael to come by plane and drive back with me. I can charge for expenses, but not such extra ones. … More later anent Turbayne. I'm using him in my Purdue piece (entitled "Rhetoric, Poetics, and Philoophy of Language"—and built around talk of analogy and metaphor, as per his book, Richards' *Philosophy of Rhetoric,* and my old-timer P&C in which I mumbled quite a bit about "analogical extension" and "metaphorical extension." I incline to wonder why Turbayne never mentioned the ingenious exhibits of Adelbert Ames, Jr. Didn't he know of them, or did they throw things out of gear?

But dooty calls me elsewhere. … And may youenz all find out what's ailing you. My prime ailment is the morbus insanabilis, old age.

K.B.

Onwards, Outwards, and UP 07821
VIII/5/74

Dear Billions,

Last night on TV when it was asked at ten o'clock, "Do you know where your children are tonight?" I realized with a shock that not only did I not know where they all were, I didn't even know where you all were.

Then it occurred to me, "Bejeez, does he know where he is?"

So I'm just asking you to check in and send in an ad interim report. And do you know any scandals?

Anything you can say to make life more worth living would be appreciated. And above all, I'd welcome the info that you've got your BP down without chemicals.

Me? E'en now, with mine own fambly all around me, I grow lonesomer and lonesomer. And while worrying about the slightest symptom foretelling my demise, I bravely wish I had died in my sleep already.

All the time we must strive to be rational; yet all the time no matter how you look at it, it's cwazy.

Yet lo! e'en as I was writing you, the lady mailman drove up, it seems, and left a lot of deposit, which Butchie rescued betimes. So we perforce go on from there.

Meanwhile, having sold a piece of my correspondence for 25 Grand, I live in terror lest the bank in which I deposited the check folds before I can extricate the sum again. Meanwhile, being as stinko a patriot as that movie guy, John Wayne, I'm gwanna invest in My Country's Bonds (doubtless at a loss such as the movie guy is not subject to).

But what with the progress of inflation, my paper-gold treasure has doubtless already shrunk to $24,001.99—and that's that.

In any case, fare forth, my lad, ever towards greater conquests. And when you win, praise God because you won. And when you lose, praise God because He has contributed to your greater knowledge, which is the knowledge of the threats of failure. And when you break even, be glad that you got by with Lady Luck.

There's only one thing I can promise for sure. I will put off slicing my jugular vein as long as there's not a grave by Shitney Hook for me to piss on. That shrewdly vulgarian apostle of Freedom ... well, you get the idee. In keeping with my theories of perfection and of itshay, I have chosen him as my ideal of the perfect bullshitter of freedom, e'en unto having breakfast with N*x*n.

Uddawise, as I was sayin, Onwards, Outwards, and UP,—and if not, why not?

> Holla! (and I speak as one who
> never touched a drop)
> K.B.

Which of thy texts didst say is O.P.?

K.B.

Under New Management ~~Nixon Nook by the~~ Heavingscote 07821
IX/3/74

Dear More and More Billions,
    'Twould be wonderf if you ended up OFFICIATING at Penn State.
And on the basis of my sound theory that, the more turmoil an educator has around the house, the greater CONTROL he is capable of at the
office, I'll gamble on the likelihood that you'd be the greatest administrator since Alexander the Great, though I don't know how things went
with him around the house.
    'Tis true that my 25 Grandlets bring tears to the eyes, as compared
with what all N*x*n has, wherewith to get pulled out of the klink. Yet,
e'en I, in the cause of Justice tempered by Mercy, uncorked a quinquain
thus (plus a trick whereby, though all five lines end on "em," the first
rhymes only with the third, and the second rhymes only with the fourth
and fifth, as I worked it all out while you were pyramiding your invest-
ments on the can:

> "White House Says Tapes
> Are Nixon's Own Property"
> (Headline, New York Timely Indoctrinator)
>
> If it's the tapes he wants, then give them him
> however they might somehow benefit him.
> With him in trouble, in this interim
> let Life at least ironically permit him
> to take unto his bosom his own records that undid him.

    Sorry that you're still grounded with the Falconer bizz. But you're
solidly right, not to give the baystards a subsidy. The job itself is subsidy
enough. Bob Zachary is probably in Europe just now, planning to be
back circa end of Sept.

My plans? To putter around until Feb., when I hold forth for a term
at Princeton. (There are to be other incidental moments.) Although, I
am told, statistics prophesy circa 6-7 more years for a guy in his seventy-
sevensies, I still go on hoping that some night I'll sooprize us all by sleeping a bit too long—and that will be the end of that.

I doan get the *New Republic,* except for two copies of a recent issue
in which I reviewed Wayne Booth's tome anent *The Rhetoric of Irony.*
All I know thereafter is that I recd. $100.00 for the review and, a week
later, a rejection slip for two poems. Doubtless that was the end of what
could have been a truly lovely engagement. My xeroxing resources here
are only slightly better than at the Poles. But I'd love to learn what you
had to say about Crane's family letters.

Psst. Courtesy: the Self-Pity Dept.:

Here's what's honest:

The multiplication table,
Allen and Greenough's Latin Grammar

an old man
staggering along a dirt road in late autumn
at sundown …

> Be fawned upon,
> K.B.

> How-Afford Ford 07821
> IX/12/74

Dear Untold Billions,

Yes, your review sounds totally convincing. As professional as could
be. Ardent felicitations!

You ask about the Booth-Burke interchange. I expect to get reprints,
and I'll promptly ship one theeward. Maybe not until the snow falls.
To date I haven't even seen galleys. Also, I hope to assail you with the
FINALIZED version of my piece on Satire (due for publication in next
issue of Michigan Quarterly Review). And I'm wrestling with one hell of
an angel; namely: the talk on "Rhetoric, Poetics, Philosophy" I uncorked
at Purdue (the trouble with it being that it was really notes for seminars

I gave at the U. of Pitt., and it was so perfectly adapted to the form, it doan quite go as a lecture to the general public). And I don't know how to make amends. So I fear I wont.

Since it's obvious that you need something to occupy your idle hours, I'd suggest that you consult the items anent Burke in the last number of The Quarterly Journal of Speech. Here I am, having to do somethinks about that (two doughty champions, both on my side, and having at each other). Wadda woild! That sorta thing shouldn't happen until a guy is dead.

And here I am, only 99 and 44/00% dead. And I just recently learned that a sweetly troubled lady reviewed my Language as Symbolic Action in the Nov. 1973 issue of Romance Philology, which doubtless taxes the resources of all Geneseo.

I write many letters that I don't send. But I keep on trying. I just vetoed one to you because it said some unseemly things about things like compassion—and it aint fair to get an Eddicator saddled with the crime of receiving such. Also it contained an item in which I burst into song anent the state of my backside. I killed that because it obviously was but the first of what should be a sequence, but I'm not so sure that conditions will encourage me to go on being songful. But I did also tell you about my joy in Butchie's still being here with me, and how he goes about things (just now overseeing a job on the dam, and such a lousy foreman that he does four-fifths of the work). But wow! he's due to leave soon—so I'll take a double beating when autumn falls upon my battles this time avec the Selph. Natheless, if my backside contrives somehow to behave well enough, I'll keep on not letting the dirty dishes pile up—and I'll crush the cans and smash the bottles. And not only will I pay the bills; I'll even remember to cash or deposit my checks. (Psst: not long ago I found one that, up in the thousands, I had in an envelope on which I had written a note. On looking at the note several months later, I decided that it was nor worth saving. I started to tear it up. But Someone Up There was taking care of. For I thought of looking inside—and therein nestled a check for one-fourth my booty while at the U. of Pitt. I had to ask for a renewal, since the check was not good after 90 days. And as a result of that transaction, I discovered that my Soc. Sec. no. had got undone.) Be sorry, felluh, for us, yes, be sad—and on thus tumbling into an iambic pentameter line, I realize anew how the love of jingling has so beset me these recent months, I 'gin wonder whether it's but a lonely oldster's symbolic return to the sexual compulsion of adolescence.

But dooty calls.

God bless F*rd and N*x*n,
K.B.

Ad Interim 07821
XII/31/74

Dear Billions,

Well, for Gawsake, here I am, packing towards a term at Princeton. (Harold Toliver wrote me as to how you had given greetings, but after I had left.)

Butchie is due tomorrow, and is to help me on my way. (Two trips may be necessary, binnuz the limits are but fifty miles apart.)

I'm truly sorry that you ne'er divulged to me just how your vocation as an Administrator has been working.

Meanwhile, e'en more death-minded than I was at age 7, I now at 77 shift betwixt thoughts of the o'er-all and the cult of particulars though (frankilee) my ideal particulars would be those that Occamize the O'er-all.

School doesn't start until early Feb. But I'm to be reachable thus: Department of Comparative Literature, Princeton University, 326 East Pyne, Princeton, New Jersey 08540. I shall be thinking of you, and let's hear from same. Do tell me if you have any advice, by way of either encouragement or admonition.

Watsamattayuh? Why no correspond like a human being? What allatime everywhere else?

Ennihow, I looks iggerly forward. (to what?!)

And with all my joyousness when thinking on that House Full of Swedes,

Holla!
K.B.

R. D. 2, Andover, NJ 07821
IX/10/75

Dear Billions,

Delighted to receive thine of 9/5. And I think that your article is quite frisky. To be sure, it broke my heart when you say, "Norman O. Brown has put this very nicely when he says, at the beginning of *Love's Body*, 'at least in the life of the mind, ventures should be carried through to the end.;' " If you have time, see in P.L.F. (unabridged edition, pp. 38n, 70, 84, 86; or in abridged Vintage edition, 33, 59, 70, 73, 74). So it's to that artful dodger I owe my emergent concern with the step from expression and communication to the "tracking down of implications." Obvious, "to the end of the line" is the better way to say it—and just as obviously, under the circumstances he had to fudge it. In that book, Brown goes to the end of *half* a line. Specifically, he tries to set up half a dialectic (unity without diversity, the one sans the many)—and it's so damned stupid that he gets away with it by persuading the students it's a vision. He doesn't answer objections for the simple reason that he *can't*. But I must hurry on.

You were kind to the three of us you ended on. Wilson, a born journalist, made the great discovery that we're used to taking anything if it's presented as *news*. Don't ask people to follow an argument. Tell 'em the *story* about how it went. I guess the method is the secularized analogue of our Savior's parables. (It's the difference btw. the NT and theology. It will tell you a story about the first three chapters of Genesis. You don't have to hang on, any more than you have to hang on when you've turned on the news. It's an exceptionally effective rhetorical device, and I admit that I'm trying to learn it, within limits. With logology, you have to hang on. So, insofar as possible, try to say it as gossip. For instance, with a talk I'm scheduled to give this coming November, entitled "Rhetoric, Poetic, and Dialectic," I think of presenting it in terms of a story about what I got into when I was invited to comment on the last chapter in W.S. Howell's forthcoming book, *Poetic, Rhetoric, and Logic,* said chapter being entitled "Kenneth Burke's '*Lexicon Rhetoricae*': A critical Examination." Heck, not only is Walter Cronkhite news. The Gospel was news. The Second Coming is at hand. Ye insomniacs, while lying awake, watch and wait.)

It's true, Frye beats me at the local game. I do believe that, as things go on, teachers will discover what it is missing; namely; the search for the *generative principle* in a given work. All schemes lend themselves to the laxity of students who are happy just to pin labels on things. Thus, I wince when receiving papers written by earnesties who tag the terms of the pentad, or hexad, or something or other, and call the job done. My hunch along those lines is that, when something gets called an "Anatomy," for instance, the job is thought to be over, whereas it had but begun. But your experience better fits you to pass on that point than mine does. For I caint see around the corner enough in such cases.

As for me-am: Though I worked like cwazy this summer (not in your healthy way, but smacking out drafts, one after another, on the typewriter) I do brutally experience the waning of my powers. For somehow or other, the garrulousness of age takes over. Everything I want to say reminds me of something else that is relevant, but tangentially so. And an argument with someone almost prods me to start writing my books all over again (ptikly in Howell's case, since he never so much as even mentions the title or any book or article I published since that first edition of C-S, 44 years ago. I took a bbl. of notes, and slapped out 60 pages on my deal loyal long-suffering QWERTY UIOP before I discovered what I was looking [for], namely: a way of not doing anything of the sort. Maybe not all will agree with my "solution" (as a "Communication" in the Q.J. of Sp.)—but at least it solved the problems of psyche and blood-pressure.

Except for two talks (one to be given later this month at Skidmore on Whitman, and one next May in Minnesota on a title not yet specified) my only involvement for the Academic Circuit is for a month (mostly November) at Seattle. There I am to be straddling English and Speech—and despite my self-admonitions, I dare hope that this foray will turn out OK.

We once had a whip-poor-will hereabouts. Though I don't know where he got his booze from, as soon as he whipped five or six poor-wills, you could tell that he was plastered. A drunken whip-poor-will tries to get ahead of himself. He tries to burst forth with another "whip-poor" even before he has decently rounded out his last "poor-will." In sum, he just tumbles all over himself, even without the slightest concern for punctuation. It's pretty much like a letter I'm writing to a friend of mine, who asked me how to spot an alcoholic style. As an *epistolary* mode, it is entitled to ask for forgiveness. Indeed, since a genuine letter requires the scribe to epistolate alone, the sense of good-fellowship communion might even require that the sender pour drinks for the two of us, and drink in thine honor. Consider it being done.

But the postman is due. So I make haste to desist.

Am besten to thee, to dear bad-girl Betty, and to the turbulent svensks.

> Holla!
> K.B.

[Postcard]

> Andover
> IX/25/75

From *The Recluse:* ... "so shall they unfailing love / guide, and support, and cheer me to the end /"

From *Elizabethan and Metaphysical Imagery,* by Rosamond Tuve [unlegible] "and the final intention of an image must be sought by following it through to its end."

Dear Billions—Maybe "end" doesn't mean quite the same as "end of the line." But N.O.B. does continue to irritate me.

> K.B.

> R.D. 2, Andover, NJ 07821
> X/7/75

Dear Billions,

Peace! I have decided to abandon my vendetta vs. N. Brown. Even groveling is a better fit for the comic frame than growling. I think my rage dates from the time when I heard him say "penis" in a chapel, and everybody appreciatively tittered. For me that summed up the quality of his bad-boyism.

Sorry indeed that Doris G. is no longer with NR. I doan no what the new policy is to be. But at least Denis Donoghue writes that he was asked to name and praise an unjustly neglected book. He suggested TBL, and they agreed. He sent me a copy of his pages (3), and they do help indeed.

Have you followed any of Harold Bloom's books, incl. my review in the NR? He has sent me advance proofs of two further books. I consider him exceptionally ingenious, and am still trying to figure out just where we agree and disagree. He does by his trick route (the Kabbalists) which

I approach via my logological treatment of orthodox theology—and the confusions as to just where draw the lines are somethinks. I read him with engrossment. He would dedicate a prospective book to me (we have been corresponding); but I have proposed that he wait until he makes sure.

I am scheduled to be at Seattle on Nov. 3., c/o Dept. of English. (I hope to get a more exact destination soon. Long live pinpointing.) I'm to be there during November. I started looking around for further possibilities for a while, towards delaying my return here until March. I have a likely potentiality for period from mid-Jan. through Feb. But where btw. Nov. and mid-Jan.? I may end up here, solo, during what promises (query) to be a mean wint.

But I should already have begun, in a big way, preparing for my trip. (Which MS-dried parts of my brain take with me?) Decisions, de ... etc.

Whatever happened twixt you and Bob Zachary? A recent letter from him causeth me to tremble. For it wd. seem to suggest that he is Moving On. Oof!

May thou and thine rejerce,
K.B.

Room 116, McMahon Hall Dormitory
Campus, U. of Washington
Seattle, Washington 98195
XI/23/75

Dear Billions,

Though my show here has been going exceptionally well, and though I'd like to think that the sudden demands upon you reflect the news of such vibrancies (incl. Denis Donoghue's gracious plea for TBL in the Oct. 18 issue of the *New Republic*, I know that big publishing mastodons never evince such promptness of response. The inquiries to you are surely the result of developments from quite some time back, incl. mellow interchange twixt Bob Zachary and me anent possibly their redoing your number. Dell is busy with his own business. But Charles Roig is evidently about to publish his stuff on me. (Unk writes me saying that a package has been sent from him, though I don't know whether it's proofs or a book or what.)

I'm not sure just what Bob Zachary is planning. Some time back I had the impression he was leaving. But when he left recently he gave the impression that he was coming back. That's all I know, having not heard a word from him since he left.

I had a pleasant eve with Arthur Oberg, just a few days ago. I had been on a panel with him and Blessing, mostly about Whitman, partly about Roethke, whose name hereabout is still magic. (He has a hall named after him.)

Though 78-yearolds in their anecdotage don't have breakthroughs, I have hit upon some clarifications recently that give me (and, I trust, the vast multitudes) somewhat the feel of a breakthrough—so although I have been working quite hard, I don't feel bepooped. And despite the exactions of an institutional schedule, I have managed sans nembies. I have probably been off the damned stuff for nearly five months.

Epic triumph: Recently a school up the line (WWSC) asked me to give a talk. I asked for 500 plus expenses. It's just the end of the term and money is scarce. But bejeez, Nine (9) departments chipped in—and I'm scheduled there to repeddle my talk on "Rhetoric, Poetic, and Dialectic," with a general haggle afterwards. Come Dec. 1. My job here ends in a few days, but I shall probably linger until near the middle of Dec., when I expect Butchie to pick me up, for Victoria. I'm to be at Ellensburg for a week in Jan. The Nevada deal hasn't yet been settled. Their terms were satisfactory, except that things were vague about living quarters. I was assured that there would be no problem, since "Reno is a motel town." But I figured that all the motels in Reno are there to divorce one from one's money. So I may end up by trekking back to And/or after all. Meanwhile, I shall probably be flitting back to NYC for a meeting, Dec. 4-5, at the Academy. (Had I been in the East today, I'd have been on a TV program, peddling my stuff anent "socialization of losses," to do with the plight of NYC. There is a guy who has a discussion show and likes my type. Too bad, I'd have had a chance to get in a plug for ATH.)

My safest forwarding number is: c/o K. Michael Burke, Room 1001, 260 West Broadway, New York City 10013.

"π∃≤&*=+ [ ] / | - Holla!

K.B.

Department of English
Reno Campus
University of Nevada
Feb. 22, 1976

Dear Billions,

Glad to hear from same. (And I thought that my recent communication had been Clarity Itself.)

Sorry you couldna find room somewhere for Macksoud. But I do grant that he aint the power I wish he were.

I'm out here getting a divorce—but from what? I'm scheduled to be back at And/or circa the first week of March. Meanwhile, know: I haven't put as much as a single nickel in one of the slot machines that in the downtown area are as lined-up as headstones in an over-populated urban cemetery. But I do like it that the freight trains go right through the center of town, right next to HAROLDS even.

There's an interesting gazette published by the Psychology Dept. here: *Behaviorism.* And I've been having some fun taking shots at Skinner in the name of Dramatism. One good thing about the Skinner lads (and lassies!) is that they help sharpen one's position. And the editor (at least in advance) has expressed a desire to have me submit a statement of my case. But I have publicly announced that, if I receive a box of candy through the mail I won't eat it. Meanwhile, actually, all seems fairly civilized, as regards my haggling.

If your outfit gets the Michigan Quarterly Review, do take a glance at my review of Steiner's *Beyond Babel.* I think that the deal about "Let's make a fire" touches on a goodthing. By some slip-up, I got no offprints. My answer to Howell is scheduled to appear in the forthcoming Q. J. of Sp. But some on my side will resent it that I warn't more scrappy-like.

I give my next-to-last class this aft. The last is on Thursday. The whole six-week job is a Summary—and this sixth week it's the Wind-Up of a Summary. Today I set up the general basis of GM; and then, in this Grand Bicentennial Year, leap from that to my stuffo on the U. S. Constitution (which you, to your eternal disgrace, DODGED). The book by the French scholar, Charles Roig, is apparently now in the pipeline. He translates large chunks of me, and applies my blandishments to the theory of Fr. constitutional law.

I'll be on the look-out for your Hussain Hidaway.

I have worked my damfool head off. And sometimes got scared (when all of a sudden dizzy). But it now 'gins look as though I might come through not too badly beaten.

Avec Universal Liebe,

K.B.

R.D. 2, And/or NJ 07821

The Copesmithery

X/2/76

Dear Billions,

Yes, come when thou willst. And bring along an undeniable Evidence-Machine if so inclined—and we'll haggle to our hearts' contents.

But you'd better hurry. For though I am, for the timebean, much less out than I am used to being, times do march on. Also, my years 'gin tell—and what they tell aint nearly as much fun as porn.

Me no fershtay the problems anent your publisher. When they discontinue a book, don't they in all traditional decency relinquish rights? Or are the further dealings involved in rights to re-use the original *printing*? That would make sense.

Bring along your godam Evidence-Machine—and betwixt us we can come pretty close to slapping out for you your whole additional chapter. And everybody will say how much more clearly you say it than I do.

But in the meantime, bone up on me on the US Constitution, in GM. Uddawise, go f-q thyself. The Bicentennial tells me that the word-world is close to unnerstanding my bleat there anent concerning—and I can tell your godam Evidence-Machine prezackly what has happened since.

I'd wince about youenz all being in disarray, except that I know you're at home there. Life must be as privileged for you even as for the likes of Patty Hearst, though at much less cost. Be ever gong-gong, that I may still know you. And you'd not be stupid enough to try robbing a bank. We know that banks are there to rob us. Hereabouts, every time a hot-dog stand folds up, a new branch-bank takes over, e'en with architecture worthy of a Williamstown. As my frenn Matty Josephson might say, they swoop down upon us at the narrows. (That poor duffer, by the way, is now in dire straits of a different sort, since his exceptionally bright wife is in the last stages of cerebral cancer.)

Obviously, my days are numbered. So yesterday I spent all day, from early morning until midnight, working at the piano on a tune. Being all alone, I worked hard on I know not what. Which is to say that, even in our seventy-ninesies, we still improvise. There was no money in it—that's obvious. But my poor Pap would have been playing solitaire. (I don't think that he ever cheated at solitaire; but Mom, his mother-in-law, did. That was a family joke. And I loved to be nearly smothered in her breasts when she so embraced me.)

But we all must hurry on.

Flowerish!
And avec Universal Liebe,
K.B.

The Copesmithery 07821
XII/2/76

Dear Billions,

'Tis 1:45 towards today.

I'm as lonely as the Father wd. be sans Son and Spirit.

Butchie has finally cleared out (he helped me wonderful-like through November). So all my childer are out prodigalizing somewhere or other.

And I am as though shivering, though I doubt that it's from the cold. I enclose, if I don't forget, the testimony of an item I got to smacking out precisely when he was leaving.

It's not meant to be a poem, for I'd never try to write a poem. It's but the makings of either a Diarism or an Epistolation, the only two modes of formal utterance I can conceive of.

I'm scheduled to be in town tomorrow. Had hoped to see the Cowleys. But Muriel phones me that Malcolm is in the hospital. If that dear slob clears out first, I'll never forgive him. I'm getting sick of being deserted. I thought that Libbie was so loyal. Yet when it came to abandoning me, she did the most radical job of all. But I assume that she meant well. Matty Josephson's wife just cleared out on him. Her cancer of the lungs had shifted to cancer of the brain (inoperable). She had always guyed me when, with a drink in my hand, I begged her to go easy on that godam weed. But now I'm wondering whether, if I went back to smoking, I could cut down on the alky. For it takes at least twenty years to get cancer from cigarettes, and I'm 79.

Could we sell that angle to the tobacco trust? "You have never smoked. You are now in your late seventies. It will take at least 20 years to give you cancer. Why not let loose? Even if you smoke five packs of our cancerettes a day, they can't kill you before you die anyhow." I now have the same attitude towards nitrites and similar poisons in food. They are all *slow* poisons, and naturally I'm racing towards death. So they can't catch up with me. Couldn't we work out some fantastic dishes, for sale only to oldsters, and to be dispensed only by prescription, since their flavor is due to chemicals that won't get you for a least twenty years? Don't you have a chemist relative who could help us set up, from the grass roots, the first enterprise of this sort?

In any case, know that if you want to do that co-verbalizing job you spoke of, you're welkim. Phone 201-347-3249,—almost that quick it's a deal. And if you do come, bring twice as many tapes as your cassette will need. I'll buy half and pay cash. And we'll both take records of the Grand Confrontation.

But it's now 1:30 of the next afternoon, and I'm expecting a taxi (binnuz I'm going to a meeting of the Am. Acad. of Arts and Let.)

May youenz all be joyous,
K.B.

An Invocation, In Principle

Great, as it were, Magistrate
Thou Kink of Kinks
Thou Principle of
Address in the Absolute.
I beg, no wars,
Have merry.

My pals,
dear non-believers all,
On learning how
in our struggles
against aloneness
I have thought of choosing
for a time
to rejoin
in a nearby male
nunnery

And so knowing
they fear for the
Next Phase of my most
immortal soul.

Thou great Principle of
Address in the Absolute,
Consider these as
Lines on Contemplating
A contract for Asylum
against this winter's (_____)?

at a nearby Abbey
which loves us all
at least
in principle ...

KB (XII/1/76)

The Copesmithery, alas! 07821
March 9, 1977 (3/9/77!)
booful date

Dear Billions,

The U. of Chicawguh guy tells me that you are to do the job. Let me not have perjured myself.

But for Gawsake, let's haggle about it beforehand. Be late, rather than barge in. Send me the thing, and lend me the book.

Of course you can get by. But I don't want you just to get by. I want you to come across as though you were writing for the most momentous gazette in the world.

You're good. And also you're fuzzy. (Who aint?) Let's try to get as much of the fuzzinees out of it as we can.

Frankilee, I wept for what I considered to be your way of *wasting* that recent opportunity as you did.

Your piece was intelligent (*logos*); it established you as a likable guy (*ethos*); and the subject concerned no less than the implications of environmental botching (*pathos*).

So much for the *rhetoric* of it. But it was weak where, after *rhetoric in general* doan meet the issue, "scientific specialization" *begins.*

Plizz, before you get all steamed up, plan for a section in which you tell us how many stages the work goes through (along with whatever notable terministic twists characterize each). No, get steamed up as you will. But give us somethinks like that along the line., incl. key equations and, if necessary, their transformations.

Heck, haggle and haggle. Meanwhile, here's a cwazy notion that of a sud. occurs to me:

There's a Frenchman who (temporarily at Brandeis) is doing a book on me for his countrymen—and we are to have a conference somewhere before he excapes. There's a possibility that it may be in May, when I'm to get my modest crowning by the Am. Acad. of the Arts and Sciences (in Boston). Or if he prefers, we may make arrangements here in April. It might be morbidly amusing if the three of us improvised some sessions here, in case the idea dint fill him or you or both with loathing. Such a tangle might add some angles.

Postim is due. (Wow! for "due" I wrote "die." Yes, my die is due.)

> Rejerce,
> K.B.

> The Copesmithery, alas! 07821
> March 20, 1977

Dear Billions,

Helndamnaysh, I'm not at all against your ecological slant as such. On the contrary!

Maybe you'd turn out to have the *administrative* genius that the whole thing needs, if we're to turn it from a prayer or a bellyache into a POLICY.

All I resented was what I took to be your notion that your prayer was gettn somewhere, — but sans an organization it's just a holier than-thou kind of bellyache-in-reverse. When I'm so godam sick of my bellyache, I'm all the more resentful of your you-love self-love "promissory" accents, along with straight lies (lies to self) about what to hope from the litry, nsech, who'd gladly rip up as many forests as necessary to sell as many copies of their books as possible.

But hold! I'm writing you at cocktail hour. And we both know that if you decide to turn that article into a book, by the time you're through you'll have added all the qualifications your statement needs. So, fare forth with my benedictions. In the meantime, take a glance at the current (March 18) issue of *Science*, on electronics. I think it is a highly reputable job, almost a milepost. If you're like I'm, it will scare out of you what one gets scared out of one—and all the more so because you'll rarely see such a technically scrupulous body of statements about anything. I'd have read every word, except that dooty called, in preparing for a trip to Texass, so I had to hurry on. But I'll help so peddle the issue that I'll never be able to have a copy of my own. (Of course, Butchie would keep his, but I might have filched my anthropology daughter's had I not already started selling the issue as the temporal equivalent of a landmark.)

I hadn't sent you my recent items because I planned to spring them on you when you came. But I'll try to catch up (ptikly binnuz there aren't many). This one on Skinner involves much more than I cd. say on the sumjick. (For instance, "Dramatism" is much closer to Behaviorism than my stance here might seem to indicate, though I am adamant in my insistence that "symbolic action" is not reducible to "nonsymbolic motion.") And fuzzily I caint remember whether I sent you my review of Steiner's *After Babel,* with its paragraphs, that I consider basic, on "Let us build a fire.")

Meanwhile, may there be a God, that He may have mercy on us all.

Holla!
K.B.

Andover, NJ
June 19, 77

Dear Billions,

Sure. Let's figure out something for July.

And bring the Swedes along, while also figuring out exactly how they are to be bedded (as I recall, they had capsules) and boarded (they must somewhat take part in the processes of feeding and cleaning up afterwards).

So far, the pond is quite wet and plenteous. And there's the tennis court if all is of a dryness by then.

Tell Dawlink Betty for me that, as I size things up, she is going through some problems all her own, and you're a guy who is just asking to be blamed. Of course you should be blamed. Everybody is a candidate. But it stands to reason that Ole Sore-Thumb Bill is sticking up there, as the most obvious thing to hit with the hammer of Betty's vexations connected with her problems of career. And alas! no problems of career can ever be settled. The goads of career are like trying to go on counting and counting until you have got the number that is beyond the possibility of adding "plus one."

But having come 80, I'm hoping this year to round things out by Saying Goodbye, in as methodological a way as poss. So far, the prognostications are not discouraging. But we could go on from there.

Avec Universal Liebe,

K.B.

Andover, NJ
VII/27/77
wadda nice date!

Dear Billions,

Libbie's Lil House on the Hill is being refurbished, not as much as we plan for eventually, but plenty enough for it to be quite viable after ten days or so are up. So there'll be plenty of room for the young Sweeds to exercise in, incl. trips back and forth. And the tennis court is workable, and the pond still is, as Wm. C, Wms. wd. say, "still wet," though not as plenteously so as earlier.

So, if possibilities seem possible, communicate avec. 202-347-3249. The only days in August that are out as at present are the oneth and tooth.

There are all kinds of things for us to consult and haggle about.

Bob Zachary was here, and we made a first weeding for the Sinballix volume. It needs a further weeding. If you have a cassette, bring it along—and your burdens would thereby be so lightened that you'd be like to levitate.

Week-middles are better than week-ends, when the young gents are likely to be here, possibly with company. (But soon after mid-August, Butchie will be returning to Victoria.) Jerre Mangione is planning to visit his family in Rochester, during August. I have suggested that he phone you. You'll like him and "Paintricia" a lot. (Binnuz she's a painter-person named "Patricia," I thus neo-etymologize her name.) Jerre is scheduled to fill in as Acting-Director at Yaddo this autumnality, while the Boss is vacating. He has been teaching at U. of Pa., in Inglese, but is being retired for age (68). In the olden dayes, Jerre used to spend summer months hereabouts.) He drinks but wine—and fittingly in a style midway btw. beer and the heavies.

I must hurry on. Onwards, outwards, and UP.

K.B.

Andover, NJ
VIII/26/77

Dear Billions,

Helndamnaysh—is it you, or me, or the nature of things, or what?

Was hoping to hear from you, about possible arrangements.

Plenty of room now. Butchie has returned to Canada. Unk is in Nevada.

I look forward to the Sept. 2-3 English Institute deal in the most dejected state of mind conceivable. I'm in a cross between a squirming tangle and total emptiness.

The only development I can even remotely imagine making me feel good would be the news that I was to have three secretaries, a housekeeper, a handy-man, and a guardian.

And to cap it all, I am caught in a fantastically indeterminate bundle of quandaries to do with the ways in which Kant's aesthetic in his *Critique of Judgement* misfits with Aristotle on poetic imitation and rhetorical persuasion.

I'm sorry,
K.B.

Andover
IX/27/77

Dear Billions,

Okay! And the hunnert more makes me happier—and that's the least they can do for an old geezer in his psychological nineties.

I remember Ned Rosenheim from away back. Nice guy.

Let's make it Wed-Thurs, Nov. 2-3. And I'll plan to get there the aft or eve of the day before. I'll arrange the trip soon, and say.

For a possible housing arrangement, I'd suggest that you phone Dick McKeon, whose gracious invitation of many months ago I warnt able to fit in with. He might have available space.

Went to Nemerov's coming-out party yestiddy. On three stiff Vodkas I yowled a plenty.

I hasten to put this in the box. Postim nearly due.

Holla!
K.B.

Andover
October 5, 1977

Dear Billions,

How's this? Arrive on American, Flight 581. 4.58 P.M. from Newark. Nov. 1.

Return from Chicago, 1.10 P.M. TWA flight 384. Nov. 4. To Newark. 3.59 P.M. If anything wrong, spick.

Yes, I remember the Windermere. "Once elegant," yes. Fine. The oncer the better.

My stuff is in a woeful scatteredness, but I'll start trying to put togidda a list. I guess I'll first try slapping out the Sinballix. A young guy (not so young) who was an understudy of Hugh Duncan now has a connection with a school in Miami. We have tentatively worked out a deal there for me, six weeks beginning last week in Jan. He was for a regla 12-week course, but I had sworn to do no more straight teaching. So we have a loose sort of arrangement whereby I don't have a class, but do various odds and ends of consulting, plus three public talks. I forget the name of the school, but it's the International something. I'm to be labelled a D*st*g**sh*d V*s*t*ng Pr*f*ss*r.

At the moment I'm trying to finish up my notes for a talk I'm to give down the line at Drew (Oct. 28): "Theology and Logology." Denis Donoghue is at Rutgers for a while. We've arranged for him to voyage hither on Oct. 20.

But I won't much relish our talking about my dreams, other than what we might be immediately engaged with during the Chicago doings of Nov. It looks as though I'll have enough trouble at best working into a viable rut.

And yes, do let me know as soon as youenz guys have worked out your schedule.

Meanwhile, I've settled on the two most epoch-making sentences in all history: (1) "Let's get together and do such-and-such." (2) "It aint my fault, it's his." Shouldn't there be a third?

Holla!

K.B.

Andover
November 7, 1977

Dear Billions,

Herewith the Stout Affirmation, amounting to $230.01.

My expeeerience at the meetings gave me some notions which I expect to develop, possibly handling on parts of it as a parting thought to your colleagues. But that must be later. In the meantime, wd. say:

Please tell Betty, on the basis of what she seems to be concerned about, that the most succint example of REVERSAL (anent women) is in the footnote, pp. 118-121, *Attitudes Toward History*.

Anent the much-needed addition of the stuff on the Dialectic of Constitutions (if you patch up your book anent me), please do consult (and perhaps xerox parts of) *An Introduction to Legal Reasoning*, by Edward H. Levi. Also, *the Supreme Court and Social Science*, by Paul L. Rosen. I would like to send you a letter (which you would include in your text) along these lines:

> I do wish I had had those books to quote from, when writing my pages on the Dialectic of Constitutions. They are made for my purposes. But they weren't yet in existence. Professor Levi told me that he had read the opening pages of my *Grammar*, but had never got to my section on Constitutions. I can well believe him. For I am sure that, if he had got that far, the point about "the Constitution-Behind-the-Constitution" would have been explicity discussed in some such terms, whereas there are but passages in which the concept is implicit. Rosen's book sharpens that aspect of the case in a way that would have been *greatly* to my purposes, as the very title indicates, since he is em-

phatically concerned with new "social" developments that are an ideal example of what I mean by "the scene behind the scene."

Please look over both those texts from that point of view, and see if you can't see quite clearly now, how those pages can be presented. (They are an ideal instance of what I mean by "circumference" with regard to scene. The pentad (or hexad) yes. It's suggestive, but flimsy, if not developed in terms of the ratios. But even that is flimsy (a mere matter of *labelling,* which students of English are generally taught to love) unless developed further in terms of *circumference.* (When taken to that stage, one can begin to work with *generative principles,* prophesying after the event, etc. I, of course, view the archetype racket as a mere matter of labelling. It's essentially inert. I think the second of the Clark U. talks, *Dramatism and Development,* helps point up that matter.) If you, on going through the Levi and Rosen books, don't suddenly see what's eating at me, and why I place so much stress upon that section of the *Grammar,* then aroint thee, knave. The *structure of the law,* here, becomes an ideal instance of textual *structure in literary matters generally.*

But I must stop now, for post-time nears, and tomorrow the mails are closed. Meanwhile, I'll go on trying to write a brief post-mortem as a farewell adress to those of your local enterprise.

Holla!
K.B.

[Postcard]

Andover
XI/7/77

Bill-

Forgot to enclose the evidence, which is herewith.

Incidentally, the reprints do seem to have been purloined. It's damned vexing.

K.B.

Clutcher's Gulch
XII/18/77

Dear Billions,

Jeez, when I run across a guy as generous as that, my first instink is to hit him for a loan. And it flows like a brook in June. E'en as I was racing off to the county hospital, at 4 A.M., thinking that this was it, doubtless the local P.O. was already quartering such words, that would encourage me to hang on. Indications are that the stuff I'm taking is working (the problem was high blood pressure, the suddenness of the rise being due to an especially vexing clutter of Unfinished Bizz—and the most vexing part of the vexing clutter.

...

Two days' interruption

The damned ailment shouldof eased up, but hasn't. I may be in real trouble. (If, for instance, the symptom involves a bodily condition still to be disclosed.) If worse comes to worst, I'll ship you the pages to read at the other session, plus some notes still to be added. I should know by later in the week. To continue:

Mine enemy might accuse your paper of o'er-attitudinizing (in my behalf yet). Minor suggestions follow.

p. 7. change "sparing" to "sparring."

p. 10 machines as "perfection of rationality." That is, a caricature of human rationality. Article on "Dramatism" in *Int. Encyc. of Soc. Sci.*, 449C.

p. 12. "every part of ... physical world ... has a symbolic ingredient." Quite misleading. World of nonsymbolic motion has *no* symbolic ingredient intrinsically. It is endowed with such by the symbol-using animal. This is major.

p. 14. I question whether the Pentad Matrix *talks* well. Best instance of ratios is in "Dramatism," 446D. Plus stuff on circumference (447B)

p. 16. should be Lexicon Rhetoricae.

p. 17. on "centrality of language." However, I all the more stress the unbridgeable division of the motion-action polarity. (as vs. Behaviorism's monistic assumption that there is no qualitative difference btw. verbal behavior and sheerly animal, physiologic behavior.

p. 27. I'm not sure that I see the "freedom" issue as clearly as you suggest. There is plenty of bondage in the realm of symbolic action. See *Language as Sym. Act.*—bottom pf p. 58.

p. 39. was amused by the dog story. But I think 'twould read better if you inserted "when I was" between "Burke the man" and "accompanied by." Thus, "Sometimes, vixiting Burke the man when I was accompanied by Burke the dog."

I'd suggest dropping the "reign...pore" flowerish since it's too visual, hence needs explanation, which makes it lame. Can't I sell you my greatest motivational flowerish? Namely: "Why does a chicken cross the road to get on the other side?" Or perhaps you weren't raised as I was on that as my first riddle, with of course the second part as answer to the first part as a question.

Sometimes you used titles as a rhetorical device (for suggestiveness), like batches of balloons for sale by a peddler at a circus.

In haste. Thanks a whole lot. If you tone it down you won't make me consider myself insulted. Meanwhile, postman is due. I'll try to let you know how things are going with this roar in my ears.

Holla,
K.B.

Florida International University
English Department
Miami, Florida 33199
1/13/78

Dear Billions,

Bejeez, I thought you were putting me away for good, and I sorta felt that you shared that sentiment avec. But by heck, the chawnces are that Big Shot has decided on lettn me do the rounding-out so obviously necessary for the first of my years in the eighties. I couldn't ask for a better sichaysh than now beckons to me for the next few months.

I owe you some money. Please tell me how much. And also please give me Dick McKeon's address, binnuz he even owes a doctor bill. Or tell him to write me. My clearings-out are always laden with lacunae.

Here I am in Kathleen Callaway's place. Haint that a sweet name, I say to my sickly Selph when crawling into her bed. She has every little thing in place here, and I feel so ashamed that so many of my ideas can't be filed in the spirit of Kathy's ways. And everything I do I feel like an intruder upon her privacy. Every spot here speaks of Kathy—and I must somehow live up to her darling primnesses. Don't you speak mean of Kathy, or I'll, well, I don't know what.

Betty called to say farewell, Gott segne sie. And I got pretty godam low. I brought a btl. of them godam pills with me, but I'm gwanna try cuttn down (seeing if I can get along with two today as vs. the adjudicated three). but I haven't yet got the water sichaysh settled, and am still drinking this progressive swill. But at least I'm eating peanut butter the way God made it.

The lad who brought me here doesn't really know how nice a guy he is. He keeps feeling guilty about taking care of me whereas I feel that I'm sittn pretty. To be south this wint is in itself enough for me, ptikla binnuz I'll be professionally verbalizing.

next morn:

Howe'er, my job hasn't started yet. It's just that I'm not up there hating myself all alone. And I still cling to the notion that my troubles there may be largely due to one kerosene stove that is operating properly. My trouble is that I'm so damned autosuggestive, as soon as I began suspecting the damned stove my heart started pounding every time I looked at it. But I will say, in this area of open windows out of town, I have been beset by no furies. I have twenty-four dollars worth of capsules—and my ambition is to share at least half of them with some poor progress-fretted alligator who doesn't know what's wrong with him.

As for my Sinballix wolume, I have a bit of a notion along this line: Instead of reprinting the various items as they stand, *talk about them,* e'en to the extent of saying why I'm leaving out such-and-such, and saying perhaps what might profitably have been added, etc. People are so used to the news, they can't follow an argument unless you manage to make it look like telling a story. At least, I'll try to do as much as I can by way of showing "how one thing led to another." I have in mind the sort of thing I did in the twenty-minute statement I read at the MLA meeting (though you, alas, dint seem to think it worked very well in that case, I'd blame the trouble on the *over*-condensation needed under those conditions). Ennihow, it's a notion I keep tinkering with. Incidentally, I think I'll begin with my *Ethan Brant* piece as an example of random note-taking, along with some gossip about how I got into my "indexing" bizz, perhaps incl. the gossip of the time when I was awakened by "zigzags" that spontaneously presented me with

—ah, shit—this is the second time that I've been fooled by this new carbon paper.

Ever forward towards Avanti,
K.B.

Florida International University
English Department
Miami, Florida 33199
Jan. 24, 1978

Dear Billions,

Helndamnaysh, I'm sorry to hear that you're engloomed. I suppose it's about you and Betty—and it's a damned shame. For as I size things up, she's in a motivational tangle that is essentially a matter of her own internal development, and you're the handiest externality on which to project it. Indeed, you may even be inviting some swats—and that's a hard offer to resist.

I salute the wisdom flowerish, but the other reminds me of my rival offering: "a good bush needs no wine."

But damn the luck, my moving around does so frustrate my sickly attempts at order. By all means, I must find you the address of Ross Altmann, who can give you an excellent chapter. He did a thesis on me which has some ideal spots. I came with the avowed intention of writing him from this end of the line, but what happened to his address? Do you know John Macksoud, who teaches at Binghamton (the NY State outfit there)? He could tell you. (He once taught in the Speech Dept. at Sanata Barbarbara, and published a book which you might locate in the Library. Since he published it at his own expense, he might well have given copies to various universities, I know not. Ross did the job under his guidance. And my only objection concerns some places where he leaned in the direction of the over-sell. What a crying shame that I can't spot the address among my disjecta membra. I'm sure to find it sooner or later, since I'[m almost certain that I brought along with me some comments I wanted to send him. I teyuh, Bill, the guy has a lot of good stuff. Also, I think you'll find much good stuff in the Jennermann MS. As for Jim Mullican, I'd suggest an angle of this sort: He is intending to give a course on me this spring. Why not suggest that he simply jot down diaristic notes as they developed? Just quickie comments on what turned up, pro or con or tangentially? Informal "happenings" of that sort can have a kind of vitality that is hard to get except thus on the run. Why not quote to him these exact sentences, and add that, time permitting, I'd be glad to come in with a bleat here and there? If I cd. sell youenz that idee, me lad, we could really do somethinks.

As for Prof. Christian Susini, please tell him it's your notion, not mine—as I take it that, although he is quite at home in English, his interest is in doing a book in French. His address is 13 rue le Verrier, Paris 75006. He had intended to be at the MLA meetings, but was deterred by illnesses in the family. Surely he would have found the journey not at all worth the trip, particularly when we add my godam ailments that turned up just when all was to be under the sign of relackussing at Year's End. He writes vaguely of problems connected with the transcribing of our interviews (some taken on cassette). And I'll tell him to send along anything whatever. This is my Summarizing-Year, and that's that, ptikly if Big Shot has decided to let me putter along as per indications so far.

I agree with your notion that my tentative twist anent the various Sinballix items was wrong. Here's the list, roughly to date:

Kinds of Criticism; Three Definitions; Othello; King Lear; Burke and Hopper on "Mysticism"; Thanatopsis for Critics; A 'Dramatic' View of Imitation; Ethan Brand; Symbol and Association; The Poetic Motive; The Carrot and the Stick (?); On Catharsis, or Resolution; Catharsis - Second View; Dramatic Form - Tracking Down Implications; Comments (?Western Speech, 68); Kermode Revisited; Poetics and Communication; On Creativity - A Partial retraction; Towards Helhaven; Doing and Saying; Dramatism and Development (probably just the second); As I was Saying; Why Satire; Dancing With Tears in my Eyes; Towards a Total Conformity (?); Invective Against the Father (possibly Words Anent Logology?); possibly comments on my review of Steiner's *After Babel*, binnuz I think that my pernt about the necessarily *analogical* aspect of language is basic, otherwise no expression could be applied to two situations, since no two situations are identical in detail. Hence, my theory of "entitlement" must be reaffirmed. I forget whether I ever showed you the stuffo on "(Nonsymbolic) Motion/ (Symbolic) Action" (which *Critical Inquiry* is to publish, and of which I believe I should publish at least portions. And I incline to feel that some of the Theo-Logo stuff should be referred to, in a kind of Summing-up. A quixotic possibility would be some pages being nice to Phil Young's book on Hemingway (as my notion of relations btw. equations in a book and equations in a life, the duality underlying Coleridge and equations in PLF). And I forget whether I ever showed you the CENTRUM article on Austin's *How to-Do Things With Words,* essential for my way of placing ATTITUDE betwixt MOTION and ACTION. (I'll give Richards credit for having pointed up the ASTTITUDE bizz, as per my section on " 'Incipient' and 'Delayed' Action" in GM. Austin's so-called 'illocutionary" utterances are purely and simply ATTITUDE words, as I think I showed purty conclusively in my CENTRUM piece.) I also hope to use some of my stuffo on Hirsch, with regard to ambiguities he introduces into the relation btw. text as object (of cognition) and text as act.

Incidentally, the items I listed are not in the order of their appearance. But I'd be most grateful for any suggestions pro or con, incl. possibility that you may have quite different emphases in mind. (Incidentally, over and under and before and behind it all, keep reminded that ultimately this job is replacing archetype with entelechy, as per the second of the two Clark U. essays on *Dramatism and Development.)*

Any suggestions for arranging the material are respectfully solicited.

Meanwhile, skate, skate, e'en unto ten miles, you ole Skate, and remember the man who "talked of a broad, horizonless lake, its water absolutely still, but with a gently sloping surface. 'Limpid moveless water,' he explained, 'tilted slightly sideways. And when it freezes, O the ecstasy of skating from the upper end.' " Would I could give you some solace, lad; but them of my age has none to spare.

Tomorrow eve my tasks here begin in earnest. Chuck has got 'em to plaguing their selves with my "Dramatism" piece (which, it seems, the Encyclopedia has farmed out to an anthology)—and we're to go on from there. The weather foretells storms. And I have not yet recd. any copies of my "Chorale Omega," which I alone, in all this world, seem at all interested about. Do you, by the way, know of a Harbinger book, *Interpretation: The Poetry of Meaning,* edited by S. Hopper and D. Miller, 1967, in ptikla pp. 98-101? I gotta work with this somewhat, in re some of my tangle with Hirsch. I recall your saying that this is standard stuff now. So I doan wanna be in the position of quoting myself when I should be quoting someone else. If you will tell me to whom I shd. be indebted, I'll squirm accordingly. I originally worked with it in a talk at Indiana State U., one of Sherry Pattison's speech conferences (which she organizes annually with considerable skill). I have a special twist I hope to give it, with regard to Hirsch. So, all advices would be dutifully appreciated.

> Avanti, whatever the hell that
> means,
> K.B.

> Florida International University
> English Department
> Miami, Florida 33199
> II/4/78

Dear Billions & Billions,

When you start feeling sorry for yourself, just remember you're disgustingly far from being 80 years old—so just cut it out.

Meanwhile, besten Dank for your notes anent the sinballix. To the best of my memory, the present versions of the *Faust* essays are all what is. The whole *Oresteia* exhibit would throw things outa shape. So keep your copy, and mebbe some day, when I'm flitten around like an angel … The Hirsch job would be but an artikkel for a gazette to which I promised it. My only worry was somethinks you said about how everybody knew about how books, like musical scores, are but instructions for performance. I eskedyuh to say where and when.

Yes, much that is in LSA belongs in the Sinballix. But as I see it, the best I can do about that is to include a few pages in which I say so, and why. Why not?

Caint I begin with the mere business of "indexing"? (Incidentally, things in my mail encourage me to THINK that the 20-minute job I done at the first MLA session wasn't as bad for them-as-dint-know-much as it was "for you and I" who knew what a slaughter it was. In fact it set one guy (who has got me a one-grand performance on the West Coast in April) to organizing a book on my sickly Self up to and incl. C-S, also incl. prior poesies nsech. 'Tis fantask how, e'en as one dies by the minute, oddments keep turning up. If I could just bring myself now to commit suicide or get caught robbing a bank, I could provide a good income for my family and all my friends. But I must hold off. For I am a man of principle, and I have sworn to one ambition. I must somehow survive long enough to piss on Shitney Hook's grave. That great champion of Ideal Freedom finally proved my point by attaining the state of Breakfast in Nixon's Whitehouse. So I must hang on somehow, though I'm growing awful tired of trying to believe in anything, even the pissandicity of Shitney Hook.

Meanwhile, please do send me a copy of the Theo-Logo bizz; and lo! we might work out somethinks just from there (if, for instance, all youenze guys chose to pitch in, and we went on from there—for that's my idea of how things might develop, with whatever haggles turned up along the way). If I caint take care of myself, then smack me down. I'm not asking for quarter. Jes give me a chance such as the conditions of your earlier collection dint give me. Let me slap back, where such seems called for. In your earlier job, you had too much respect for my opponents. You could do an artikkel discussing such things now, I'm sure sans breast-beating. It cd. all be civilized, along the lines of my hopes anent Jim Mullican. To hell with the way slobs are turning out books. Let's slap this one out as things develop, by all mean incl. epistolation. But I do hope that you can find Ross Altmann's address. I'd of sworn I had it.

*v*nt*

K.B.

Florida International University
English Department
Miami, Florida 33199
February 17, 1978

Dear Billions,

First, before everything else: Please do get in touch with Prof. Charles Roig (University of Geneva, Dept. of Political Science, and author of 160-plus pages entitled *Symboles et société: Une introduction à la politique des symboles d'après l'oeuvre de Kenneth Burke.* Now, through Feb. 28, his local address is: c/o Prof. Terry N. Clark, The University of Chicago, Dept. of Sociology, 1126 East 59th Street. If the liberry don't have a copy of his book, so much the worse for the liberry. I ptikly hope that you'll get along grand because he stresses the Constitution bizz, nsech.

Next, are you sure you gave me the right address for Dick McKeon? I had the feel that it shd. have N. or S. or some such, but not so with the address which you gave me, and which I used, sans to elicit response, though I owe him a doctor bill (of what amt. I know not).

I know nothing of GLYPHs.

Nor of Cary Nelson's fancy, cum the quite likable scheme of your being a part of it. I think I cd. at least get Chuck to send you copies of the Freccero and Fletcher papers, though I'd incline to imagine that the authors themselves wouldn't exactly view them as powerful contributions to world history.

AND THANS ONE HECK OF A LOT for the copy of the THEO-LOGO bizz. Binnuz I'm free for several days (with nothing but my sickly selfness to contend with), I'll give the item a last-over, and report accordingly. Schemingly, I cd. get Chuck to xerox my copy as modified, if modified, and send you a copy of same. The damned thing should be good for something, at least as a "point of departure."

Last eve I did a job that went over gratifyingly well. Built around the Emerson-Bentham texts I use in my "(Nonsymbolic) Motion/ (Symbolic) Action" routine, that is slated for publication by Columbia U. Press and *Critical Inquiry.* I shall probably try it again in my one-night stand, March 3, at a Dallas, Texas convention, though a couple of questions from the audience helped a lot. My relations to an audience change immediately, the moment I can get someone to pipe up with something—and some such aid was forthcoming. Did you, by the way, take a glance at my notion in the current *C. I.*? (Things got botched up, so that I haven't yet recd. reprints.)

Happy to learn that you're feeling better. Here's a recent quatrain to read and weep for me about: "After the maples this spring/ things will go on until when/ after the maples this spring/ will my sap ever flow again?" To be read, I guess, as my first thoughts of returning north (which, I am sure, will be quite plentiful by mid-March, though I fear And/Or before April, since I still think that some of my troubles are due to a defective kerosene stove there). Lectures in California and Washington are shaping up for late April, but our pal at Northwestern has lapsed into silence, after talk one a one-grand job.

Aimlessly,
K.B.

Florida International University
English Department
Miami, Florida 33199
February 21, 1978

Dear Billions,

'Twas a neat copy, hence herewith the corrections are few.

But wouldst thou agree to prefix this Foreword, which would require no repagination?

Nacherly, I could go on and on—but this shd. do for the timebean.

And would you allow me three copies of the whole project? Also, if convenient, a list of whom sent at? And, of course, a record of any bleats, towards a creative curse on my part?

And for my Grande Finale show, when I do naught but versicles and some bits of rhetoric-slanted prose (scheduled for the eve of March 2), do please suggest some items you think Most Likely to Succeed, and what by all means to avoid. And any sales angle for our announcement.

That will be the end of my official duties here. The next day I fly-flit to Texas for a one-night stand. Then I hope to linger here in March as long as is feasible, when the occupantess returns to kick me out. (I'm hoping that I may stay through at least the first three weeks of March.)

Every wunst in a while I decide that I'm in a new groove (doubtless the last) to be entitled "Operation Nondescript." Forgive me if I don't try to describe it, beyond saying that, even if someone gave me a fantastic chunk of money, I'd have not the slightest idea how to have fun spending it. ... But no, I'd hire Strawinski, if we was still around, to help me write down my tunes. Meanwhile, I have expeeerienced no inspirations greater than that quatrain I sent you when, on a warm mid-Feb day in Miami, I bethunk me of dormant maples in the snows of Vermont.

And oh, yes—I'd write anonymous attacks on my novel, and hire Anita Bryant to sign them.

Somewhitherwards,
K.B.

[Postcard]

II/23/78

Dear Billions,
   Please note in margin, p. 36, fifth and sixth lines from bottom:
I must verify that point later, from my books at Andover.
   It does not figure in Freud's article on Negation (*Verneinung*). The
point he makes there is wholly O.K.

                              In haste,
                              K.B.

                         Florida International University
                                  English Department
                                  Miami, Florida 33199
                                     March 15, 1978

Dear Billions,
   Sorry, paper shortage.
   Delighted to receive thy cheery one of March 10. Go Adam, go
Eve. Sorry about Roig. I may still be seeing him. He proposed coming
here. But I've asked him to make it Andover. To be carless in Florida is
worse than being Eyeless in Gaza—and to have entertainment trouble
besides!
   I have scheduled my flight north for the 28th. So don't send the
Theo-Logo pages here. Rather, hold 'em for a while, then send to And/
or, with note: "Hold Until Called For."
   Tell me: Did you get in touch with Ross Altmann? That thing of his
has some damned good stuff in it. When and if I get back home, I think
I can find some other items, among the things I recd. from dissertators
nsech.
   Linger for a while, on sending the Theo-Logo piece around. I've got
some talks to give on West Coast in late April, and at Northwestern in
May. The Jennermann wd. be OK, but I'd like to negotiate further with
Griffin before your sending it to him. I need to see how we organize our
schedule. I'd love it if we cd. work from such a MS, on the basis of the
studentry having read it. But since my "(Nonsymbolic) Motion/ (Symbolic) Action" routine may be twice-published (half-hanged?) by the

time of our meetings in May, I still gotta get my assignment clear. Wait for a lil bit yet (at least until I learn how the CI deal works out: whether they are publishing the item in the issue as planned, etc.). I should know in a few days. For if their plan went through, I'll be receiving final copy in a few days. Jim Mullican has picked up consid. Do you think of sending him a copy?

Had one hell of a calamity here. Fell asleep with some yams on the stove. They boiled dry, and one thing led to another, entelechially culminating in frizzling a bakelite handle to a frazzle. That was a couple of days ago, the place still reeks of the fumes—and I gather they're loaded with cyanide. I don't yet know how it will all turn out—but in the meantime I've added some further symptoms to my vexatious syndrome.

Uneasily,

K.B.

Abiturus soon (FIU, III/21/78)

hence, send reply to And/Or

unless, for some reason, a hasty

phone call, to (Residential) 305-

226-4190

Dear Billions,

Besten Dank for thine of III/13/78, and for the Theo-Logo reproductions.

All is to the good. But I'd feel easier if you sent me a xeroxed copy of your friend's comments in toto. Your comments anent footnote one seemed all to the good. But they seem to need ultimate sharpening in terms of the "(Nonsymbolic) Motion/ (Symbolic) Action)" dichotomy, *hoffentlich* to be published in the summer issue of *CI*, though clearly formulated in GM. But I do not ground this distinction upon its way of saving the world for "freedom," the "ethical," etc. I ground it upon a *theory of language as symbolic action* (in contrast with such a world of sheer nonsymbolic motion as must have preceded the mutation whereby our anthropoid ancestors developed the necessary physiological structures, and will go on after all such symbol-using animals have disparooed from this planet).

When your friend asks, "why may not purpose or scene receive the primary stress?" your frenn presumably has the advantage of not having read my stuffo in GM on Philosophic Schools. So far as I can glimpse, from your quotes, your frenn is *turning against me* as a theorist of symbolic action what I have *tried to stress* in my GM analysis of such resources.

Once you make the distinction btw. symbolic and nonsymbolic, on the symbolic side our whole vast "universe of discourse" arises, with as many transformations as are possible to as many distinctions as can be revealed by asking about the resources of dialectical transformation. I take it that your pal has never bothered with my discussion of dialectic in GM, as one Billions Rueckert dodged the whole (ESSENTIAL) section on the dialectic of constitutions. (Whereat, incidentally, I am reminded. If all goes as planned, when I arrive at the airport in Newark come next Tuesday, we are to pick up Prof. Charles Roig, author of *Symboles et société: Une introduction à la politique des symboles d'après l'oeuvre de* You-Know, savant from the University of Geneva, and scorned in Chicago by a love-torn academic wildman of our mutual acquaintanceship. How do you THINK he will take it, out there our way?)

But I admit, I squirmed about that godam pentad matrix, and wished I had never been born. I do wisht you'd drop it. For I doan see that it adds a godam thing.

As for Emerson, if I were allowed but two, I'd take Emerson and Mark Twain. But in the cause of accuracy with regard to present issues, (please, I beg you, please) bring to the fore my paragraphs regarding Bentham's theory of fictions, LSA 196btm-197tp.

There's one basic distinction I build from: "Is it a *tree,* or is it a *word* for tree?" And my "Dramatistic" position can correspondingly end up as the distinction between "is-aint" and "do-don't" as the two (obviously interweaving) approaches to the definition of the peculiarly human animal (as interweaving as epistemology and ontology).

As for Jameson, I sizes it up thus: If a guy says that you stink, you caint answer. But if the guy says that you didn't do what you did do, have at him. In this instance, our Yaley was inadequately informed. And Godwilling and Deo volente, I'll respond accordingly.

> Nacherly, more anon, and
> rejerce,
> K.B.

R. D. 2, Box 393
Andover, NJ 07821
April 3, 1978

Dear Billions,

Jeezoos Keerist. I gotta somehow pull this place together, or I can never again put myself together. "Operation Nondescript" it is indeed. Charles Roig was here. (He met me at the Newark airport when I arrived March 28, and he left this morn.) He was gettn to be like me, putting things down and not being able to find them. They disappear among the clutter, like animals that resemble their environment.

Reading Theo-Logo, he found three errors: Page 13, line 10, number shd. be 3.1416; third line from bottom of main text, should be "psychogenic"; seven lines from bottom, "by" should be "without" (an error that could have downright tragic results).

I'll write Lee Griffin. and tell him to show his students the article (duly corrected) if he wants to. I don't see any point to your taping the main talk, which will probably be my "(Nonsymbolic) Motion/ (Symbolic) Action" routine, scheduled for publication in Summer issue of *Critical Inquiry.* But there might be a discussion period, of some newness. And I assume that the other talk will be largely impromptu discussion, which do take if the speeerit so moves you.

The entelechy stuff has turned up with a new wrinkle—and I'll try to send you a copy (It's still in handwriting)—which is to say, cryptic, so far as public consumption is concerned.)

If I can manage to get together the various items that fit the Stern case, I'll write you about it. I'd like to get into that. Yes, by all means send Jim Mullican a copy of L-L, avec corrections, ptikly the third. (I found a batch of notes I had written but not used for TBL. I have some badly xeroxed copies. If I can find them in time, from among this morbid clutter, I'll send the item along, in case you take a morbid interest in such exercisings.) I doan mind about the Jameson artikkel being published; for I think that the Editoriality would welcome a bleat on my part, since they welcome the gore of controversy. And unless J. has modified things a bit, I THINK I can charge him simply on *factual* matters, the best situation for an aggrieved author would defend his Selph in poison.

Ross Dean Altman is addressable thus: Lincoln College, Lincoln, Ill. 62656. You might write him a note to the effect that I am delighted with much in his thesis. But I didn't see how you could use it all, and maybe he wouldn't want to yield but excerpts. There's a lot that he has nailed down quite right, and from an angle that gives his presentation a special raison detter. If he thinks he could part with parts, I'll dig the unbound copy (he has since given me a bound one) out-from-in-under the several layers of civilization that have piled up here, and send you same.

The Betty-Sichaysh is very distressing, but I'm not in a position to throw stones at either of youenz, even if I wanted to. Sometimes, in my more morbid moments, I imagine incipient developments whereby Libbie might have broken with me (for a guy who is full of himself is a damn-nuisance in many ways, ptikly if he's around the house all the time. And not only was I full of myself all of the time, every now and then I was full—and having heard myself on a record taken here, at my request, when I thought I was winning like cwazy in an argument with a frenn, well, that's exackly what I was doing: winning like crazy, and let the participle dangle as it will).

But there are only two ways to get out of being eighty years old; namely: to konk off, or drag on into becoming 81. Wadda dilemma!

Rejerce,

K.B.

The damned thing is illegible so I send not.

[Postcard]

IV/11/78

Dear Billions,

This is to say that I have heard from Ross Altman.

I shall try to find and send you a copy of his MS. (I have bound and unbound copies)

He'd be willing to cut his down, with some rewriting. I think you'll like it consid.

More soon.

In haste,

K.B.

Here 07821
IV/14/78

Dear Billions,

You know that joke about the two black girls (I suppose it has to be ethnic to be a joke) who were going to put two dollars on a race horse, and went around to the stalls, hoping to see him before they placed their bet. The keeper told him where he was. A few minutes later they came back and said they weren't going to bet on that stallion. He asked them why they changed their mind. They said, "He aint got his mind on no race."

I incline to think that, this spring, you aint got your mind on no race, so far as the Logology Sweepstakes is concerned. But ennihow …

By now you shouldof received the Altman MS. Recently I sent Lee Griffin a batch of page numbers anent "entelechy," "perfection," "end of the line," "tracking down of implication," etc. Maybe we could get Ross to use some stuffo like that for his revised ending. (I think 'twould fit if he presented it as a place where my notions on poetry in particular and language in general come togidda.)

Was happy to learn of Hayden White's decision about your essay. That shd. make an ideal songful starter.

I'll try to say more about the Stern bizz. But can't until after the present doings. I'm scheduled to leave on the 20th, return on the 30'th. I must also write a commemorative tribute on Matty Josephson, who as you may have heard recently died of a heart attack.

We might get Roig to suggest some Constitution excerpts from his monograph. Trouble is: It would also require translating, except of course for its quotes from me. I'll bring up the matter when I hear from him or see him (he talked of passing by this way again this summer).

Binnuz you have done so much on Faulkner, I wonder if you settled with John T. Irwin's *Doubling and Incest - Repetition and Revenge*. I have just read Cowley's new book, *And I Worked at the Writer's Trade*. It has a chapter in which he gets quite exercised about what he calls Irwin's "meta-Freudian" interpretations of Faulkner's work. It looks to me as though I shd. get the Irwin book and put it through the Logology wringer.

I'm hoping soon to write up the notes I have used for a Whitman lecture. When as and if I get around to it, I'll send you a copy. Howe'er, it but trims up and points up what I have said already (my most unwieldy offering being the chapter in *Leaves of Grass One Hundred Years After,* M. Hindus).

I'll also mention your project to C. Susini, when I get around to writing him. He stresses my litry side (how favorably or unfavorably, I'm not sure; his last letter, sent to me some months ago, asked me somethings which I thought he should be doing himself).

My copy of Brooks on Faulkner got stolen soon after I received it. Do you know if it is now in paperback? 'Tis too expensive (as I recall) for me to invest in hard-coverly.

> Ear-ringingly,
> K.B.

07821 IV/14/78

Dear Billions,

Phone call from Gambier. The plans for renewed Kenyon Review have eventuated.

So, in answer I suddenly bethunk me: That wd, be a good place for the Theo-Logo bizz, because of the pages on Miller.

So, wouldst kindly slap a copy in that direction: Address thus:

> Ronald Sharp
> English Department
> Kenyon College
> Gambier, Ohio 43022

I note, by the way, that Helen Vendler is giving four talks on the Keats Odes later on this month. At Kenyon, that is. They sent me a notice.

They promised me a quick decision.

> Ear-ringingly thine,
> K.B.

Charlie Marcus' and K.
Burke's Birthday 78
07821
May 6, 1978

Dear Billions,

Have been back after the trip West. Just recd. letter from Lee Griffin. Begad, he has been doing quite a job. And he has set up for me some sessions which I welcome. I do hope you can be there.

Also recd. letter from Ronald Sharp, who is quite enthusiastic about the Theo-Logo bizz.

All went quite well except for Wash. State U., where they had one of those disconcerting arrangements whereby I go on talking, and twice students leave for other classes. I must make sure to avoid those. (I had one such once before, and they are damned disconcerting. But the guy who piloted me to and from was very nice.) But the Seattle and Bellingham deals went grand—and ditto the SCU sessions.

I got my pay for vocalizing, but still need reimbursed for travel expenses—and may have had a hunnert dollars in travelling checks lifted, though I can probably get that back, after much stew.

Recd. Betty's zealous feminist paper on WT. But haven't yet been able to do my homework.

Meanwhile, I'm having one hell of a time trying to write the commemorative tribute on Matty Josephson. Problem: How make it *personal* without getting into the act? Ideally, I should write one about him and me, then konk off, and have Cowley read it.

In any case, at least I'm cured of eighty, though it has left some damned bad scares on my insides somewhere. Still pillulating.

Am hoping to send in a brief bleat on the Jameson piece, confining my complaints to the charge of faulty reporting.

The Rutgers savant is still after me to do a one-term Burke-on-Burke job, but I doan wanna make up my mind about anything, at least not several months ahead. And I had vowed ne'er again to take on a regla class.

But I desist, I talk too much.

Holla!
K.B.

Andover
May 11, 1978

Dear Billions,

Helndamnaysh, bob seemed oke when I saw him (April 23). I must write him pronto. (I believe I may be able to dig up his home address, perhaps not). Does everything just go *down* in history? And what a dismal consoler I am ... Here's hoping all's well, by now.

Meanwhile, yes, I'd be glad to have you have at me, anent the selections for the Sin-Ballix. But I don't think that the appearance of some parts in the collected volume, LSA, makes much difference. I intend to do a bit of editorializing, referring to many things that could be included in SM for *one* fragmentary reason or *another.* For instance, the quote from Darwin (C-S, pp. 160-161) could well be recalled, at this late date, and with but slight restatement with regard to my comments. (Perhaps I should refer to Stanley Aitch's tugging-at-the-leash along those lines in *The Tangled Bank.*) I was thinking generally of noting how, ideally, I'd split the subject-matter into two aspects of identity, or character: the "equations" of the poem as poem and the "personal equations" of the human individual in his nature as citizen and taxpayer. Among the texts I wanted to mention in that later regard would be Phil Young's book on Hemingway (with perhaps, in the appendix, an article that I wrote on "A Clean, Well-Lighted Place," but never got around to typing up for publicaysh). The problem of the shift btw. the two kinds of identity comes to a focus in my *Hudson Review* article on "Symbol and Association." (One wd. be under "Poetics," the other under "Ethics." Here my term "Attitude" wd. burst forth grandly, as the specifically human midway pernt twixt Motion and Action—yes? no?)

But I do very much want to hear wherein you agree or disagree, with corresponding suggestions along the way. All told: Grammar ("substance," the universal modes of placement); Rhetoric ("identification," centered in partisan relationships); Symbolic ("identity," unique bundle of equations, but there are the ov'er-all "laws" of such uniqueness, ptikly with regard to rules of thumbs as to what we should look for, how, and why; here even a morbidly "split" personality would be treated as a "unit," with internal motives inclining to be "perfectly" at war).

I'm scheduled to get a plane back at 5:10 PM Friday. Might we work in something btw. 12 o'clock and then? (It looks to me as though my school-work ends at 12.) There would be certain advantages if I postponed that departure until the next morn, owing to a damned awkward schedule late at night on the Andover end of the line. It's conceivable that I might shift the time, if the company would agree, and if you could let me have a comfortable chair to recline in for the night (in my work clothes, a kind of sichaysh I have often managed during my travels) and my presence wouldn't interfere with your reborn trysts. That all could be negotiated when I get there.

Meanwhile, characteristically, I have replaced a letter from a friend anent a book entitled somethinks like *Poetics* (Poetry?) *and* (or) *Sociology.* I gather the gent says he is thinking along my lines, or some such. Do you know of same. I have written asking for more details.

I'm scheduled to arrive at O'Hare on Wed., May 17, Leaving Newark 7:00 PM, Chicago 8:21, United Flight 117. Griffin and his pal are to meet me. It occurs to me that that info might somehow fit in with your modus vivendi.

At least, bejeez, them lads is doing this thing right—and if I flopsy-mopsies, it's my own godam fault.

Recd. nice letter from Roig, who apparently survived the rigors of the tangle here, on my arrival back. Also, he tells me that he has been in touch with Susini (who has written me that he has been about to suffer my RM). E pur si muove, or something like that.

Beginning tomorrow, I'm to spend my time (for my public talk at NWern) trying to sum-up my year of summings-up by beginning with the gist of Motion/Action, turning next to the gist of Theo-Logos, thence to the entelechial drive that comes to a focus in a would-be total *anthropomorphizing* of nature (brilliantly accelerated by modern technology), whereupon, lo! there arises the Realm of Counter-Nature (an ironic vision quite fitting for a guy who began with a book entitled Counter-Statement). I must be careful not to drop dead precisely then, e'en though such a formally perfect act would do for me and my doctrine precisely what Herostratus hoped to do for Herostratus by burning down the temple, and what all our poor poets, and poetesses, and poetasters, and poetostriches aim at when, by killing their selves, they attain whatever immortality it is, to become for a time a subject of conversation at cocktail hour.

I ache,
K.B.

Lingerlag 07821
VI/9/78

Dear Billions,

Wayne Booth phoned me yestiddy—said he had recently co-verbal-
ized with you.

When you move on, let me know exactly whither.

I have written a far-too long uncorking anent the Jameson item. I'm
planning to submit it, with understanding that the editors can cut it. I
wanted to say it all; but after getting it said, I don't feel the pressure to
publish it all. I got interested in the enterprise because it sharpened the
diff btw. an approach via Dramatistic Logology and analysis via Marx-
inspired critique of Ideology. In sum, my way of dividing things arrives
at a statement like my critique of Darwinism (which, in making the
choice purely btw. nature and the supernatural, underplayed the role of
symbolicity, which is neither supernatural nor reducible to natural motion). In the same way, Marx's flat reversal of derivation (the choice being
btw. Hegel's unfolding of the Absolute Idea in nature-and-history and
the evolution of nature-and-history being reflected in ideology) deflects
accurate treatment of the middle realm as a power in itself, regardless
of how it arose. As a matter of fact, the adjective "dialectical" by which
Marx modifies the noun "materialism" smuggles in the needed function
ambiguously. (Incidentally, on the side I'm piling up some notes for my
twirp anent counter-nature, with much anecdotal illustrations, but the
attendant machinery being entelechial principle, fallacy of instrumen-
talism, the human organism's progressive "anthropomorphizing" of the
nonsymbolic ground by bringing it, in one way or another, within the
realm of symbolicity—an over-all human Purpose which could also be
called a Compulsion. That wd. be asking Schopenhauer to move over.)

And —— would you will willing to consider being an executor of
my litry remains? I'm having Butchie o'ersee things in re administrative
decisions. But I think you'd be ideal with regard to editorial decisions,
etc., incl. comments, etc. that you might consider relevant. And I'm also
thinking of Ross Altman, around the edges somehow. I hope to get all
such matters definitively settled this summer, incl. a final version of my
Will in general. Would you consent to be Billions Nachlass R.? I have
not said anything to Ross.

Meanwhile, don't forget: I'd welcome any of those notions you have about the Sin-Ballix Motivorum volume, which I want to get to final work on, as soon as I have typed up the Jameson bleat.

And damn, I haven't heard a word of Bobbert Z. I wrote him another letter yesterday. He seemed somewhat subdued when I saw him recently. I guess that that damned business was coming on, partially I suspect in response to vexations of his job.

How goes?
K.B.

Han gin gon 07821
VIII/7/78

Dear Billions,

The latest Newsletter of the Chicago Nat. Hum. Inst. tells of your hunnert pp. anent my sickly Selph. Here's hoping that somehow we can find some time to talk over all them things generally.

And I liked the nice tribute to your Ms. Barbara Fields.

Here's hoping that your tangles, if not getting ironed out, are at least getting ironed down.

I continue my temporary sojourn in the ancient Chinese citadel of Han gin gon, a genuine survival from the early days, when gunpowder was still used but for fireworks.

Meanwhile, I wonder if it would be convenient for you to send a copy of my Theo-Logo pages to:

> Professor Lee Thayer
> Division of Humanities
> University of Wisconsin-Parkside
> Kenosha, WI 53141

I gotta start negotiating with him about some verbalizing I'm to do at the U. of Houston, come Oct. And I'll probably be using part of that. (Incidentally, it now seems definitive that the piece is to be published in the first (December) issue of the gazette redivivus.

Butchie will be leaving soon now for Canada, so I'm quite on the Slope of Glum-Glum. And in trying to do some pages of tribute on Matty Josephson I have stirred up the depths of my morbid memories, with the damnedest dreams—for I'm almost immobilized.

Yet the genius of technology still pulsates in me somehow. Hence, even while immobilized in Han Ging On on the Slope of Glum-Glum, I wanly closing-phase thus:

> Yours for the principle of an ever-more
> cost-effective ideology of biofeedback,
> K.B.

I'd be nauseatingly grateful if you could give Lee Thayer a copy of that item. (Incidentally, it seems that the Inst. Encyc. of the Soc. Scis. is getting out some kind of new edition, and is including an entry on me. Would that be at least a bit of an excuse for ha ngi ngon? Do you get *Critical Inquiry?* Or do you need a copy of the Burpian Motion/Action routine in the current (Summer) issue?)

When is that Camden deal? Might you swing around here then? —And please tell Betty I hope to catch up soon.

Ever Onwards 07821
VIII/30/78

Dear Billions,

Begad, your case is seeerious. They wrote, telling me so, and asking me what the hell about you. Singing clamorously in they behalf, I tried three times to do so in a letter-perfect letter—then decided that there was no such possibility in me, so sent the third along, with a slight stutter at one point. Here's valiantly hoping, to the greater glory of you, me, and Penn State.

And here's somethinks. This morn I recd. a letter from Christian Susini, whose thesis on *Kenneth Burke et le Dramatisme* (he says that his countrymen will be intrigued by the word "Dramatisme" in particular, and are always partial to isms in general) is up for *soutenance* at the Sorbonne, Sept. 25, 2:00 p.m. He sends me a ten-page summary of his thesis (a copy of which I'll send you, if you are interested, when I have time to get some x-xeroxed).

And binnuz the Theo-Logo bizz won't be out until circa three months later, he asks whether he could see a copy now. I beg of thee slavishly: Could you send him one? Youthfully hoping, wd. say, his address is: Prof. Christian Susini, 11 rue des Capucins, 43000 Le Puy, France. If you are shouldering any costs, spick, and I'll disgorge. His summary tells what he's talking about rather than what he says about it; but his way of doing so convinces me (a) that he knows what he is talking about, and (b) whate'er may be his reservations his attitude is benevolent. His last paragraph divulges thus: En conclusion nous essayons de montrar les prolongements de la réflexion de youknow dans le demaine d'une méditation (I likes the word) sur le langage ainsi que les éclaircissements apportés par le Dramatisme à ce que Paul Ricoeur nomme une sémantique de l'Action. La démarche dramatiste nous paraît, à cet égard, plus pragmatiste. Elle ne s'élabore pas seulement dans la direction d'une sémantique; elle offre plutôt les prémices d'une recherche plus vaste, l'amorce d'une synthèse dont notre temps a le plus grand besoin. And he quotes in English, anent Lévi-Strauss, my avowal that "all his terms are on the 'action' side; he has no words for 'motion'." I'll plead that my motion-action dichotomy is pragmatic, empirical, not metaphysical (it wd. be the same whether the world metaphysically is all "idea" or all "matter," or even all in my own head); but I can expect to go on getting pushed around about that, for I myself admit that metaphysics is in our blood and bones. ... I also like it how he puts togidda both my part and my frank deals with the best of collaborators, from away back.

I felt purty gloomy this morn. And then comes Frenn C. Susini's epistle. So I feel as though it's worth hanging on for another day.

Did I say? Critical Inquiry is printing, sans omissions (I agreed to make such if asked) my Reply to Jameson. I also sent a copy to Hayden White. Do you know anything of J's forthcoming book? Has it forthcome? I'm tremenjously interested in seeing how his use of the term "ideology" exactly fits and misfits with my uses in C-S and RM. And I'm so vexed that I have lost my notes on the passage in a letter by Marx to his publisher (it was printed in the edition youenz guys were using, of the XVIII Brumaire) saying *exactly* what his contribution to the theory of the class struggle was. I wanted to press it, you wouldn't help me, and now I've lost even the quotation.

Otherwise, rejerce,
K.B.

as from
The Copesmithery
Lingerlag Lane
Clutchers Gulch 07821
X/24/78

Dear Billions,

Heck, no. Me no Srong Silent Man. Me be verbalizing like cwazy. But though I'm 81, I still remember the Compelling Empire of Young Love. So I have taken it for granted that history must stagnate for a while in your areas.

As for the disposal of myself this wint, though various fragmentary possibilities have turned up, nothing for the whole season looms. So, for all I know, I may drag on here. Who knows? Certainly not I.

In the meantime, I have decided that what I'd most like to do for book-publishing purposes would be, not the Sinballix, but a third *general* book (like PLF and LSA). I think of some such title as "Constitutions—Behind-the-Constitution," though that may be overly local to my nomenclature. I keep looking for a suddenly looser way of say it.

I had nearly everything I wanted to include. It was, to the best of my memory, all in one carton. And looking, I find that much is missing—and that's one hell of a thing to find. It can all be reassembled, but would involve one devilishly much work xeroxing in some big library. I'll show you and Bob Zachary the list—and maybe among us we can assemble the lot without much anguish.

You meantion doing somethinks on Whitman. Do you know my references to him in that "Towards Looking Back" piece I published in *Journal of General Education?*

The recent (Autumn) issue of *Critical Inquiry* winds up its articles on Metaphor with a 40-line "Doctrinal Strain" of mine (à la Platonic myth). I'll send you a copy when my reprints arrive.

May your turbulencies ease up before not too long. Meanwhile, please hand on to your sons these solemn words of proverbial wisdom from their Uncle Ignatz:

Always Face Reality

Be better than
those tips of icebergs that

like ostriches
with five-sixths
(or is it seven-eights?)
of themselves submerged
hide what their head
should admit to itself
in the sand ...

It looks just about definitive that my Theo-Logo item, along with my "Invocation for a Convocation" (a one-page "Doctrinal Strain"), is to appear in the first (Winter) issue of Kenyon Review redivivus.
Still somehow, like a damfool, hoping somewhat,

K.B.

as from
The Copesmithery
Lingerlag Lane
Clutchers Gulch
I/15/79

Dear Billions,
Here's hoping that your silence indicates happy involvement in your Progress Towards Avanti.
Me, I won't bother you with my bellyaches.
But herewith the Definitive Response to Jameson. As you will see at a glance, most of it was but a waste of time, except insofar as I necessarily seize opportunities to combat the Quietus. But please do read the paragraphs I have marked on pp. 414-416. As you probably know, that's what I'm building around now.
Also, I'm quite involved in the *Psychoanalysis and Language* volume (edited by Joseph H. Smith, Yale U. Press).
And I have recd. a copy of Susini's thesis (L'Oeuvre Critique de Kenneth Burke: Langage et Logologie). O'er six hunnert pp. - quite a workout. I shall write him in homoeopathic doses.
Meanwhile, come this Wednesday, I'm to attempt a trip to NYC (Plaza Hotel, for lunch in auguration of *Kenyon* revivivus). The first number, just due, begins with my "Invocation for a Convocation" attitudinizing, and ends on my Theo-Logo bizz. I am also vaguely expected to somethinks at lunch, and am still uneasily trying to decide what.

Maybe clowning would be best, since then I might be forgiven? How does clowning line up with cloning?

Ennihow, let us know some day that you are going

AVANTI,

K.B.

Tell the young gents that Uncle Ignatz has beautified his Inspirational Poem thus:

> Always face reality
>
> Don't be the mere tip
> of an iceberg that,
> like the ostrich
>
> with five-sixths of the self
> (or is it seven-eighths?)
> submerged,
>
> hides his, or her
> head in the sand …

Note also that the improved version takes care of possible feminist resistances to my earlier version -

Back at the Old Stand
II/21/79

Dear Billions (amongst megabillions of troubles),

Jeezoos, youenz settlers *do* confront a lot of unsettlednesses. I'm sorry indeed. Here's hoping things will ease up.

My trip to San Francisco and Asilomar turned out purty good. The principle of individuation that me and Tommy Aquinas worked out between us (him doing it theology-wise and me logologizing it) is proving to be an excellent way-in to my Tangle of Implications. And my poesy-reading was as successful as my December show at NYU.

But there was one amusing contretemps. On the occasion of a banquet at Asilomar, I sat on a dais with fifteen others, looking down upon the tables of the hoi polloi. The two middle dignitaries were the Governor of the State and Ignatz de Burp. I sat on His Right. During the entire meal, He talked to the Lady on His Left, and never so much as acknowledged my existence. The whole show was in honor of Gregory Bateson, whom I had come to join in the honoring of. He is a quite gracious guy whom I have known from quite some years back and it's my suspicion that he told the Organizeress to put him next to his wife on one side and me on the other, whereas the Guvnr had wanted them on both sides of him. Bateson, by the way, is dying of cancer—and it is astounding how blithely (on the surface, I'm naturally inclined to think) he takes it. Cancer of the lungs—he was a chain smoker. Light up. (I was a chain smoker, up till about forty years ago. I guess it's alky that is hurrying me on my way. But though it has tricked me into quite a few costly blunders, it also helped me a lot, whereas tobaconism was just a damned nuisance.)

The freezing rains set us in the middle of a glacier, even to the extent that the wheels of the car were as though set in concrete, and had to be gouged out (the floor of the garage being several inches deep in ice). Howe'er, at least I got a good poem out of it, and I'll send you a copy when I get some more xeroxed. Theme: "Age in the grip of Ice."

The feed-line from the kerosene tank to the boys' room has got clogged, so that's all closed off. Also, I have abandoned the upstairs entirely, and am sleeping in the bedroom downstairs. And whereas I always thought that the expression "a dirty old man" had moral implications, I can assure you that all it means is: "an old man who lets his house get dirty and needs a bath." (Fortunately my trip West got me out off that groove for a bit, but now that I'm back, who knows? What is the difference between being in a rut and being in a state of B9 Continuity?)

> As the felluh says,
> AVANTI (typed upside down)
> K.B.

[Letter typed on the back of a copy of C. Susini's letter to K.B.]

From the same ole severe
monastic cell
IV/5/79

Dear Billions,

Greetings to Lover Boy from Old Man Envy, who at least can congratulate himself that he suffers from other entanglements, though in any case we necessarily live but in the sign of Unfinished Bizz.

T'other side is self-explanatory. The writer's name is Christian Susini. I do hope that you'll feel inspired to bubble forth with all sorts of suggests. (I've had good luck in the two Frenchmen who have chosen to get involved in my line. The other, Charles Roig, is in the Dept. of Political Science, U. of Geneva. He features my stuff on Constitutions, which all you local yokels don't dare touch. And recently he sent me a 20-page article subtitled "Leninist Dialectic Seen From the Point of View of you-know's Dialectic." And Youknow is purty happy to be associated with it, which is to be in a Moscow conference on political science.)

Christian S. piled up a voluminous doctoral thesis on Knowknow, Language and Logology (near 600 pp. in all, though XXX of them are a transcript of what we said back and forth in the presence of his Cassette—and they are in English). It is indeed a job to be grateful for, though I've been so godam run-ragged with Unfinished Bizz, I have but found the time to sample it random-wise. But everywhere I look, that guy knows what he's talking about, and what I'm talking about. And we'll all be in, unless you have by now moved on.

Ennihow, with love to all,
K.B.

Still somehow clinging on - 07821
V/12/79

Dear Billions,

Recently returned from four oratings at the U. of Cincinnati. I'd rate the two (midday) ones as infelicitous, the two (evening) ones as grounds for feeling good about.

Meanwhile, your silence e'en to the extent of not returning my self-addressed and stamped postcard with the requested info anent the whereabouts of Hayden White causeth me no slight uneasiness. For I take it that, busy as though mightest be, the info could have been tossed off—unless thou art supervexingly involved, or perhaps did not e'en receive my letter. The latter possibility wd. be a considerable cause for distress for it contained a poem which I'd hate like cwazy to have fallen into alien hands (I mailed it to your office address—if I don't get an answer from this one I'll scrounge around and find your new home address, which is in one of your letters). And by all means, I must fear e'en more if you did receive it and are exceptionally entangled.

As for me uddawise, I somehow get the feel of going into a new (and doubtless FINAL, short of total senility) phase, beset by an evermounting sense of ever-mounting incompetence, along with, every once in a while, a neater way of saying something for a line or two (this sentence not being an ideal example of what I think I mean, unless maybe alas! it's only too accurate an instance).

But that effort leaves me exhausted, so I desist, and take this through the frail drizzle (make it "dim drizzle"?) to the mailbox.

Best luck to thee and thine,
K.B.

Andover
August 26, 1979

Dear Billions,

It looks as though, if I survive that long, I'll be at the MLA meetings this December. Norman Holland asked me to join the "Self in Writing Forum," Dec. 28. And I understand that there's to be one on De Burp's Rhetoric and Logology on the evening of that same day. Just now, I admit, I don't feel as though I'll last till sundown. I don't think 'twas the Alky that directly did me in—but it led me to be careless of my eating.

In just a few days now, Butchie will be leaving. I almost wince at the thought. I grow older and gloomier by the minute.

I have slapped out quite a batch of notes towards my three public talks at Buffalo (in month-middles of Sept., Oct., Nov.) But now I have to whip up the old nag, for the typing and arranging. And I'm gettn tired, I'm gettn tired.

Meanwhile, let joy be unconfined,

K.B.

Andover
Sept. 4, 79

Dear Billions,

Helndamnaysh, I'm sorry that the turbulence keeps on having
turned into disturbance in that "Country Full of Swedes." That's tough.
I wisht I knew how to be of some help. I wrote you a letter suggesting
that youenz all, incl. Betty and Barbara, come down for a Grand Conference, with the idea of seeing whether it might be possible to bust the
malign continuity that seems to be perpetuating itself out of itself, and
mainly to the end of maintaining a tradition or some such—then undid
same. (It had seemed so wonderful, but it all came out of a bottle.)

As for my doings at Buffalo, I am (was) scheduled to appear on the
17th, but I hadn't yet heard the date of my talk. In fact, I don't know
from nothin. Some time ago I recd. a full statement of the conditions. I
wrote accepting same—and I have heard nary a further word.

I assume that I'll be hearing soon, binnuz Labor Day is such a notable moment of change in most Academic shedyuls.

Meanwhile, like the whole world, I'm running low on feck—and
even talk of synfuels, despite the sound of the term, doesn't stir me any
more than, at my age, out-and-out porn could.

Ennihow, rejerce.

Avec Universal Liebe,
K.B.

Andover
November 26, 1979

Dear Billionth,

A miserable day, and me alone with my sickly selves. But at least,
when Unk and his Julie were here Thanksgiving-Sunday, they recovered
a room that had been a hopeless wreck—and now it looks entrancing.

The doings at Buffalo are done, though there are still left-overs to
be disposed of. I think I sharpened some of my positionosities whereby
I can more directly and assertively ask: "Just what does it mean if an
animal that grows through nine months of total wordlessness, is born
totally wordless, and then gradually learns an arbitrary conventional
symbol-system, beginning with some equivalent breast-feeding?"

. . .

Some hours later. A guy came who would interview me. Then came the need to open a can of tuna, listen to the news, etc., and now 'tis 9:30 P.M. Also Tim Crusius lingered here for a couple of days, while his wife and her brother saw some of the sights in NYC. No history was made.

I do grow considerably a-gloom.

...

Next morn. Brightnsunny, but more dullness on the way.

Do write and tell me that things are improving, in re your family-vexations.

Me—so far I envision no way of making do with the first ten-week stretch of the New Year, so I may end by being right here, gambling on the chawnst that this winter won't be so damned mean as last year's was. I have plenty to busy myself with and about. In the immediate future, I must prepare my talk for the 28th, in San Francisco, also write some new forewords or afterwords for the U. of Cal. Press editions of P&C and ATH. And my three talks at Buffalo shd. be FINALIZED, along with several incidental obligations. (I don't know when the session takes place at which the body of my work is to be anatomized at the MLA sessions. I enclose a postcard in the hopes that, in case you know, you divulge same.)

Logologico-polygraphically thine,
K.B.

LETTERS
FROM
1980 TO 1987

Andover
January 6, 1980

Dear Billions and Billions,

Please do tell thy pals for me how grateful I am for their worryings about me.

But when asked to say something, here's what I shouldof said:

> You can't know what it is to be a mussed-up guy like
> I'M, sitting there listening and wanting to chime in
> at almost every sentence, with a comment around the
> edges of what got said. And through it all, I was inter-
> ested in how (as it seemed to me there the first time
> I heard your placement of something or other) you
> sometimes seemed to get there by a route different
> from mine—yet all to the good.

But that should have been ongra noo; for there we'd have been wash-ing quite clean linen in public, and that wasn't the kind of conference that should turn up at the last minute, and with Lanham gone besides.

So I improvised two dodges.

(1) How sweet it was to hear the Selph discussed so friendly-like. (2) I confessed as to how the principle of "sacrifice" first engaged me in a big way when I had ten cents to spend for fun, and I had to choose between ice cream and beer, my choice of either involving my sacrifice of the

other. Whereat the "entelechial principle" leads (as per religion, tragedy, etc.) to the "perfecting" of such trade, for trade is the essence of them all (binnuz if sans trade, then no communicaysh), at least where going beyond borders is concerned). But the "perfecting" angle I dint mention, for that's too ongtra noo for introducing it out there.

Thy Betty turned up. I had to dodge her at first, in connection with other jobs. But I owed her some personal communing of some sort. And when the opportunities offered, I tried to get in touch with her by phone, six calls in two days. No luck. The poor woman knows that I'm on your side, yet I did not dodge her for that reason, since I have great respect for her problems, too. I did see her after my talk; but our definite dates had to be later, and that's when things fell apart, through no fault of our eithers'. I wrote assuring her that I had had at least seven hours for us to share, but she probably doesn't know how sorry I am (through a deal of my own) for both sides of all such controversies (and I could make a good accusative case presenting what a shit I was in my rebirth).

There's a cwazy poem I wanna send you, about my decision to stay here this wint. But I must delay until I go to the County liberry, maybe as much as two gallons of gas away. And the effusion also happened before I recd. news on the basis of which I may end up basking at least as low down as Atlanta.

Good!

K.B.

Andover
March 6, 1980

Dear Strong and Silent,

Nearly nine of my TEN DAMNEDST WEEKS for this year are over, but sans any of the horrors that beset me last year, though the one sizable snow was enough for the County Snowplow to rip up my mailbox.

I write you because I just recd. a note from Susini, who writes sending me a list of the articles anent my Sickly Selph he has assembled for the RANAM issue (I don't know the gazette, but I apparently should)—and I grieve to note that no Billions R. is among same.

For my part, I hope to write a kind of epistolary item discussing some notions that occurred to me in connection with Wayne Booth's pages in his Critical Understanding volume.

Greatly depressed with the discovery of my frightfully increasing inefficiency, I confess that the pages I hoped to do for the new edition of P&C (U. of Cal. Press) still dangle. I had promised myself that by now I'd have gone ahead and be finishing up my pages for the new edition of ATH.

Also, I grow more garrulous. Everything spins into a volume, so that I have to throw the whole godam thing away and start o'er.

How go things with youenz? I saw Betty at the MLA meetings, but things didn't work out very well about a meeting. By the time I was free enough to arrange somethinx, she seemed to have vanished. At least I phoned her six times sans to get an answer. I wrote her an apology, but I fear she may hate me.

Did you get things settled about your book for Bob Z? And do you know whether anything ever happened with regard to the volume that was being assembled anent me? Or were there two? Or is there none?

Here's hoping that your vexations anent the fambly are easing, have eased vastly.

I have plans for sessions (quickies) at Gainesville and Notre Dame, but no others. And I hope to write up my Buffalo talks. (One of my troubles with the new pages for P&C is that the material of my Buffalo exercising keeps intruding. Damnear everything I ever think of fits in somewhere.)

Say somethinx.

Best luck,
K.B.

Andover
July 2, 1980

BILLIONS!

Could you perchawnst help me?

When I attended those sessions in Chicago (so many stages in history have happened since then!), youenz all were using a paperback copy of The Eighteenth Brumaire (International Publishers) which contained the copy of a letter from Marx to his publisher. In it Marx said that his ptikla contribution to the cause was not the lore of class struggle, English bourgeois economists had contributed that. His contribution was in showing the inevitable triumph of the proletariat, thence the step from dictatorship to the class society.

Then at Buffalo I got a xeroxed copy of that letter, but it is where?

Is it possible that you have a copy, and could send me a xeroxed copy? And could you and would you? And get it to me, for sure, not later than July 10? (I'm scheduled to fare forth to Notre Dame on the eleventh, and I'll need the item there.)

Have been much entangled, but still dare hope that I'll get things in tolerable order. (I have gone from the state of gridlock, to a still worse one of gridlockstepping, but now I'm in hopes of gridlock-stepping-out. As soon as I get the Notre Dame sessions out of the way, I hope to trim up, quite quickly, my Last Words, "In Retrospective Prospect," for the new U. of Cal. Press editions of P&C and ATH. I have written bbls. of first-drafts, at least 150 pp., but things always got tangleder and tangleder. But I now see a way of quickly hitting the high spots, jes that.)

I e'en 'gan seeing double for a while—literally. But changed some of my habits, and now I have the great joy of looking down the road and seeing just one car coming. It's a truly ecstacatic expeeerience.

> Best wishes to all, and
> hoping that all is clearing
> up,
> K.B.

> Andover
> July 31, 1980

Dear Billions,

After a fashion I do dare believe that my doings at Notre Dame were the Crossing of a Divide. And the reports are all to the good, towards backing me up. I'm now on a slope away from Gridlock.

But there are many Steps Along the Way. One is to discuss thy MS, for which I am grateful indeed, but I am uncertain also on many pernts, binnuz I doan think that I'm the guy to say whether others go along avec.

I wanna talk over many details. Any chawnst that you could swing down hither sometime during Dawg-Daze? Nacherly your austere silences don't help much, but I must assume that you know your business.

At this here moment, just now, I'd like to askyuh this:

Did I send you, or do you have, or can you locally locate a copy of the now defunct Psychocultural Review (Winter 1979) containing my artikkel "Symbolism as a Realistic Mode: 'De-Psychoanalyzing' Logologized"? You are entitled to disagree with me, but at least you should state my statement of the case, as you decidedly do not. Then you could proceed to prove me wrong. But as things now stand, you are simply telling the world the wrong story about me and the from-the-top-down, from-the-bottom-up theory of language as a motivational realm in its own right. Smattera fack, you got me scairt; for if you still see it your way, you've missed the whole point of my distinction between homo sapiens and the "symbol-using animal." From-the-bottom-up is Marxist naive-verbal-realism. If you agree with that position, then your dooty is to ATTACKT me.

I'm scairt because your presentation is piece-meal, as thus considered, sans the basic pernt about symbolicity as a realm of motive in its own right, regardless of its derivation. We aint just bodies that learned language. We happened to learn a kind of medium that behaves in its own way, and our quotes "minds" are entangled with that miraculous instrument. The distinction btw. words and Word is on the way, but with regard to the whole story, I felt that you o'erdone the Word angle. In the meantime, for Gawsake, at least try to locate that gazette. (It's now defunct, and maybe my artikkel killed it.) I had several copies, but they have disparooed. Howe'er, the nature of things has left me with one. And I can send you a xeroxed copy, if your resources of research fail in your areas.

Each of us after a fashion has been trying to extricate from somethinx or other. Indications are that things are easing up for both of us, correspondingly somehow. But to an extent we gotta improvise about this bizz, and also I caint afford, either moneywise or timewise (I'm gettn older by the minute, and still trying to hurry up and get things cleared away with regard to MSS around the house), to neb much in this job— for your job is one that, for the best relations between the two of us, I shd. certainly neb out of. (Oof! mebbe I'll get a copy of this unexpected letter xeroxed, and send same to Bobbert.)

Yes,

K.B.

Andover
August 10, 1980

Dear Billions,

Dern the luck, I can well unnerstand your desire to slap it out and relackuss. My battles with a kind of Octogenarian Gridlock (when everything I started out to say "In Retrospective Prospect" gets in its own way, and in trying to write twenty pages, I have already thrown away more by far than you offer DEFINITIVIZED, and Punktum), said doings of mine in grid-lockstep doubtless ... etc. I mean, I'm nowhere yet, as regards my intended twenty.

It's a morbid sichaysh—and binnuz you are now clear of you personal one (and felicitations indeed, to youenz both, with best of goodwill towards all the others), I grant that you are totally entitled to say your say as you already saw fit, and ptikly inasmuch as I can spare neither the time nor the effort to neb in.

Yours is a gracious statement—and you have my thanks indeed. All we need do is leave it as what it is; namely: your considered Last Words concerning some of my near-to-last words. Written as a Baedeker, it might e'en require, not just revision, but Later Words to do with some of the earlier items as originally commented on. But there, obviously, I'd be visiting upon you the curse of my senescence, whereas you are rearing to have gone.

My latest crisis is likea dissa: The tripartite design of P&C is obviously: Unity-Disunity-Reunity, or Orientation-Disorientation-Reorientation. But what exactly make of the fact that the middle section shifted from the Orientation set to Perspective (by i.)? A very lot, happened indeed! So much so, in fact, that (as I interpret the implications of p. by i.) the Intermediate Stage is only now full upon us. As per my notions anent the self-perpetuating nature of Technology-produced Counter-Nature, even the attempts to control Technology must resort to more-and-better Technology; and Environmentalism is but Technology's best Self-Criticism.

Meanwhile, damnit, I've been going back over Nietzsche's Wille zur Macht, the whole tangle of analogical extension and perspective by incongruity coming to a pre-focus in his subtitle anent the "transvaluation of all values," which leads into my section on "Metabiology," with references to Strachey and Lawrence, all, heck—hence into my Last Words on just what happens when language that begins in word-magic, myth, poetry, priestcraft leads finally to the slaying of all that as per computer-ology, nsech—or does it?! What drops out? What but gets transformed? I hold that to be the final solemn (and often hilarious, usually but clinical) speculations of Logology anent the anthropomorphized by-products of Counter-Nature's "unintended by-products." The whole ranging perhaps from recording of the deepest emotions as per Biblical assumptions that at such times the bowels are moved, to new substitutes for what was once technically known as the "fear of God" (while we have in mind the fact that, just before his book ends, Nietzsche's neo-infantilism comes to fruition in vague restorations of pagan DIVINITY)! Incidentally, on the side, every once in a while there is a fragmentary axiom that reminds me of my last chapter in TBL (which I wrote when I was much in his groove somehow), but where my Representation was cracking up, his was becoming more and Aristocratic. Oof! For I do believe that my borrowings from him as per the middle section of P&C were right (also incl. the many incidental ones throughout TBL). I avoided the worst by admitting to myself that I'm a mutt (but, psst! a mutt-with-a-twist—so maybe I'm trying to sneak in the same way after all).

Ah, heck,

K.B.

When I came to that show of yours in Chicago, there was a guy the week before who irritated your assembled company. Do you remember his name? Was it some name like Lasch? I ask because there's a guy of that name who did a trick review of Cowley's last book. What Cowley told about himself simply as facts, the reviewer repeated, but saying the same things with a stinko slant. (Incidentally, I slavishly read all the subsequent reports of that year, having been assured by you that I could be happy, binnuz the time there did turn out quite well, I thought. But I shall go to my grave remembering how badly I showed, as compared with all them great guys that Ned Rosenheim o'ersaw. I could have had the solace of having read about what all them great minds said—but damn the luck, I've forgot it all. The curse of age.

Next morn: shame on me—mere petty irritability here took over

Andover
Hallowe'en, 1980

Dear Billions,

An ideal day for writing letters.

Also, it looks as though I may be briefly in your environs, within a coupla weeks or so. So, wouldst kindly send me your phone number, on the chaunst that we might commune a bit?

I'm to be thereabouts in connection with a bit of surgery (minor, I dare hope). I don't know exactly what the arrangments will be. Tentatively, Butchie will be piloting me there and back. A hernia that I had managed to live with for years started acting up (after a fantastic several days of acute diarrhea). So a decision had to be reached, e'en by glumly Undecisive Me. And Watson has suggested a likely solution.

I forgot whether I told you: I shall probably EXcape the TEN DAMNEDEST WEEKS here this wint, by going to Atlanta (Emory), though the stipulations are still in need of specification. Not teaching, but rather co-meditating, nsech, I think.

My talk at Notre Dame went well. My Poesy Reading and (in the evening of the same day) my Talk, at the U. of Maryland went exceptionally well. Title: "Bodies that Learn Language," the trick being that that formula allows for three loci of motives (Bodies, Language, and the Learning, which combines two kinds of infancy, not just the step from total speechlessness, but also the step from maximum immaturity, with both kinds leaving their mark). Nay more, a Fourth locus enters and takes over, owing to the relation btw. symbolic action and Technology. The mythic step from Nature to Supernature (be it so or not) has here the empirical step from Nature to Counter-Nature (as determined by the productions of symbol-guided Technology). Could anything be more damnably trim?

An immediate vexation is that I keep deciding and redeciding (with much throwing away and repeating what I threw away) just what to say about this in connection with my pages for the new editions of P&C and ATH.

What gives with the RANAM enterprise I know not. What says Susini? Quite some time ago he wrote as though I should already have recd. a copy, but in a later letter makes no mention of my telling him that no such turned up. I have written him again, asking what the heck.

Do you know anything of the Hayden White project? Perhaps he dropped it. Did the deal at Houston fall through? 'Twould probably be better if it did. Can I get attention without either getting caught in a bank robbery or shooting myself?

Maryland sent me a tape of my talk there. If it is clear and not botched, I may ship a copy around. I'll check on it soon. But my distrust of engineers—well, I don't know what to say.

Best to thee and thine,
K.B.

Did you find anything usable or pardonable about the item I sent you, anent symbolicity as a realm of motives in its own right, regardless of materialist or idealist theories of derivation. (Incidentally, there's a sociologist at Maryland, Richard H. Brown, whose book, A Poetic for Sociology, was published by Cambridge U. Press, 1977. As you might well imagine, it overlaps considerably with a book which, on p. 65, proclaims "A Humanistic, or Poetic Rationalization." The major difference is that it parades a whole army of publications which didn't exist when De Burp wrote. (Also, ironically as per my "Dramatism" article in the IESS, I'm laying claim to being literal, along with my ways of using analogy.) If you can get The American Sociologist (Vol. 14, No. 1, Feb. 1979) you'll find an item by him there. Also I note that he has a 1978 publication, "Bureaucracy as Praxis" (Administrative Sciences Quarterly) which could conceivably somewhat parallel De Burp's ATH on "bureaucratization of the imaginative" (which C. Wright Mills went along with, as per his book on The Sociological Imagination). And I've been in contact with two Canadian sociologists (Michael A. Overington and Vito Signorile) who did some nice verbalizings on me, sans my knowing of same. (Signorile also writes for The American Sociologist.) I can't write my Last Words for the P&C and ATH editions because so much stuff of that sort seems to need some kind of treatment—and everything goes askew.

Emory
Feb. 8, 1981

Dear Billions,

Yes, here I am, quite comfortably housed, but there's quite a parking problem on the campus, which I'm beyond moderate walking distance from. So I don't use my car, except for shopping on Sunday morn. (The traffic war here is tremenj.) But there is a student assigned to me as an assistant. He's very competent and willing. Yet there are still morbidities about my placement, where when, etc., though I've been here for a month. And my tangle of Unfinished Bizz also pursues me, though I did finish the Last Words for P&C, and have got through quite a bit of the writing up of my lecture (part of it given at the U. of Maryland) anent "Bodies That Learn Language. And Bob wants me to hurry with my lastwordings on ATH, so I may have to lay "Bodies" aside for a while. I think he'd like to publish both the reprints at the same time.

Your tangles rebirth-wise, and Malcolm Cowley's healthwise, and our country's economic "mess," all put together almost make me feel not wholly abiturus. But I feel damned problematical, and on principle quite incompetent. And I have no arrow to shoot into the air, though I sure am pushing a rock uphill.

And in trying to help Logology juggle all togidda Plato, Spinoza, Kant, Nietzsche, and K. Burke, Esq., I considerably add to my spells of actual physical dizziness, aided by the gas fumes of the avenues I perambulate on, in absurd attempts to be taking a "constitutional." (If you can get a copy of U.S. News for August 11, read the interview with Jerome Wiesner. He there says it for me on a single page, how Technology is a self-perpetuating, destabilizing way of life, though there's no indication at all that an authoritarian political structure could solve its problems. I rassle with two eschatologies, two sciences of first and last things, two departures from nature: (a) at death, into an imagined world of Supernature; (2) via Technology, empirically, right here on earth, into an actual man-made realm of Counter-Nature.

Deo volente and God willing, I'll be back at And/Or circa the end of March. I had luck on the way down. The guy who drove down with me loves to drive as much as I loathe it, so he drove the whole way (with both of us loving my new VW Rabbit, the contract being that it didn't matter about us, but he must take good care of that car). All went perfectly, except that every once in a while, when gesturing during a discussion, he took both hands off the wheel. That made me scairt.

My Boss tells me that he has, and is going to show me, a book by one Janet Brown, Feminist Drama (Scarecrow Press, 1979) whereby I am enlisted in the cause of feminism. I don't recall any theoretical pronouncements of the sumjick. I wonder if it's in my verse or stories.

Best to thee and thine,
K.B.

Andover
June 26, 1981

Dear Billions,

It'sgoodtohearfrom same. So I'm slipping this outina hurry. For I've been negotiating with a snake. On the back porch there's a fambly of wrens, gettn noisily ready to fare-forth. And there's a snake. I won't tell you the story about how I got hold of the snake and then fell off balance, and then in trying to right myself I let go the godam snake. And I dint scare the animal away, and it's back again. I'm trying to make Papa and Momma Wren understand that I'm on their side, this side the kill unless it's absolutely necessary. I 'gin suspect that the snake has an idée fixe; and e'en though I might frustrate it all day today, it'll do its appointed job before I awake tomorrow morn. (Hold! Of a sudden I note that all is quiet. No. they're chirping. They haven't got the signal to SHUT UP.) In the meantime, by heck, I've written a good paragraph on the difference btw. transformation and abolition.

And only yesterday, I got news-of-the-death of the woman towards whom, in the back of my mind, and totally sans scandal, I had all these years especially loved the name of Florence. And in my anti-novel I had done that dear word so dirt, I kept the secret of it from her. A friend's news-clipping tells me that in death she was exactly my age. In recalling her and my profound respect for her, I feel positively pious.

As for your delays publicationwise, don't by any means blame anything on Bob Zachary. Start with me, whose goodluck was the best part of it, yet but added to other impositions from my side—for it's truly a saga to tell of what all I went on slapping out and getting nowhere avec, in my LASTWORDINGS for P&C and ATH. You're fantastically entangled with your family; but we're so close in our thinking, you can slap out anything about me off the top of your head. To this day, while you're wrestling with your Swedes, I'm tangling with godam sentences, just them—and you can tell the world how much better I could write if I could. I think we need us both and there's room for both; but from outside us both, wow! how, in their details, differenz! All told, our books are getting held up mostly because I, whose only slogan is HURRY, HURRY, HURRY, have been tangling with Internal Swedes in the twists and turns that the absurdly simple Last-Wordings for P&C and ATH after all them years.

Yes, I do remember having had good fun co-verbalizing with a guy you say was Henderson, and along them lines, being civilizedlike, avec. and yes, things have been working towards something or other, or maybe e'en two things, in the MLA sessions, where my Fifteen Grand might help, at least by gettn people out or in for a fight. You might get in touch with Mack Rosenthal whom I had already agreed in principle with, about somethingx or other, Symbolickswise.

Tim Crusius is due next Monday. Which reminds me: Yes, the RANAM issue did come out, incl. an artikkl of his—and I hold it against YOU that there's not one in there by ( ). Shits is Shits, and like the Swedes I love you anyhow.

> Hurry, hurry, hurry,
> K.B.

Andover
September 23, 1981

Dear Billions,

Jeez, that fall of thine (which I hadn't realized) sounds hellacious. And then you had a fall into despondency. And now, Godamt, here it is, the first day of Fall.

I'm entangleder as hell, but I owe you a beep. The title, "Prospectus on Kenneth Burke's Works in Progress" has an odd symmetry with these damned everlastingly delayed Last Words I'm writing for P&C and ATH, "In Retrospective Prospect."

I plan (God willing and Deo volente) to be present at the processing of me. (Did you, by the way, ever get in touch with Mack Rosenthal? And I suppose you know that Howard Nemerov is to be there is some role, having got some funds from MLA and his local Dept. to ease the anguish.)

Here's what you could do that would be quite helpful, by the way: Get some of you guys to write Notre Dame English Journal asking when the article by me is to appear, etc. I have already returned Galley Proofs, but the man who was in charge of that project has moved on (going from Indiana in summer to S. Dakota in winter—wow!), and since he left I have heard nary a word. The item ("Variations on 'Providence' ") wd. be quite relevant to the meeting as you describe it.

Meanwhile, I enclose a copy of a thing I sent to Wayne Booth, as a not wholly likely candidate for use in CI. I also enclose a copy of a letter suggesting an addendum. And I enclose a copy of my bow when receiving the Medal cum the Fifteen Grand.

And with regard to my Definition of Us in LSA (as rephrased to dodge the rebukes of the Feminists) memmer that I have inserted (not added; I want to end as before) is "acquiring foreknowledge of death." And that whole project has been further self-occamized by my title, "Bodies That Learn Language," the substance of which I gave in a public lecture at the U. of Maryland circa a year ago, and which I am circa 4/5ths of FINALIZING.

And at least in one sentence, I'm being gallant envers the Gays: "To homo sapiens and homo faber, add homo homosexualis." I sorta feel that that has possibilities, but the bare entitlement is the extent of my vision. But its ingenious etymologically. The homo of the noun is Latin, the homo of the adjective is Greek, with the rest of the word Latin.

Best to thee and thine,
K.B.

There are some guys that taped some interviews with me last Fall. I'll try to learn how that project is faring.

184 Amity Road
Andover
October 3, 1981

Dear Billions,

Wow! Lupus—and you were out there mopping up the sunlight! As I understand it, that you should have scrupulously avoided, from the day you knew you were so inclined. Here's hoping. Bah! our godam vexations.

Me, I doan no whether there's such a word as "abiturient," as in an expression like "abiturient mood, or attitude." But this Fall (yes, Fall, I give up my dodges such as "autumnality"), this FALL is after me in a Big Way.

Uddawise, in quickie style taking up your letter's problems in-the-order-of-their-appearance:

(1) I grieve that you dint cotn to my "Sensation, Memory, Imitation - and Story" exercise in self-occamizing (reducing but, I hope, not beyond propriety). I dint think of it as somethinks new. As per the Addendum (which I forgot to send you and is enclosed herewith), I thought I

had done a neat job in putting those four old-timers togidda, just bing-bing-bing-bing, just like that. But I forgot to send my STATUESQUE finale. In any case, your demurrer helped me point up better the Grand Step from the sensation of something feeling hot to the words, "That feels hot," at which point Story enters the world of what is otherwise wordless nature. I loved the final trimness of it all—and lo! your sluggish response has helped me make it neater, thereby also giving us greater hope to believe that there really may be a God after all.

(2) But you identify yourself in free (?) fancy with a tolling sound, a knell, which in turn is identified with burning and ashes, which in turn—but I hurry on.

(3) I'm still hoping that your book and mine can come out togidda. More on the pernt later, in connection with a different entry.

(4) A favorite graduate student of a pal from away back, Henry Sams, attended Hartman's course which referred to me in the Catalogue. That graciously humane colleague has recently died of cancer (this is Ole Abiturus speaking), but not before reporting that she had gone to take the course with the stout intention of speaking in my behalf, but he had been quite friendly. I have not yet had an opportunity to see his book.

(5) I don't know whether "the Frenchman" filed a copy of his thesis anywheres in the U.S. I have a copy (it's two sizable tomes). And I'm sure that Arminius can give you some leads Germany-wise.

(6) Try Prof. M. L. Rosenthal, Dept. of English, NYU, 19 University Place, NYC 10003. I don't understand why our correspondence is not in the file. And I cannot even imagine some morbid reason why it shd. be missing.

(7) If all goes as planned, I shall mail the finished lastwords anent P&C not later than Monday, Oct. 5. But I do wish that you would re-lent and ask Bob Z. to show you a copy. Perhaps read it en route? There is no haggling with thee at all. What I have been doing (in the cause of Story) is to make my Demise as anecdotal as poss. But my agonies are over—and I can knock of the pp. anent ATH almost totally sans the GRIDLOCK (or rather COUNTER-GRIDLOCK) that has had me enthralled in wrestling with the non-angel of P&C. By COUNTER-GRIDLOCK I mean: Instead of being like in a traffic jam, unable to go backwards, forwards, or sideways, I kept going every-which-way. And I have literally piled upon more than 200 pp more than the pp. I am retaining. And I cd. still go onandon, but I think that I have wangled things in a way whereby I doan needto, for my finisher-upper in ATH.

My prime anecdote there concerns C. Wright Mills's The Sociological Imagination. It's name-droppingly there, but not at all lugged in. And it's a dern shame, but there's an article by an anthropologist in Papua, to be published in The American Journal of Sociology (which published Louis Wirth's humdinger on P&C in your collection), checking on how that text got treated (non-treated, so far as acknowledgement is concerned) over the years since then. You'll also see my artikkel references to two Canadian sociologists who did quite well by me and whom I think you should mention.

But time's up. Best to thee and thine,
K.B.

And do you know anything at all about Howard Nemerov's role in all this MLA biz? He's at 6970 Cornell Avenue, St. Louis, MO 63130, in case you have any interest in communicating avec. I intend to write him about it all soon, but I was hoping to get the lastwords stuff outa the way first. Whereat I repeat: I do most zestfully hope that our doings can come out at the same time. So, I'll be slapping away for about 20 pp. to wrap up ATH (P&C took more than twice that, but its very excesses have eased things for what's left to be done). Incidentally, I plan them for EPILOGUES, perhaps with an introductory note begging the reader not to read the beforehand, and even not then maybe perhaps.

154 Amity Road
(same residence, but a bit more progress-wounded)
November 16, 1981

Dear Billions,

Thine, with its many disgrunts, recd. Welkim back.

Notre Dame English Quarterly has notified me that the issue is scheduled to appear towards end of this month. If it threatens to be delayed much longer than that, I can send you one of my typed copies. I was hoping you'd ask Bob for a copy of the P&C pages. (He hasn't even acknowledged the receipt of them.) Did you see my introductory pages to the RANAM issue? I still intend to do somethinks with that "Sensation, Memory, Imitation / and Story" piece. (I note that CI has an issue on Narrative. And I have a hunch that my prime logological way of drawing the line between the taste of an orange . . . . . . no narrative

and

"the taste of an orange" . . . . . . narrative

will lead to differences throughout. At least you have fired me with a burning ambition to try. My Epilogue for P&C hinges about the notion that whereas it was presented as a tripartite structure, actually the middle section ("Perspective by Incongruity") took over and will never get out as long as technology keeps on expanding the realm of Counter-Nature (as I assume that it will).

Last week was probably the verbalizingest such of all my life (two days at Andover, MASS, four at Terre Haute Indiana, going day and night, avec and sans alky, and surviving surprisingly well, doubtless as a relief from the Return of the Repressed that has plagued my Epilogues for P&C and ATH. (The latter shd. be shorter, only 20 pp., and that's already half done.)

In Indiana I learned that Hayden White's collection is on the way (probably by Johns Hopkins). But the man who said so was astonied to learn that I had not been asked to contribute one word. And Tim Crusius says that the So. Cal. one is on the way (also sans word to me). I must try to get you at least an index of main points in the "Bodies That Learn Language" routine, still in need of both completion and revision. I enclose a bit of local gossip which might interest you, though there's nawthin in it for you (except perhaps the bit in the last four paragraphs).

But time's up.

Love to all,

K.B.

The Graduate Institute of the Liberal Arts
Emory University
Atlanta, Georgia
January 13, 1982

Dear Billions,

As the felluh says, any ill can wind up to sombody's good. In this case, I was scheduled to give my first Seminar today; but the exceptional morbidities of the weather are such that the School has shut down. So I am holed up in my Residence here, and can make at least some effort to catch up with my mail.

FIRST, I owes you great gratitude for undertaking the job of getting that Show together.

I have but one regret. I think that if I had been scheduled to comment (for a certain minimum number of minutes) immediately after each paper, I couldof done much better by youenz guys. As it was, I had to jumble the Response indeterminately to all three, so no one got specifically answered. I couldn't remember the positions clearly enough; the need to hurry on made it impossible for me to ask for specifications; and my notes were too fuzzy for me to take them up in an orderly fashion. To proceed as we did, in my Eighty-Foursies I was not competent to do the job right without having seen the papers in advance and picked out (plus quotation) what I took to be the main point of each. But proceeding as we did, one doesn't do as circumspectly as one could uddawise, ptikly if one is the likes of I'm.

Robert Wess gave me three papers: Two versions of "The Entelechial Motive," one the shorter version of his talk, and one on "History and Rhetoric," (bearing,. Gott segne ihn, on Jameson). I hope to write him about them soon, prombly today. They're good. Any chawnst of my seeing yours and our pal's in Illinois?

My Residence address here is: 827-9 Clifton Court, Atlanta, GA 30322. Phone: 404/321/0464 (private). If you are sending me anything of any size, better send it to the ILA address.

Here's hoping that things are oke about the Swedes. My car got battered a lot, but sans a scratch to me (except to my Psyche, which continues to feel quite humiliated).

I'm sorry that the post-sessional communing with youenz was so brief and nondescript. Do say somethinks, assuring me that everything is alright. If I stop this now, it may go out on today's mail, in case anything goes out on today's mail.

Avec Universal Liebe,
K.B.

Atlanta, GA
January 28, 1982

Dear Billions,

Thanks much for assurances; I droop readily, hence am always in need. Wess gave me two versions of his paper (one long, one short) and a copy of some stuff he did on Jameson. All v.g.

I think the Symbolic has all been published, and merely needs a few editorial connectives. In going back over P&C, I see the lineaments of the stress upon symbolic action "Aristotelian," the "Perspectivism" Kantian (but largely by one of Kant's bad boys, Nietzsche, with Bergson also figuring, and Kant's other bad boy, Marx). The action slant would be ontological, and the perspectivistic slant wd. be epistemological. The latter would later come to a focus in the dualism of the motion-action pair. The Order doings in RR would seem to be in the middle of both.

If you get going on Rhetoric next year in LA, for Gawsake let me give you some leads. I'm probably going to La Jolla circa early June, to pal around with a group there. One, Helene Keyssar, I met when at Pittsburgh. Another, Joseph Gusfield is giving a course on me and writing a book on me. But he's in sociology, and may not be to your fancy. (In fact, I suspect that where you thought my IRP epilogue languishing was when I was dealing with the material in the two issues of The American Sociologist.) And there are some lively ones in San Francisco. But maybe it would make the MLA more like a Teamsters Union, stealing members from other outfits. Incidentally, your mention of Hayden White reminds me that my haggle with the CI people got me to reading On Narrative, which begins with an article by him on Annals, Chronicle, and History proper, and I'm thinking of writing to him about it. For I want to add Eschatology (as either the Christian or Marxist designs), and I'm wondering what he'd say to that. But he never acknowledged the copy I sent him of my Rejoinder to Jameson's article in CI.

Got an exceptionally friendly letter from Wayne Booth, and a typically amusing one from Haitch Nemerov (in connection with his fun-having to do with my getting celebrated at). It ends: "I even had a (one) fan letter anent my posy reading (Nemerov's one-man show) at MLA; it was a charming note, only the chap forgot to detach his booklength manuscript before mailing."

Avec Universal Liebe,
K.B.

I gave my first colloquium yesterday. It got me so stirred up, when I got back to my severe monastic cell I partook of too much medicament. I awoke at 3 A.M., to stay awake until now, 8:51 P.M. the next day. And circa early afternoon, I'll swear, I thought I had made the fatal blunder this time. I felt so damned low, and cardiac.

Andover
March 29, 1982

Dear Billions,

How goes?

My Collig, Don Burks, gave me a copy of these [list of dissertations on Burke attached]. You prombly already have 'em.

I expect to be in Rochester, and may be seeing youenz somewhere along the line. After three days of verbalizing, I'm to get a minor carving job at Strong Memorial Hospital.

The Company is gettn interested in other offerings of mine. I'm interestee in your suggest about a collection of the general artikkels. Wadda yuh say? I've always hankered after using the title, "While Everything Flows" (partly, I think, because when I'm most productive I must leave the typewriter proportionately more often to pee). but obviously, that must be but implicit. How, then, thus: "On Human Relations: A Gathering, While Everything Flows." Or, macaronically, we could give 'em somethinks trivial to talk about (always a shrewd device for the current short attention-span) by saying not "gathering," but "Gatherum," as per "omnium-gatherum."

There's a guy, Bert States, who plugs for a book of my Shakespeareana. I'd like him to do that, and consult with me about the unpublished notes I have on such. I wouldn't fill those out; I'd say simply what I wanted to do but didn't, a good "educational" resource in itself.

And if your godam vexation leaves you inclined to hurry up with me and my impending abiturient predestination, we cd. slap out a contract of that sort, with regard to finishing up that job. (Perhaps e'en requiring of me only a dialogue with thee, anent whatever we might have to consider as still dangling.)

I think that Tim Crusius and I have invested a lot in him with regard to the Oily Boik, and should slap the rest of that togidda.

I glimpse some further feasibilities about other things still but hanging around as a possible Nachlass. I think we could get your frenn Wess interested in some of that. And if things turned at least somewhat as well as they conceivably could when I'm finishing up my tourette this Spring in Lahoya (combining Helene Keyssar's work on my side in Communicaysh with a seminar that Gusfield is giving along the sociology angle). I inclines to feel that, if one other possibility that's in the air materializes, LOGOLOGY is here to stay; and some Shakeable Downable Big Shot in the Transcendent Realm of Money will endow a Chair in Logology

But I subscribe to Lucretius; hence I take it for granted that I'll never be around to worry at all how all that gets botched by the Next Phase. I expect to be in the same Circle of Hell with Charlie Marcus. (Kierkegaard will be in Paradise; but still, without ever having to know it, he'll be looking for a course in Froyd.) And that takes care of birthdays on May 5, except that in principle Charlie and I (despite my great sympathy with him for what the Marxists did to him) we just caint get together. For he wants to (re)volutionize what I just want to (e)volutionize). and that's the hell of it. For neither will work. At least so far I see not the slightest hope either that Technology will (r-e)volve the sociol-political system capable of controlling it, or that at the very least there can ever prevail (as Logology MUST opt for) an educational system designed to help us all teach one another how we're all damfools together, rather than educating one another how to take advantage of one another's tomfoolery. It can't be did—and what with the homisuicidally "advanced" stage of "defense" (grotesque misnomer) now ... but I can't finish that sentence.

Heck. All the time this got loose, I'm trying to hurry up and pack.

Avec Universal Liebe,
K.B.

Andover
June 18, 1982

Dear Billions,

Sure, I expect to be at And/or all summer from now on. so we can arrange a time when Amanda can come out here, too.

I'd like to so arrange things that the Sinballix and Human Relations While-Everything-Flows appear togidda.

My Ten Days at Lahoya were busy-busy-busy in a big way. And I had fantastic living quarters (in a penthouse atop an eleven-story dormitory, with the Pacific my horizon on one side, and right outside my window on the other side on the roof whenever the sun shone sprawled a scattering of bodies, an ideal setting for the definition of us as "bodies that learn language"). On the fourteenth I attended the graduation exercises at Emory, and am now out from behind the eight-ball.

Yes, I have had quite some dealing with Hillis Miller. (Incidently Emory is trying to wheedle him away from Yale.) He has written a sketch of me (with a strongly biographical slant), for some Encyclopedia. And we path-crossed in connection with Hopkins and "logology," which he had agreed to define by.

Let's plan for some time in July.

> Avec Universal Liebe,
> K.B.

> Andover
> July 26, 1982

Dear Billions,

In unseamly haste I wd. depose:

Amanda Mecke phoned. Is all ready to voyage hither, if we give her a few days notice in advance.

Say when.

I expect to be here all along for several weeks at least. Say how long you expect to stay, and I'll let Amanda pick her day within that range.

She tells me I'll be getting proofs for the 1935-37 volumes within a couple weeks.

> Rejerce, just as though there
> were no Regan,
> K.B.

> And/Or
> Nov. 16, 82

Dear Billions,

Heck, doan worry, me no know.

I'm told that the whole biz is being held up because they can't get a second copy of P&C to tear apart. I told Amanda that I found a second P&C copy, but she says it needs a second Bobbs-Merrill one. Bob Zachary writes:

McClung should examine his conscience. They make
capital of your name & go on squandering really big
money on non-entities; this month the Press is giving
a big feed to all comers to celebrate putting out some
archaeological monograph. Est. cost: $20 K; adjunct
to the Muses's diadem: zero. They have been making
some reckless advances, etc.

Meanwhile, dawdle, dawdle, dawdle. I'm told that they must type up
my typescript—yet that, too, lingers. Why? You tell me.

The damfools are gwanna ruin my rhythm, by simply not taking advantage of it. (Or are they at least minded to give your text a drag? My
poetizing and my theorizing, both go over gratifyingly, and even my Ten
Damnedest Weeks, come January, are in the cards, with THREE offers
for next April. (I had some ecstatic days recently at Yale, and have a joyously promising deal looming soon at Amherst.) Every minute when I'm
not dying I'm doing jes grand. (Not just towards 83; I'm also invited to
indenture the Sickly Selph for a deal in 84. Yet, now that Bob Z. is gone,
where next?

Love, love, love, love, love—killkillkillkillkill,

> Holla!
> K.B.

> Groove 154 ... 07821 ...
> xii/8/82

Dear Billions,

My Amherst job, performance-wise went quite oke so far as audience reception went, but one spot may have not been just right for one
of the depts. that joined in subsidizing my One Grand plus expenses.
My "Bodies" angle suggests that just as Marcel Marceau as a mime is all
body, no words, so some litry analysis sees us as all words, no body. Adolescence, in its role as a purely physiological (i.e., nonsymbolic) locus of
motives, is particularly important as a critical stage in the development
of the human hulk that is becoming a votary of the litry vocation. And a
passage in which another Marcel, Proust, was writing about his Marcel's
initiation did not strike me as being analyzed from that point of view
(particularly with regard to the emergent including of the psychogenic
asthma as an integral aspect of symbolic action, his style). My complaint
was that overly an litry characterizing of the passage makes the analyst a

Marcel Marceau in reverse. A burst of applause made me realize that my position had been made to seem more adversary than is the case, to the satisfaction of some other dept. that had pitched in to make up my pay. (However, in a sense I am quite adversary. For I suddenly realized that my view of "symbolic action" in such situations is a variant of the hagglings in connection with my point about the symbolizing of opium's effects in Coleridge's Mystery Poems.)

Incidentally, do you know my essay in Rhetoric, Philosophy, and Literature: An Exploration, edited by Don M. Burks, Purdue U. Press, 1978? Nawthin new, but ptikly towards the end there are some usefully pointed observations, along the lines of the closing pages in the Notre Dame piece. And there's a gratifying essay anent my Sickly Selph in The American Journal of Sociology for July 1982.

How went things with Amanda?

Towards whatever,
K.B.

Emory
Jan. 13, 1983

Dear Billions,

Damn, I'm most sorry to hear about the troubles with Quentin. But I realize how hopeless such things can be. Of our clan there's one who goes in and out of Halfway Houses. All the others seem to have dodged troubles of that sort, though some (inc. Harry Chapin) turned up with asthmas that seems to have no part in our families' past.

I suspected somethink like the botchery of our session. The detail that it was scheduled for the same time as the U. of Cal. Press party is ptikly tasty. And the MLA one, too! I'd ascribe it to no "blunder," but to an inside bit of "Administrative Rhetoric."

You ask whether I have a preference for the next time. I'd say, Yes. Let them go to hell, and please tellem I said so.

I have seen neither your volume nor Hayden White's. But I have recd. from the press a copy-edited version of my epilogues for P&C and ATH that just about enrages me—and I haven't yet decided what I'll do about it. Please tell me: Is Wayne Booth still Head of the Outfit? I have been building up steam for a letter to him on other matters. I'd like to resign as an Honorary Member of the whole outfit, and put an advt. in some place or other saying that I'm doing so. But I will say one thing about it all: Rhetoric as a topic fits the Speech people better than the MLA.

Incidentally, my "Dramatism" is to my "Logology" as, in the traditional line-ups, Ontology is to Epistemology. We are the symbol-using animal; we know "reality" via the dualistic perspective of (nonsymbolic) motion and (symbolic) action. But though I hover ever about theology and metaphysics, my approach is wholly secular and empirical. I consider my relation to humanism as analogous to William of Occam's relation to scholasticism: The schools had built along the Anselm principle of fides quaerens intellectum: beginning with faith and deriving from it the corresponding realm of reason. But Occam, without attacking the Faith, would abandon the attempt to reconcile them; each was a realm of its own. Similarly, in proportion as "science" becomes Technology, I'd abandon the notion (since the Renaissance) that "Science" (Technology) is in the same groove with Humanism. Language made possible two ways whereby humans departed from "the state of nature." One, the personalistic; two, the instrumental. The first "flowers" in stories of the Supernatural; the second comes to fruition in the ever-extending realm of Counter-Nature. Aristotle's concept of the "tragic pleasure" is humanistic; the meter-readings of the body's behavior during such an expeeerience are in a wholly different realm. The clinically analagous record of the poetic exaltation is a perpective by incongruity that is "perfectly schizoid."

The student who piloted me around when I was here last year became somewhat of a fan (to my considerable surprise), and is giving a course on me. I'm trying to work out ways of being helpful without nebbing in his classroom performances. Being fully aware of the awkwardnesses built into the sichaysh, I'm gwanna try and see if we can handle that. My ambition is to work out a way of our relating whereby the whole thing will end by our being a batch of mellow fellows.

But heck, I shouldof written about five letters by now.

Avec Universal Liebe,
K.B.

[Postcard postmarked Atlanta, Feb 2, 1982]

Dear Billions,

Are you sure that the "Creativity" piece was in Shenandoah? If so, can you without trouble say when? They never sent me a copy, or asked for permission. My copy is in a Monograph Series, No. 12, published by U. of Tulsa.

Do you know my "Doing and Saying" piece? Salmagundi, Winter 1971.

There's a book On Narrative, edited by W.J.T. Mitchell, U. of Chicago Press (material originally in CI). Opens with an essay by Hayden White. I'm thinking of haggling with it, though White;s piece can, I think, be fitted into my groove (if to Annals, Chronicle, and History we add Aeschatology).

> Holla,
> K.B.

> Emory University
> March 28, 1983

Dear Billions,

Helndamnaysh, I'm sorry about your vexations.

I haven't seen Hayden White's book. How many bottles of vodka would it cost me? Whom should I address, and how, in asking for a discount? Would it irritate me? Who says what?

We have been having some pleasant meetings here, but not a one of us has, to my knowledge, seen e'en the title of Hayden White's book.

Incidentally, next March I am also to be doing a job at the U. of Nebraska, Lincoln. All around Pluralism. Wayne Booth will be there, of course, and McKeon, and quite several others. I have taken as title "When Pluralist (necessarily), When Decidedly Not." Incidentally, the Head of it all, James E. Ford, Chairman of the English Dept. there, wrote me about his zeal anent my article in October 1961 issue of Poetry, anent my stuff on Poem on "The Raven." Going back over it, I realize that my excerptings in LSA really botched it a bit.

Recently I tried on my pals a "sympathetic" analysis of TBL, a strongly formalistic discussion that, at the same time, tried to give the feel of the poor slob's predicament. I worked in enough of the plot to end by reading straight through, the last chapter. By heck, it worked. The various jottings call forth different tonalities, and several get an effect by "flash-back" (thereby serving to "integrate" the book even at the very moment when it, and the guy, are falling apart). But there must be a brief pause btw. each fragment and the next, along with the contrasts of attitude. The guy was such a stinker in his treatment of Genevieve, and at the end he knows how wretchedly he needs her. But the "jottings" are not for an eye-reader. They must be imaginatively heard.

...

next morn. Fantastic nightmares. Some kind of awful tabu had been violated. Not sexual. Rather, something had been said wrong—and apparently by many, who knew one another and seemed to suspect one another. Yet there were definite sides somehow.

Leave at an ungodly morning hour on March 31 for San Francisco. Address during April: % Professor Carol Wilder, 765 Josine Avenue, Palo Alto, CA 94306. I'm scheduled to end in Oregon, thanks to Bob Wess, on May 5, historic birthday of me, Kierkegaard, and Charlie Marcus. I'm delighted you got to going with Trevor the Meliorist.

> Bestest,
> K.B.

> Back at Clutcher's Gulch
> May 24, 1983

Dear Billions,

'Twould seem that I survived, but a bit the worse for wear.

Tim Curtius sent me a review he did of the Representing volume (I mean a MS copy of the review). He gives you quite favorable comment. I guess I'll encounter it somewhere along the way.

John Gage told me that he is now doing the bibliography deal. (Incidentally, I had grand times with both of the Oregon stops, though cruelly beset by spectacular bouts of insomnia and parlous conditions with regard to my body's plumbing.)

I gather your book is out. I 'gin fear the Outfit is being quite evasive about my two reprints. It goes out of its road to muss my rhythm.

How go things with thee and thine?

> Bestest,
> K.B.

Back at Clutchers' Gulch
154 Amity Road
And/Or 07821
06/20/83

Dear Billions,

By heck, your new stuffo in your book anent my Sickly Selph, and your friendly exercising in the Representing volume do make it look as though somethinks is going on. Thanks slavishly.

I'm sorry to hear of your new ailments. Is something that you are taking for your other vexations turning up with side-effects?

I'm still trying to unkink things a bit here, extra troubles being that we had a considerable plasterfall last wint, and the work on the job is still not quite finished. Also, Butchie hasn't yet arrived—so, all told, the gainliness is on the un-side.

I may have an extra copy of the "Bodies" draft. I'll keep on the lookout as my unpacking moves on. (It's now among the jumble caused by moving out the stuff in the room that took the worst beating.)

Yes, let's put that Panta Rhei volume togidda for the next U. of Cal. offering. (I note that, in yestiddy's NYT Book Review, they attest to a policy of having me among them as they keeps in print permanently.)

Suppose I ask Bob Zachary if he has any idea as to how we shd. go about it properly to divvy up the take? Or might we ask McClung to make suggestions? Or both?

I'm getting another modest honorary award this coming autumnality, though I'm still avowed to secrecy as to whence where from.

The interview with me in ALL AREA NO. 2, Spring 1983 is out. P.O. Box 492 Canal St. Station, NY 10013. I'm told that it has been advertised in the NY Review, but I'm behint in everything. So far at least I have but one copy. It's a quite ambitious manufacturing job they put together, but they're working financially on a piece of string for a shoestring.

I think you'd be interested in Walter J. Ong, SJ, Orality and Literacy: The Technologizing of the Word, Methuen. I can get along quite handsomely with it. For it enables me to both salute it and say exactly wherein we part company. He mentions me not, but it bothers me not at all. (He knows my stuff; we have corresponded, at his suggestion and his discontuance; but my notion of "symbolic action" cuts things a different way from his division btw. word as "event" and word as "thing." I can well understand why either he or his editor or both would decide it would be more convenient if his book got no nearer to me that Austin's "speech-act theory." Do you, by the way, have a copy of my comments on Austin's book? Probably not. For you most decidedly should have discussed that piece at considerable length. And if you don't know of that piece, it's my own damned fault.)

But I must hobble-cobble back to my last, while I last.

Bestest to thee and thine,
K.B.

The Copesmithery
Lingerlag Lane
Clutchers Gulch
August 20, 1983

Dear Billions,

Herewith a copy of the TLS review. Also a CANONIZED copy of my answerve.

Bob Zachary thinks you might oughta wanta get into the fray, binnuz your book is the "occasional cause" of the review.

Kindly return the two pages I carved out of the TLS.

Two days later, 08/22/83

Intended to say much more, and enclose more. But am in a jamby-wamby. Tomorrow I go to Maine, where I join until Friday in a Wm. C. Wms. commemoration.

Rejerce,
K.B.

Andover
May 11, 1984

Dear Billions,

Wow! your enthusiasm is so infectious, it damnear convinces me. In any case, even readers who would say that you're all wrong would grant that you really meant it—and such generosity is there to be grateful for, as I decidedly am.

Don Burks writes that the Govt. has recognized the identity of the "Society," has given it a number, 35-1598666; and already one membership-check bounced for lack of funds.

The news that Searle (a follower of Austin's "speech-act" line) has received a grant from the MacArthur Foundation makes me wince for our outfit's frailty. (I think of that twist about the group whose members survived by taking in one another's washing—and I guess we must fit in with a supply-side economy of that sort. But I do keep trying to think up some way whereby something of moment could be put out now and then—along with a winsome sales pitch for more members.)

And damni tall, I owe a vast no. of letters thanking the many guys and girls who contributed towards getting the enterprise started. In fact, my behintness in such matters is truly morbid. Also, I agreed to write some friendly words for Nemerov's forthcoming collection of his critical prose—and as usual I am in a jam with that, while I should be valiantly at work writing up my activities at the Pluralism deal in Nebraska, and I'm not yet clear of the aftermath from my recent doings at Penn State.

This aft. I attend church in celebration of a local wedding (with dwinks elsewhere afterwards, I think). Last eve I fell asleep listening to a news program—and it so threw me off schedule that I wasted nearly the whole night tossing.

With best to thee and thine,
K.B.

[Postcard possibly from Andover]

Sept. 9, 1984

Dear Billions,

Any chance that you could send me some suggestions for the complimentary copies of P&C? (Not the obvious ones, the Joshuas who organized the whole biz. My problem is that I keep gettn those, which I had on my list already.)

And wow! Jim Chesebro writes that you show signs of dubiety, anent the whole project (if I interpreted him correctly). Please do tell me anything along that line, for it could help me plan against.

Bestest to theenthine,
K.B.

R. D. 2
Andover, New Jersey 07821
January 7, 1985

Dear Billions,

'Twas good to hear from same. But I do wish you had been more joyous.

And I did rejerce at signs of your team-mate attitude.

There's one notion you might think of, in a winding-up mood (which is what I keep lingering on with (and by)). It's what I wept to see you hadn't done with the revised edition of your book anent my Sickly Selph.

In your comments on the writers in your Pro and Con Compendium anent said S.S., you could have retrospectively evaluated their evaluations and your then evaluations.

A mature discussion of how things looked then, etc., in the light of how they look now would be a wholly independent contribution to matters of this sort. You could do it as no one else could - and you could put the focus upon the issues, not upon me.

Others, like Frank Lentricchia and Phil Tompkins, can tell us about the Derrida, Gramsci connections, etc. (I forget whether you have suffered the All-Area interviews.) And since, as you say, you are already ahead of Paul Jay along that line, we could all profit by your shaking a leg thuswise.

Meanwhile, with regard to the De Burp Society that I am now at 87 saddled with the responsibility for (thus belatedly, after so many years besnooting bureaucracy, now having an organization as a problem child, I who only once in my life changed a diaper) I keep figuring out how we can put together newsletters with comments by members corresponding on joint logological enterprises. And thereby, I dare hope, I won't merely be asking that people subscribe as a way of paying for a wreath on my pre-grave. Yes, Trevor the Meliorist is a great gift - and I have told him that if we can't get the membership to newsing back and forth about their projects, I'll RESIGN.

Holla - and the bestest,
K.B.

Andover
May 16, 1987

Dear Billions,

No, me no grouch. In fact, I very much liked the piece you sent me, And have some notes for a letter. But I was so far behind on my schedule, I had to pack them for my return to the Copesmithery. And I haven't yet got that jumble unjumbed. I'm delighted with your having dragged a class through TBL. And I have been taking notes for quite some time with the trick conceit that I would round out my opus totum by a tract on that, perhaps with the story of my operation (the last piece in my Collected W.O. volume) as a kind of sequel. Here's a possibility: Keep a record of all the students' papers and any discussion in classes. If I bump off before putting my papers in final shape, I already have the design and its rationale completely clear. You could put it all togidda, then as an extra twist, add a section noting how it bears upon the responses of your students.

You might use a title such as "Towards a Better Life: its Form and Psychosis." Or at least this title could be referred to as the "methodological" title. I shall begin by discussing the book purely as a literary form, as "poetic action." And the "psychosis" would concern what was eating at the author "as citizen and taxpayer," involving the theory of motives as discussed in the prefaces, plus the acrostic design of the first preface, the first letter of each paragraph (read in that order, revealing the name of the person to whom the book is dedicated).

There is one copyright hitch. Do you know of, or did you refer to, my chapter in a book, "Why Man Takes Chances: Studies in Stress-Seeking," edited, with a foreword, by Samuel Z. Klausner, Anchor Books, Doubleday & Company, Inc., 1968? It's a good summary of the goings-on as a story, incl. themes I have more notes on. A lot of that could not be better said. So there would be the need to make a deal with editor or publisher for the inclusion of that material just as it is. For the subtler aspects of the form, I borrow from Macbeth, which has two kinds of endings (1. recapitulation, as in Lady Macbeth's reenactment of the murder scene; 2, to the end of the line, Macbeth's fight to the finish). Then I deal with the "psychotic" ambiguity, the shift between the total end in the last jotting of the last chapter and the "resurgam" theme (which, you may recall my gossip, was flitting about the author's PCS when he wrote the last jotting, as he recalled in retrospect.

If you don't have a copy of the "Stress-Seeking" piece, I could lend you one, which you could copy if you cared to, and return the piece to me. Denis Donoghue has done some good work on TBL besides the thing he contributed to the Seton Hall show, and which I liked, though Paul Jay seemed to be against it. I thought that his selections made a kind of "Beatitudes" in reverse, for which I have invented the term, "have-at-titudes." Paul talks of trying to put the Seton Hall pieces into a single volume.

Golden has written Vic-Vit suggesting that he might publish my Watson tribute in Pre-Text if I agreed. I like the idea except for one detail: I'd want to give that publication only "first serial rights," and later have it in the On Human Relations/While Everything Flows collection that shd. be a kind of match with LSA. What say about "Definitivizing" that batch of stuff? Then talk to Bob Zachary about presenting to U. of Cal. Press; how much % do you and he decide should go and on what terms? I'll agree to what youenz judge, then we'll present that, with the Table of Contents, for negotiatings with the Press. Punktum.

You speak of Dale Davis, whose personal address is also the address of an organization of some sort of which she is presiding official. I recently failed to get her a Guggy for her Dial project, though from the start I feared that said outcome was in the cards. But she brings both devotion and savvy to her enterprise. And now, having only a few days ago received a letter from Carroll Terrell (of Orono) I now aim to get him to let Dale Davis take over the role I had tentatively thought of taking on as a participant in the forthcoming " M M Centennial Conference" slated to begin June 12. Since Terry had already engaged her in connection with these doings, and since I had already told Dale of the approach I would exemplify (as the result of a student's work on MM I had encountered during my winter sessions as a Verbalizer in Residence at the Emory U. Graduate Institute of the Liberal Arts (which initials turn out monstrously bad on a college T-Shirt), I zealously liked the idea of asking Terry to hand that job on to Dale, with the notion that we could correspond gossip-wise if she felt the need. And in any case, I should say that poems like "To the Memory of e.e. cummings" and "Poetic Exercise on the Subject of Disgruntlement" are totally indebted to her "librarian" primnesses, as vs. my ways of moving-in-on, like the profile in her Steamroller parable. That student's thesis inclined towards the view of her as sex-less. I never saw a more womanly woman. One colleague who inclined to such inside info asked me, while we were drinking togidda, whether she had been my mistress. I wrote a letter to Watson, "Now I have seen everything," for nothing could have been more inaccurate, as both he and I took for granted. And both she and I resented Hemingway's cult of the bullfight, (see my Steamroller way of saying so, in the lines, "I am Toreador" C.P. p. 226)

But what of the drama that (as per pp. 25-27) MM knowingly permitted to be described, as thus tortuously presented? The sichaysh was thus: The occasion was the party after the first night of the play, when Anthony and Florence sat drinking in their costumes as the Greek poet Alcaeus and the Hebrew Mary, they and her husband Joseph, while the "vulgar supernumeraries" in their costumes carouse. The theme is a vulgarization of Matthew Arnold's design, Christianity as a union of the Hebraic and Hellenic, Florence as the Mother of God sitting there drinking with Anthony as the fiery young Greek who had successfully courted her, while her much older husband, like the Magi, "who appear at the incunabula (cradle) of this new faith (reflecting the incest-taboo between parents and offspring) felt "compelled to do homage to a purely mental aspect of virginity." I think if I had said all that as bluntly as here, it could not have been said at all, and not just with regard to MM, but with regard to the nature of the book. I felt that this had to be done twistedly, and not just pains-takingly, but (for the readers) pain-causingly. Incidentally, the last sentence in the second paragraph on p. 28. But in the last sentence on p. 9 (I realized in going over the work's "psychosis") I had already characterized the high-blood pressure style my body was letting me indulge. I look upon my "when I had my operation" story, the book's "sequel," embodying a deliberate attempt to "take it easy" attitudinally, hence stylistically, bodily. Is this stretching things?

It's now V/19/87

… Alas! it's now V/24/87

One thing after another intervened, and every one brought up stuff I wanted to talk about to you. And now, this being a big weekend, my nonagenarian garrulity is peopled by both new doings that are notable.

V/25—sudden chance to get this letter mailed in NYC this morn.
Holla!

Index